THE WORDS

THAT MADE

AUSTRALIA

Published by **Black Inc. Agenda**
Series Editor: Robert Manne

Other books in the Black Inc. Agenda series:

Whitewash: On Keith Windschuttle's Fabrication of Aboriginal History
ed. Robert Manne

The Howard Years ed. Robert Manne

Axis of Deceit Andrew Wilkie

Following Them Home: The Fate of the Returned Asylum Seekers
David Corlett

Civil Passions: Selected Writings Martin Krygier

Do Not Disturb: Is the Media Failing Australia? ed. Robert Manne

Sense & Nonsense in Australian History John Hirst

The Weapons Detective Rod Barton

Scorcher Clive Hamilton

Dear Mr Rudd ed. Robert Manne

W.E.H. Stanner: The Dreaming and Other Essays ed. Robert Manne

*Goodbye to All That? On the Failure of Neo-Liberalism and the Urgency
of Change* eds. Robert Manne and David McKnight

Making Trouble: Essays Against the New Australian Complacency
Robert Manne

THE WORDS

THAT MADE

AUSTRALIA

✳

*how a nation
came to know itself*

✳

edited by

ROBERT MANNE

&

CHRIS FEIK

Black Inc. Agenda

Published by Black Inc. Agenda,
an imprint of Schwartz Media Pty Ltd
37–39 Langridge Street
Collingwood VIC 3066 Australia
email: enquiries@blackincbooks.com
http://www.blackincbooks.com

The National Library of Australia Cataloguing-in-Publication entry:

> The words that made Australia : how a nation came to know itself /
> edited by Chris Feik and Robert Manne.

> 9781863955782 (pbk.)

> Australia--Social life and customs.
> Australia--History.

> Feik, Chris.
> Manne, Robert (Robert Michael), 1947-

> 994

Printed in Australia by Griffin Press an Accredited ISO AS/ NZS 14001:2004 Environmental Management System printer.

FSC
www.fsc.org
MIX
Paper from
responsible sources
FSC® C009448

The paper this book is printed on is certified against the Forest
Stewardship Council® Standards. Griffin Press holds FSC chain
of custody certification SGS-COC-005088. FSC promotes
environmentally responsible, socially beneficial and economically
viable management of the world's forests.

Contents

Introduction ... ix

OVERTURE
Miles Franklin
1

THE WORKERS' PARADISE
Albert Metin
3

THE ANZAC LANDING
Ellis Ashmead-Bartlett
15

THE GALLIPOLI LETTER
Keith Murdoch
22

WOMEN IN AUSTRALIA
Maybanke Anderson
27

KANGAROO
D.H. Lawrence
36

THE AUSTRALIAN DEMOCRACY
W.K. Hancock
43

THE FOUNDATIONS OF
CULTURE IN AUSTRALIA
P.R. Stephensen
56

WHAT IS SIGNIFICANT IN US
WILL SURVIVE
Vance Palmer
69

THE FORGOTTEN PEOPLE
Robert Menzies

72

THE CULTURAL CRINGE
A.A. Phillips

80

RE-WRITING AUSTRALIAN HISTORY
Manning Clark

86

THE AUSTRALIAN LEGEND
Russel Ward

102

A NICE NIGHT'S ENTERTAINMENT
Barry Humphries

111

THE AUSTRALIAN UGLINESS
Robin Boyd

114

THE LUCKY COUNTRY
Donald Horne

124

AFTER THE DREAMING
W.E.H. Stanner

127

RACISTS
Humphrey McQueen

136

AUSTRALIA AS A SUBURB
Hugh Stretton

148

MANZONE COUNTRY
Anne Summers

157

THE REAL MATILDA
Miriam Dixson
159
THE SPECTRE OF TRUGANINI
Bernard Smith
167
THE END OF CERTAINTY
Paul Kelly
179
FROM THREE CHEERS TO
THE BLACK ARMBAND
Geoffrey Blainey
193
THE FUTURE EATERS
Tim Flannery
204
A SPIRIT OF PLAY
David Malouf
213
HOME-GROWN TRADITIONS
Inga Clendinnen
221
OUR RIGHT TO TAKE RESPONSIBILITY
Noel Pearson
229
THE NEW LIBERALISM
Judith Brett
245
THE FIG, THE OLIVE AND THE
POMEGRANATE TREE
Ghassan Hage
250

Sources ... 257

Introduction

Several popular anthologies of Australian essays, speeches and historical documents have been published recently. There is, however, so far as we are aware, no book that collects those illuminating passages – in novels, histories, polemics, magazine or newspaper articles, radio broadcasts and even theatrical revues – that opened the eyes of Australians to what was peculiar or particular to one or another aspect of their society. Sometimes phrases associated with these passages – 'the workers' paradise', 'the forgotten people', 'the cultural cringe', 'the lucky country', 'the Australian ugliness', 'the great Australian silence' – remained in national consciousness long after the details of the arguments from which these phrases were drawn had faded from memory. Through these passages, the nation came to understand itself. This is why we call them 'the words that made Australia'.

This volume brings these passages together for the first time. We hope that in doing this the anthology will offer its readers more than the sum of its parts. The passages in *The Words That Made Australia* not only reveal a series of influential but separate claims about the nature of Australian society. In our view, in addition, they form a record of some key moments of what the former prime minister John Howard used to describe as the perpetual Australian symposium on national identity, or what we prefer to call the century-long Australian national conversation.

The anthology begins roughly at the time of Federation. As an overture, we offer the fresh and delightful closing passage of *My Brilliant*

Career, written when Miles Franklin was a young countrywoman in her late teens. In our reconstruction of the conversation that followed, however, the opening gambit is a bold claim advanced by the Frenchman Albert Metin – Australia's more modest Tocqueville – in his *Socialisme sans Doctrines*. In essence, Metin argued that despite the absence of socialist theory, Australia (or Australasia, for he included New Zealand) was the first society on earth where the working classes truly flourished, where in practice the social experiment of trying to create a roughly egalitarian society had succeeded, and where as a consequence the 'workers' paradise' of which socialists had long dreamt was to be found. Metin was scarcely interested in the place of women in the workforce. Maybanke Anderson's 1920 essay, 'Women in Australia', provides a valuable addition, entirely consistent with Metin. According to Anderson, class division in Australia was far less salient than in Britain; working-class women avoided domestic service if factory work was available; by international standards they were generously paid.

The idea of the workers' paradise did not provide material suitable for a national myth of origin. In his dispatch from the front line of Gallipoli, published throughout Australia, the English journalist Ellis Ashmead-Bartlett galvanised the new nation with his report that on 25 April 1915 the young men of Australia had for the first time been tested in combat and had not been found wanting. At that moment, the nation's myth was born. Its hold on the national imagination was not threatened by the terrible suffering of the Australian soldiers at Gallipoli or the failures of the British military command, which the Australian journalist Keith Murdoch observed at first hand and conveyed in his long-remembered letter to the Australian prime minister, Andrew Fisher. Nor was it threatened by the subsequent retreat. Ellis Ashmead-Bartlett's words instilled pride in the Colonials; Murdoch's spoke of the suffering and the folly that followed. In combination, these words helped ensure that the story of Gallipoli, which has remained Australia's myth of foundation, was untainted by jingoism or swagger. This left its mark. As Inga Clendinnen observed movingly in her 1999 Boyer Lectures, *True Stories*, Australians had continued to pay solemn tribute to their war dead without a hint of military vainglory.

Following the war, the conversation about Australian society and Australian nationalism took a different turn. In 1922 the English novelist D.H. Lawrence visited Australia briefly. His novel *Kangaroo* suggested that he was repelled by both the shapeless and classless democracy he encountered and what he took to be the attempt to create a European society without roots in landscape or in culture. Lawrence's challenge was not easily shrugged off. In her defence of the temper of Australian democracy almost eighty years later, Clendinnen still recalled with anger Lawrence's aristocratic contempt for Australian egalitarianism.

In 1930, perhaps the greatest of all Australian historians, W.K. Hancock, provided the most serious alternative to Metin's version of Australia as the workers' paradise. Hancock was struck not only by the material prosperity of the egalitarian society, but also by its sameness and mediocrity. He believed there was something distinctive and peculiar about the way Australian individualism was expressed through reliance upon the state, which was seen by Australians, in Hancock's memorable phrase, as 'a vast public utility' for the satisfaction of needs. He observed the degree to which the society was built on the assumption of the availability at time of trouble of the Royal Navy and behind three great protective walls – the White Australia Policy; the manufacturing tariff, which Hancock regarded as economically irrational; and the delivery of the idea of the just wage through the centralised industrial arbitration system, which he likened to the medieval concept of the just price.

In 1935, in a muscular and prophetic tour de force, *The Foundations of Culture in Australia*, the publisher P.R. Stephensen provided the most persuasive answer to Lawrence's earlier unnerving questions. Stephensen claimed that the basis of an authentic Australian national culture already existed. He argued for its consolidation along lines he somehow was already able to imagine. Stephensen saw that the fear of colonial cultural inferiority was the greatest impediment to the foundation of a distinctive national culture in Australia. This aspect of his argument was taken up after the war in A.A. Phillips' amusing and extraordinarily influential *Meanjin* essay on 'the cultural cringe'. Forty years after *The Foundations* was published, when Stephensen's manifesto was long forgotten, the creation of the kind of confident national culture he advocated and imagined became one of the projects of the Whitlam government.

Far more than most writing from Australia in the 1930s – like the recently published arch and crusty essays of Walter Murdoch – Stephensen's seems to us remarkably contemporary. It was also alive to the threat of fascism, which he describes as 'the *Heil Hitler* buncombe' and 'a schoolboy bully, armed'. Yet within a few short years, in one of the more remarkable political reversals of Australian political life, Stephensen was to become the nation's leading exponent of the fascist world-view. For this he was eventually interned for three years. In 1952 Manning Clark visited the reclusive Stephensen to discuss *The Foundations* with him and found only a 'wreck'.

Until the Second World War, most social and historical analyses of Australia were, like Metin's, preoccupied by the egalitarian democratic working-class achievement or, if written by those further to the Left, by the struggle in Australia between capital and labour or between the bourgeoisie and the proletariat. In 1942, at a time when fear of Japanese invasion was still alive and intellectuals like Vance Palmer were wondering anxiously whether the young Australian society would or should survive, the former prime minister Robert Menzies, already looking to post-war peacetime, added a dimension to the national conversation. In the first of a series of radio broadcasts aimed at resurrecting his political career, Menzies argued that it was neither labour nor capital but the modest, thrifty, diligent, family-minded, home-owning suburban middle class – the so-called 'forgotten people' – that formed the true moral and social backbone of the nation.

In the post-war years, discussion of the forgotten middle class was indeed taken up as a theme in the national conversation, but not always in a manner that Menzies might have approved. At the beginning of his career, Barry Humphries, perhaps Australia's greatest social observer, invented the character of Sandy Stone, the respectable, sexless, house-trained suburbanite – in whom the heroism of the Anzacs had been reduced to pottering in the garden at Gallipoli Crescent and 'a nice night's entertainment' at the RSL. In his *Australian Ugliness*, Robin Boyd provided a complementary image that was long remembered – of the fast-spreading fussy suburban ugliness where the forgotten people lived. Strangely enough, it was a man of the Left, the social scientist Hugh Stretton, who, in 'Australia as a Suburb', a chapter of his seminal *Ideas for Australian Cities*, deepened Menzies' intervention with an attack on the shallowness of much of the aesthete's anti-suburban condescension and an original and eminently practical defence of the possibilities for a satisfying and varied life offered to the family by the suburban house and garden set on the intelligentsia-derided quarter-acre block.

In 1958 the historian Russel Ward published what would turn out to be one of the most significant contributions to the national conversation, *The Australian Legend*. Ward provided an historical account of the creation of the character type that had metamorphosed into what he called the Australian 'mystique' – the rough, independent, practical, hard-living, hard-drinking, loyal 'mate'. In his view the mystique was founded on the lives of the nineteenth-century nomadic bush workers, and then elaborated and mythologised in the work of the popular turn-of-the-century national poets, like Henry Lawson and Banjo Paterson. Implicitly, Ward drew upon Metin and the early historians of the Labor Party or the working class, such as Brian Fitzpatrick and V. Gordon Childe, for his suggestion that Australian culture was naturally egalitarian and working class.

Ward's intervention in the national conversation was not only influential, but had also already been recently contested. At the time when Ward wrote, Manning Clark, on the eve of embarking on his six-volume history of Australia, had just announced an altogether different vision. In his history, he promised, the preoccupations of the labour historians would be transcended. He would cast a cold eye on the illusions of the radical tradition regarding the convicts and the supposed Antipodean origins of mateship and democracy, and acknowledge the achievements of the nineteenth-century bourgeoisie – the building of the cities and the creation of the universities. Clark also promised he would write a history of grander themes – on the struggles between Tradition and the Enlightenment, and between the Roman Catholic and Protestant worldviews. Even more, he would seek to find in Australian history some deeper purpose, some spiritual meaning.

The extraordinary success of Donald Horne's scathing 1964 critique in *The Lucky Country* of established elites and their habits of mind was a sign of an unsettled country on the verge of cultural change. Russel Ward had written on the Australian mystique a decade before the arrival in Australia and in all Western countries of a revolution in sensibility, at whose centre was the reconsideration of centuries-long attitudes to gender and race. The Marxist historian Humphrey McQueen, in his *New Britannia*, now attacked Ward and the labour historians for turning a blind eye to the racism which he claimed was at the very heart of their own tradition and indeed the culture of the nation. The feminist historians Anne Summers and Miriam Dixson likewise both implicitly and explicitly challenged the masculinist assumptions of those who had preceded them.

Half a century earlier, Maybanke Anderson had provided a sophisticated Australian version of the movement of ideas that scholars would eventually call first-wave feminism. Anderson took quiet pride in the movement of women into higher education and the professions. She offered a subtle and profound analysis of the many ways the early acquisition of the female vote in Australia had reshaped gender relations and therefore the nature of society. Miriam Dixson in *The Real Matilda* now wrote rather about how little the female vote had transformed Australian society. Even more importantly, as a second-wave feminist for whom 'the personal is political', she analysed the ways in which the masculinist assumptions of the mateship tradition sketched out by Ward had impoverished and deformed the most intimate personal relations between men and women.

Sometimes national conversations are punctuated by the discovery of something that is obvious but for some reason previously invisible. In 1968, the great anthropologist W.E.H. Stanner delivered the Boyer Lectures, which he called *After the Dreaming*. Before Stanner, generations of anthropologists had studied the culture of the Australian Aborigines. Some had written about the problems contemporary indigenous people faced. No one before Stanner, however, had identified the unwillingness of Australians – both the historians and the people – to incorporate the story of the nineteenth-century dispossession of the indigenous people and its tragic aftermath into their understanding of Australian history. Stanner provided a name for this national habit of radical forgetfulness: 'the great Australian silence'. He reminded his fellows that asking the Aborigines to 'assimilate' was asking them to 'un-be'. Most profoundly of all, he asked them to remember that while much had been written by non-indigenous Australians about 'the problem of the Aborigines', scarcely a thought had been given to the problem the behaviour of the non-indigenous had created for them.

Stanner's words played an important part in creating a new way of seeing that began to change the way Australians looked at their country. They helped inspire a new school of historians, a policy alternative to assimilation through acknowledgement of the right to self-determination, and eventually a national search for some form of reconciliation. There were some scholars who interpreted the meaning of 'the great Australian silence' even more radically than Stanner. Bernard Smith is regarded by many as Australia's most significant art historian. In his 1980 Boyer Lectures, *The Spirit of Truganini*, he argued that without a pained and unambiguous recognition of the genocide that had first been enacted and then repressed in national memory, Australia would lack the kind of foundation in truthfulness without which no national culture could flourish.

W.K. Hancock's brilliant analysis of the Australian political economy had never been forgotten. It is referred to in several essays in this anthology. In 1992, in his *End of Certainty*, the most influential political book of recent years, the journalist Paul Kelly returned to Hancock's framework to demonstrate how globalisation had washed away what he called the Australian Settlement and created the conditions for the modernisation of the Australian economy and society. Kelly's book, in praise of the Hawke–Keating economic reform program of free trade, financial deregulation and privatisation, marked the effective end of the Australian labourist tradition.

In the following year, the most popular of all Australian historians, Geoffrey Blainey – who had fallen into conflict with the left intelligentsia with his warning about the dangers of the pace of Asian immigration and its philosophic accompaniment, the theory of multiculturalism – published a lecture that was a harbinger of a new conservatism. Blainey drew up a new 'balance sheet' on Australian history which centred on the Aboriginal question. He told his audience that he had been brought up on what he called a 'three cheers' version of Australian history. He had gradually seen its replacement by what he called the 'black armband' version. Blainey did not denigrate the culture of the indigen-ous people or deny the tragic nature of their experience in the way Keith Windschuttle, a later, more polemical, historian would. Rather, he returned to an earlier position, held by previous generations of Australian historians, including W.K. Hancock, who had regarded as inevitable and therefore as morally neutral both European settlement in Australia and the collapse of a hunter-gatherer society when confronted by the ambitions and resources of an industrialised empire.

Three years after the Blainey lecture, the Howard government came to power. In the final intervention in the national conversation stimulated by *The Australian Legend*, the political scientist Judith Brett pointed out that the conservative leader of the Liberal Party, John Howard, now embraced a de-proletarianised version of Ward's idealised national character in which the virtues of loyalty, pragmatism, independence and mateship were made central. Until Howard, *The Australian Legend* had been monopolised by the Labor Party. As Brett pointed out, it was from now a standard part of the rhetorical style of a new conservative populism. In effect, the traditions associated with Menzies and Ward had been married.

During the Howard years, an indigenous intellectual, Noel Pearson, complicated the national conversation about the past and future of indigenous society with a radical intervention. Pearson was a lawyer and a member of the Cape York Land Council. In a series of papers and essays, he argued that despite the best intentions of the left-liberal friends of the Aborigines, a new tragedy, based upon passive welfare and the curse of alcohol, was taking place in remote indigenous communities throughout Australia. This was a tragedy that both the recent generation of indigenous leaders and non-indigenous Australians who had been influenced by Stanner – and who had sought reconciliation with the indigenous people on the basis of truthful history and support for the idea of indigenous self-determination – had somehow either failed to notice or refused to discuss. Pearson's ideas were widely resisted on the Left and embraced on the Right. No one, however, could dispute both his courage and his independence. Gradually his words reshaped the debate about the Aboriginal future.

A concern for the natural environment is an even more recent thread of the national conversation than the question of the indigenous past and future. In his very successful and original ecological history of the Australian continent, *The Future Eaters*, Tim Flannery revived, in a quite different form, the haunting questions about the rootedness of Australian society and culture posed by D.H. Lawrence more than seventy years before. By replicating so many of the cultural practices of Europe in Australia – by overpopulating, by overgrazing, by our insensitivity to the native environment, by our indifference to the lessons learned by the ancient culture of the indigenous inhabitants of the continent – are we not in danger, Flannery asked, of destroying our future? In recent years Flannery has become the most significant Australian Cassandra regarding the potentially catastrophic threat to the earth posed by the burning of fossil fuels. This is no accident. Climate change is the global version of Flannery's concept of humans as insatiably self-destructive devourers of their future.

The novelist and poet David Malouf is the child of an assimilated father of Lebanese descent and a Sephardic Jewish mother. Serendipitously, he grew up in a post-war Australian-Irish Roman Catholic milieu. In his Boyer Lectures, *A Spirit of Play*, Malouf captured as precisely and delicately as anyone ever has the transformation of Australia since the 1960s, from a dour Anglo-Irish to a warmer, looser Mediterranean culture. The world of Malouf's boyhood was shaped by puritanism and sexual shame, and by bitter sectarian hostility between Protestants and Catholics. Malouf now gloried in the fact that he lived in a world of tolerance and urbanity, of sexual and bodily freedom, of uninhibited delight in fashion and cuisine. The symbol of this new world, whose arrival he celebrated, was Sydney's Gay and Lesbian Mardi Gras. As we have seen, Hugh Stretton in 1970 described the heart of Australia as the suburb. In Malouf's Australia, the new spirit and the centre of gravity had moved to inner-city Melbourne and Sydney.

Sometimes immigrants can see a society more clearly than the native-born who tend to take everything for granted. In the wonderful essay with which we end the anthology, we hear the words of a Lebanese Christian immigrant, the radical anthropologist Ghassan Hage. Like Malouf, Hage offers a kind of celebration of the new Australia but from a different angle. Visiting his grandparents' old house in Bathurst, Hage tells us he stumbled upon the three sacred trees of the ancient Mediterranean culture they had once planted – the fig, the olive and the pomegranate. The presence of this other world of meaning on Australian soil revealed to him, in a moment of epiphany, the reality of Australia's embrace of a world of genuine plurality. Hage now felt something that had previously escaped him: that he had roots in this country, that he really was an Australian. Just as Malouf's lecture opens our eyes to the new space of social and sexual freedom that has been created in recent decades in this country, so does Hage's essay capture as clearly and truly as anything we have read what goes deep in the contemporary idea of Australian multiculturalism.

The principles governing the editing of this anthology can be stated simply. The beginning point for the selection is the time of Federation. Because the material constitutes in our view a conversation of sorts, the passages selected are published in chronological order. Some of the passages are published in full. Most are edited, some very heavily. We hope, however, that in all cases the meaning has not been distorted. At the end of the anthology we provide details about which of the passages have been edited and which have not. We also provide details of the source that in each case has been used. We accept that the selection of passages in an anthology of this kind is inescapably personal. An attempt has been made, however, to represent the national conversation fairly. Passages that we think to have been important have been included, from across the political spectrum. Most but not all of the passages were at one time or another well known. Some have passed into obscurity, some have not. All seem to us of high intellectual quality and of intrinsic interest still. There can, however, be no claim that this anthology is definitive or authoritative. Other editors would no doubt choose different passages. To our knowledge no similar Australian anthology – of the passages that revealed the nation to itself – presently exists.

OVERTURE

Miles Franklin

1901

I am proud that I am an Australian, a daughter of the Southern Cross, a child of the mighty bush. I am thankful I am a peasant, a part of the bone and muscle of my nation, and earn my bread by the sweat of my brow, as man was meant to do. I rejoice I was not born a parasite, one of the blood-suckers who loll on velvet and satin, crushed from the proceeds of human sweat and blood and souls.

Ah, my sunburnt brothers! – sons of toil and of Australia! I love and respect you well, for you are brave and good and true. I have seen not only those of you with youth and hope strong in your veins, but those with pathetic streaks of grey in your hair, large families to support, and with half a century sitting upon your work-laden shoulders. I have seen you struggle uncomplainingly against flood, fire, disease in stock, pests, drought, trade depression, and sickness, and yet have time to extend your hands and hearts in true sympathy to a brother in misfortune, and spirits to laugh and joke and be cheerful.

And for my sisters a great love and pity fills my heart. Daughters of toil, who scrub and wash and mend and cook, who are dressmakers, paperhangers, milkmaids, gardeners, and candlemakers all in one, and yet have time to be cheerful and tasty in your homes, and make the best of the few oases to be found along the narrow dusty track of your existence. Would that I were more worthy to be one of you – more a typical Australian peasant – cheerful, honest, brave!

I love you, I love you. Bravely you job along with the rope of class distinction drawing closer, closer, tighter, tighter around you: a few

1

more generations and you will be as enslaved as were ever the moujiks of Russia. I see it and know it, but I cannot help you. My ineffective life will be trod out in the same round of toil, – I am only one of yourselves, I am only an unnecessary, little, bush commoner, I am only a – woman!

THE WORKERS' PARADISE

Albert Metin

1901

In Australia and New Zealand labour legislation, at least in a radical form, is of recent origin. Up to 1890, in fact, protective legislation for works in these countries merely echoed English laws in the field (granting of legal personality to trade unions, limitation of the working day for women and children, factory inspection). Since 1890 labour protective legislation has become more frequent, more radical and in many ways more advanced than the latest schemes of European parliaments. For example a shorter working day for shop assistants is being established in all the colonies, New Zealand has compulsory arbitration, Victoria a minimum wage. Thus it is that Australasia, and more particularly New Zealand and Melbourne, are beginning to be known, not without some irony, as *the workers' paradise.*

It is the fruition of an evolutionary process which began about the mid-century with the tide of immigration following the gold discoveries. At that time workers arrived in vast numbers, bringing with them from England the tradition of combination which they put to use against their employers. In 1856 building workers in Melbourne won the eight-hour day and for long afterwards the trade unions obtained all they wanted from a series of negotiations and private agreements with employers. In this period they neglected politics and put their trust solely in trade union activity; but the employers combined in their turn against the unions, and in 1890 the associations of capitalists won a significant victory over the workers after the defeat of an almost general strike. Then the workers' leaders changed tactics, formed political parties, were easily elected thanks to universal suffrage and came, in almost all the parliaments, to hold the balance of power between the two parties which hitherto had contended for office. They took no part in government and Labor members rarely accepted a portfolio: thus the recent inclusion of a Labor leader in the Victorian ministry was considered quite an event. But without holding power the Labor parties vetoed its exercise against them or without them, except in the new and thinly populated colony of Western Australia, in little Tasmania and in only one important colony, Queensland.

To a certain extent then, governments depend on the Labor Party, but they are not Labor Party governments. When they introduce a bill on working hours or factory inspection they almost always yield to the views of those on whom they depend for their majority. In colonies where the ministry has not systematically opposed the Labor Party, labour legislation has come to form a comprehensive and orderly code of laws, but they have been passed piecemeal according to changing circumstances.

Australian politics are concerned with practical affairs. They may be socialist in their results but they are not always so in inspiration. It would be an exaggeration, then, to hold that Australasia is moving systematically towards the extension of government services. Undoubtedly a trend in this direction may be suggested by the at least tacit recognition of the right to work, by restrictions on the rights of property, by the establishment of old-age pensions and by many other measures now being considered. Again we need not look beyond New Zealand which, alone and only very recently, seems to have deliberately concerned itself with state socialism.

On the other hand, New Zealand, like the other colonial governments, has the strongest reasons for not giving all its attention to labour legislation. Its main aim is to develop agriculture and encourage settlement in the countryside. No doubt rural legislation in the progressive colonies is inspired by a democratic spirit: enactments tend to favour small and medium farmers at the expense of the great pastoralists, and since the financial crisis of 1892–93, particularly strong inducements have been extended to unemployed men who wish to try their luck on the land. Yet if these laws succeed, the result, in the end, will be to create a numerous farming class which could very well act as a check on the urban workers.

The real influence of the workers springs partly from exceptional causes. Normally mining and the processing of agricultural products are the only important industries in Australasia. The country is not, nor does it seem to be becoming, a manufacturing nation like the United States. In Australia factories are relatively few and small. These conditions do not appear to augur well for the triumph of labour's cause. But it happened that the gold rush and assisted immigration suddenly drew large numbers of wage-earners to Australasian soil. It also happened that English capitalists stepped up their rate of investment in the country, creating important assets there, assets which have become even more important since the boom has been followed by crisis. The investors quarrelled with their workers, offering them outrageous conditions. Numerous enough to organise themselves in stable trade unions, manual workers were not however so plentiful as to be competing ruinously with each other. Wage-rates prevailing during the gold-rush period remain legendary: the building workers' union won the eight-hour working day in Melbourne in 1856.

Undoubtedly wages have fallen a little since, in line with the cost of living: they remain quite fantastically high only in Western Australia, the site of a new gold rush. Everywhere living standards for working people today are still better than they are in Europe. In fact the population has grown only slightly in recent years, for European emigrants prefer the cheaper passage to America. Moreover, to guard against competition, Australasian workers have had subsidies designed to encourage European migration abolished and step by step they are bringing to an end yellow and Polynesian immigration. The advantages they defend are assured to them by the relatively low level of unemployment in a new and rapidly developing country. These advantages spring from the economic conditions of half a century ago; they have been prolonged not without artifice and, though not incompatible with the present development of Australasian capitalism, neither are they a direct result of it.

It may be said, a little bluntly, that the struggle between supporters and opponents of labour legislation is almost always concerned with material questions. On both sides equally, the poverty of theoretical notions is astonishing to anyone accustomed to European polemics. One hears from the employers simply affirmations of inflexible resistance to change, based on the defence of their profits. There is no argument whatever, only a declaration of war. Publicists who take up the capitalist cause confine the comments to the plane of practical affairs or, if they do venture into the realm of theory, betray their ignorance of it. Thus, during my stay in Melbourne, the conservative newspaper was vigorously criticising new labour legislation, especially that providing for the recently introduced minimum wage. Invoking the findings of political economy, it reproduced the theory of the *Wages' Fund* according to which the capitalist should set aside a certain fixed sum for wages, and would be unable to do anything if his wages bill should exceed this fixed sum. But the theory of the Wages' Fund, exploded by English trade union experience, has now been abandoned.

On the other side theoretical arguments are no better, or rather, they simply do not exist: people ignore or run away from them. The word 'socialism', pleasing to many European reformers because of its philosophical and general connotations, displeases and perturbs Australasian workers by its very amplitude. One of them whom I asked to sum up his programme for me replied: 'My programme! *Ten bob a day!*' I dare not affirm that this answer is typical, but it reflects an attitude of mind very common among Antipodean workers: they see their own interests so clearly and pursue them so persistently that they fear anything which might make their aims seem even less clear-cut. Here, as throughout the English-speaking world, practical considerations are prized above everything else. Demands on government are for practical concessions rather than declarations of principle. Western Europe is richer in theory, Australasia in practice. It is to England that the most well-read and intellectual of Antipodean reformers turn to seek theoretical bases for their laws, when they take the trouble to support practical considerations with abstract ideas. On the contrary it is to Australasia that we should turn to study the implementation of advanced measures, frequently debated but never actually put into practice among us. Australasia has contributed little to social philosophy but she has gone further than any other land whatever along the road of social experiment.

Short hours, high wages

The term 'eight-hour day', used to indicate the shorter working day in Australasia, is not quite correct. Here are the facts: almost universally today the working week consists of from forty-eight to fifty-two hours with Saturday afternoon and Sunday off. Shop assistants enjoy almost the same conditions but with their afternoon off on some other day, usually Wednesday. The day's work begins later than with us, at about seven-thirty in the morning on the average, and ends between five and six for the evening meal. In this respect wage and salary earners in Australasia enjoy the best conditions in the world. Are shorter working hours beneficial for the individual and the nation? All social reformers agree so completely in an affirmative answer to this question that to me any debate on the matter seems superfluous.

Higher wages cannot be evaluated in figures as easily as can shorter working hours. This is because wages differ from one colony to another and from one district to another in the same colony. Moreover wages may be paid either for hours worked or for piece-work, and finally in country areas wages are paid partly in the form of board and lodging. Thus it is impossible to present a general picture of the wage structure. However the annual statistics of each colony, to be found generally in the reports of the labour bureaux (free, government labour exchange offices), give interesting and accurate information on this subject. In New Zealand wages range from four to twelve shillings a day in the city, and from fifteen to thirty shillings per week, plus keep, in the country. We have seen above that, after the introduction of compulsory arbitration, the average wage for skilled workers in Christchurch and Dunedin was ten shillings a day.

Wages are not so high in the other colonies. In South Australia the premier declared in a public speech that he wanted to guarantee a decent wage to all workers. Pressed to give a figure, he said that six shillings a day seemed to him a reasonable sum, and this coincided with trades hall opinion. In Brisbane the trades hall complained that, according to the official figures published by the labour bureau, skilled workers' wages were only five or six shillings a day. In Sydney and Melbourne a skilled worker's wage is between eight and nine shillings a day. In accordance with the most recent legislation, this figure has risen in Melbourne.

To sum up, pay for a shorter working day is almost the same as the prevailing rate in England in the primary producing colonies of South Australia and Queensland, and a little higher in Sydney and Melbourne, while in New Zealand, since compulsory arbitration, it has reached the United States figure.

High wages and industrial development

It is often said that the benefits of high wages are illusory because employers, faced with high costs for labour, will invest their money elsewhere. Thus, when they claim too high wages, workers kill the goose that lays the golden eggs.

The wages' fund theory, referred to above, is invoked to back up this argument. If it were valid, the sum ear-marked for wages by the employer would be fixed once and for all and there would be no way of increasing it without endangering profits. Yet experience has often proved the contrary.

Do the highest wages in the world inhibit the development of American industry? Quite the contrary: America competes successfully against countries with lower wage rates and produces cheaper cotton goods, machine-tools, railway lines, bicycles and so on. The fact is that, being unable to count on long working hours and low wages, American employers look for their profits to more efficient machinery which in turn speeds up the production rate. Moreover, improved conditions keep in the factory keen and hard-working men who, in the old days, would have been the first to leave their jobs. Thus the manager can select first-class mechanics and skilled workers to operate the improved machines efficiently.

In countries with low wage rates, on the other hand, in India, Egypt and Mexico for example, workers are unreliable and clumsy and machinery is out of date and badly maintained, for the manufacturer does not think it necessary to improve its design. In these countries I have often seen factories idle because of a breakdown, or not working because of absenteeism in the workforce. To say that capitalists in such countries hate high wages would be less than the truth, but I have heard Mexican engineers deploring the low wage rates. 'At the rates we offer,' they said, 'we cannot have a European-type workforce, and we should have to offer vastly more money to achieve any real morale in the productive process.' Those with whom I spoke recognised that higher wages would benefit not only the worker but also the engineer, the works manager and in fact all the executive personnel who would be forced to improve the machinery and organisation of production. The theory is proved in the United States where high wages, considerable profits, and a good market for manufacturing goods are all found together.

Secondary industry in Australasia is very far from being comparable with that of the United States. In the colonies I studied, factories are relatively fewer and less important, and the opponents of labour legislation stress this backwardness as a proof that enterprise is inhibited by it. The argument is false, for production in Australia and New Zealand has not stopped growing, though it has increased particularly in the rural sector and mining. The fact that butter and cheese from these countries competes successfully on the English market with the produce of Brittany and Normandy, in spite of distance, transport costs, passage through the tropics and the different wage rates is a convincing demonstration that maintenance of low wages is not the only means of encouraging a nation's industrial and rural production.

High wages and the cost of living

Many people believe that raising wages would not benefit the workers, because the cost of daily necessities would rise correspondingly. It is even stated confidently that such is the case in the United States. This view is confirmed neither by statistical studies nor my own experience of the cost of living in America.

In Australasia it is completely wrong. Indeed, if we take the colony with the highest wage rates, New Zealand, we find that the price of household necessities there is not very high and that it has fallen continuously over the past twenty years, from 1878 to 1898. Between 1898 and 1899 there was a slight rise in the price of tea, an imported commodity the cost of which is very unstable, and two other equally slight rises in the prices of mutton and butter, both due to the development of exports to England.

Prices in the other colonies would be rather lower than those in New Zealand, but the differences are not great. We should notice the extraordinary cheapness of meat which Australasia produces so abundantly. On the 'stations' they think nothing of giving a sheep to shearers or other itinerant workers who ask for board and lodging overnight. Indeed this should be taken into account with the price of food, rent, domestic servants' wages and other items contributing to the cost of living. Even in the reputedly more expensive places, for instance in outback mining towns or the great cities of Sydney and Melbourne, workers' restaurants serve a complete meal, a plate of hot meat and vegetables, pudding, bread and tea, for sixty centimes. I have frequently sampled these meals: they are copious in quantity and quite good in quality.

The low cost of living is demonstrated by the proportion of the total salary spent on food. In Australia this figure is 34.4 per cent compared with 42.4 per cent in England and 44 per cent in France. And yet the total annual expenditure per head on food is higher in Australia than in the latter countries – £33.19.5 as compared with £29.14.6 in the United Kingdom and £23.19.4 in France. The Australian figure is even higher than that of the United States (£32.16.2). In 1894 Mr Coghlan, an Australian statistician, gave the average annual expenditure per head on food for the whole of Australasia the figure of £43.12.10. The colonists consume more meat (254 English pounds per head per annum as against 109 in Great Britain and seventy-seven in France) than any other people, more tea, and more coffee except for Holland, the United States, the Scandinavian countries and Belgium. Yet Australasians drink relatively little coffee. Tea is their national drink: they are the greatest tea-drinkers in the whole world. They consume relatively little alcohol.

All these figures come from Mulhall's *Dictionary of Statistics*, except for the Australasian ones which are from Mr Coghlan, the eminent government statistician in Sydney. It may be thought that Australasia has received very favourable treatment in these comparisons. My own experience of Australian life leads me to believe that Coghlan's estimates are not significantly exaggerated.

To complete this picture of the Australasian worker's living standards it must be said that luxury goods, especially imported ones, are very dear, as are all those commodities produced by skilled labour: tailor-made clothes, for example, and domestic service. The effect of a high standard of living is obvious in the realm of luxury goods and services; just as it is in the United States. The tariff in a first-class hotel, the goods in a novelty shop or a fashionable milliner's are more expensive than in France. It is this fact that leads superficial observers to say that the cost of living is high, a statement the exact opposite of the truth if one considers basic necessities, especially food.

It must also be remembered that, in the colonies as in England, indirect taxes are not imposed on the same commodities as in France. Thus beer is heavily taxed as a luxury and is expensive, while sugar, considered a basic necessity, is free of all taxes and three times cheaper than in France.

For the rest, the Australasian worker, like his English or American counterpart, is a free spender. He does not agonise over the cost of an article or a pleasure he wants: he does not grudge any treat to his family, and so what is left over from his living expenses often goes on pleasure or on luxury goods. That is the explanation of my earlier statement that average expenditure per head is higher in Australasia than anywhere else.

This tendency to free spending has many advantages. The Englishman, the American and the Australasian think less carefully than the Frenchman of paying to join a society, of subscribing to a periodical or to one or several newspapers. Working-class organisation in English-speaking countries has certainly been facilitated by the fact that workers are little given to saving money. In every country, moreover, organisation has been restricted among manual workers in proportion as low wages have compelled them to exercise the strictest economy. Skilled workers are everywhere better organised than labourers, and this is another strong argument advanced by labour supporters in favour of higher wages.

Working-class consciousness

The standard of living is higher in Australasia than in England, but it would be a mistake to attribute this solely to the results of labour legislation. Up to the present these laws have not succeeded in abolishing unemployment, poverty and prostitution in the great cities where conditions are the same as in Europe. Such ills are less troublesome than they are with us in the sparsely populated rural areas where, consequently, it is easier to find work or land. But it is just the maintenance and development of these favourable conditions which is the aim of all recent land and labour legislation. In the most advanced colonies, if not in all, the goal seems to be to guarantee to every citizen the right to work and the right to land, if necessary by limiting the number of immigrants.

Is the growth of material well-being matched by moral and mental progress? Yes, without any doubt: and if the way forward for the working class consists of putting itself on the same level as the bourgeoisie, the Australasian worker has advanced as far as it is possible to go. He has in effect joined the class of comfortably-off persons, of *respectable people*, and he carries himself with that assurance, so useful everywhere, but more influential in Anglo-Saxon countries than in the rest of the universe.

The Anglo-Saxon worker has become a *gentleman*, a monsieur. He lives in his own house, changes his clothes after work and conducts himself like a member of polite society. If he has to go to a meeting he will be clean, neatly dressed and freshly shaved. He will be conscious of his behaviour, will speak only in his turn and respect the authority of the chairman. If he is a member of parliament, deputed to attend a conference, he will maintain his position during the journey, booking a berth in a sleeping-car and staying at the most comfortable hotel, and his constituents will approve of the expenses necessarily incurred to maintain the dignity of their representative. More and more the exterior differences between worker and bourgeois are disappearing, except during working hours.

With the manners of the English middle class, the worker is adopting its opinions on all matters save *Factory Acts* and universal suffrage. He would not like parliament to be elected on a property qualification as in Great Britain, but he manifests utterly unequivocal attachment to the monarchy and the most profound reverence for the sovereign and the royal family. At trade union banquets, the royal toast precedes all others. In this connection, a little while before my visit, an English socialist was disgraced for having declared that he respected the Queen as a woman, though he was unable to discover in what way the workers were indebted to her.

Religion and its outward forms are, if possible, the objects of even greater respect. Many partisans of *labour policy* say grace with every meal, attend church on Sunday and rigorously observe it as a day of rest. They will not allow any questioning of Christian principles: they feel obliged to observe a puritanical reserve in their conversation, avoiding certain subjects altogether and replacing certain words with euphemisms.

Religious tracts are, along with fiction, the most popular of the exclusively English-language books available in Australasia. Literacy is universal and libraries plentiful. Newspapers are also popular: they are more numerous than in Europe, though just as substantial, and all are provided with foreign and diplomatic news by the same one or two London agencies. Local news is well covered and positively presented, the papers being full of practical hints for settlers, farmers and businessmen. There is always a gossip column and a sporting section.

Literature and reading in general are by no means the only pastime. Other forms of relaxation are those of the English bourgeoisie which, in turn, borrowed them from the aristocracy. Cricket, football and sports of every kind are the most popular. Cricket has become the national game and the enthusiasm aroused by an important match in a capital city has to be seen to be believed. Every year an Australian team goes to play the county teams in England: the results are cabled out every evening and enormous crowds wait for the latest score to be posted up outside the newspaper offices. I was in Melbourne and Sydney during the test match and the populace was almost as absorbed in its outcome as in that of the Federation referendum which was being decided at the same time.

Horse-racing is extremely popular. Twice I found myself in little New Zealand towns at race-time: I have scarcely ever seen such crowds, it was impossible to find a bed and all the trains, including specials put on for the occasion, were full. There were plenty of working people in these crowds. The Saturday or Wednesday afternoon holiday allowed them to travel, high wages put money in their pockets and they gamble freely.

On the other hand, many are shocked by certain amusements which to us seem more interesting than racing and other sports. Thus in one New Zealand trades hall I scandalised some unionists when I mentioned that socialist municipal councils in two French cities provide manual workers with free theatre tickets.

Many Australasian workers are advocates of temperance in the English sense: that is, they would like to prohibit the manufacture and sale of all alcoholic drinks. This is particularly true of New Zealand which produces no wine. Prohibition is less popular in vine-growing colonies.

Australasians are for the most part enthusiastic supporters of *Greater Britain*, of colonial expansion and even wars of conquest. I may report in this connection a small but characteristic fact. In the great industrial city of Melbourne, two statues stand in front of Parliament House: one is in honour of General Gordon and the other of the achievement of the eight-hour day. The first, I was told, symbolised particularly resentment of Gladstone, the peace minister, who hesitated too long about sending reinforcements to Khartoum. Gladstone, with his policy of *Peace, Retrenchment, Reform*, seems made for these democratic colonies with no standing armies, but he is not by any means popular in the Antipodes. On the contrary, imperialism is very popular. It is true that several labour organisations have protested recently against colonial expansion, or rather against one of its results: they complained that the financial supporters of conquest were at the same time the greatest exploiters of black labour and therefore enemies of the European worker. Even in this form, the motions of protest were passed only with difficulty and were by no means unanimous. At the time of my visit, pacifist sentiment was by no means as widespread or as rapidly increasing among Australasian workers as it is among European ones.

The ideal of international labour solidarity did not seem to be as strong as it is in Western Europe. Australasians are too remote from other peoples and too exclusively a part of the English world whence they draw all their books, news and information of every kind. That is why they have quite naturally set out to realise English middle-class ideals. They have had no other models before their eyes. Even those who fled England to seek a freer life on the goldfields or in the bush did not revolt at all against the society in which they had been unable to live; rather they re-established it in almost unaltered form in their new country.

It is then English society which exists in the Antipodes, but with two very important innovations: democratic institutions and labour legislation are coming into existence in the mother country, but they have been fully developed only in Australasia. The first give rise to independent attitudes and egalitarian feelings, the second ensures to the worker leisure time and resources for his mental and moral development. Throughout the universe, however, spiritual improvement progresses less rapidly than material well-being.

THE ANZAC LANDING

Ellis Ashmead-Bartlett

1915

It required splendid skill, organisation and leadership. The huge armada got underway from Mudros Bay, on the Island of Lemnos, without accident. The warships and transports were divided into five divisions. Never before has an attempt been made to land so large a force in the face of a well-prepared enemy.

At two o'clock on 24 April the flagship of the division conveying the Australians and New Zealanders passed down the long line of slowly moving transports, amid tremendous cheering, and was played out of the bay by the French warship.

At four o'clock the ship's company and the troops on board assembled to hear the admiral's proclamation to the combined force. This was followed by the last service before the battle, in which the chaplain uttered a prayer for victory, and besought the Divine blessing for the expedition, all the men standing with uncovered, bowed heads.

At dark all the lights were put out, and the troops rested for their ordeal at dawn. It was a beautiful calm night, with a bright half-moon. By one o'clock in the morning the ships had reached their rendezvous, five miles from the intended landing place. The soldiers were aroused, and served with their last hot meal before landing. The Australians, who were about to go into action for the first time under trying circumstances, were cheerful, quiet and confident, and there was no sign of nerves or excitement.

As the moon waned, the boats were swung out. The Australians received their last instructions, and these men, who only six months ago were living peaceful, civilian lives, began to disembark on a strange, unknown shore and in a strange land to attack an enemy of a different race.

Each boat, which was in the charge of a midshipman, was loaded with a great rapidity in absolute silence and without a hitch, and the covering force towed ashore by the ships' pinnaces. More of the Australian brigade were carried aboard torpedo-boat destroyers, which were to go close inshore as soon as the covering force had landed.

At three o'clock it was quite dark, and a start was made towards the shore with suppressed excitement. Would the enemy be surprised, or be on the alert?

At four o'clock three battleships, line abreast and four cables apart, arrived 2500 yards from the shore with their guns manned and their searchlights in readiness. Very slowly, the boats in tow, like twelve great snakes, moved towards the shore. Each edged towards each other in order to reach the beach four cables apart. The battleships moved in after them until the water shallowed. Every eye was fixed on the grim line of hills in front, menacing in the gloom, and the mysteries of which those in the boats were about to solve.

Not a sound was heard, not a light seen, and it appeared as if the enemy had been surprised. In our nervy state the stars were often mistaken for lights ashore.

The progress of the boats was slow, and dawn was rapidly breaking at 4.50 when the enemy showed alarm for a light which had flashed for ten minutes then disappeared. The boats appeared almost like one on the beach. Seven torpedo-boat destroyers then glided noiselessly towards the shore.

At 4.53 came a sharp burst of rifle fire from the beach. The sound relieved the prolonged suspense which had become almost intolerable. The rifle fire lasted a few minutes, and a faint British cheer came over the waters, telling us that the first position was won.

At three minutes past five the fire was intensified. By the sound of the reports we could tell that our men were in action. The firing lasted for twenty-three minutes, and then died down somewhat.

The boats returned, and a pinnace came alongside with two recumbent figures on deck, and a small midshipman, who cheerfully waving his hand said, 'With shot through the stomach.' The three had been wounded in the first burst of musketry. The boats had almost reached the beach when a party of Turks, who were entrenched on shore, opened a terrible fusillade from rifles and Maxim guns. Fortunately, most of the bullets went high.

The Australians rose to the occasion. They did not wait for orders, or for the boats to reach the beach, but sprang into the sea, formed a sort of rough line, and rushed at the enemy's trenches. Their magazines were not charged, so they just went in with the cold steel, and it was over in a minute for the Turks in the first trench had been either bayoneted or had run away, and the Maxim guns were captured.

Then the Australians found themselves facing an almost perpendicular cliff of loose sandstone covered with thick shrubbery. Somewhere halfway up, the enemy had a second trench strongly held, from which there poured a terrible fire on the troops below and on those pulling back to the torpedo-boat destroyers for a second landing party.

Here was a tough proposition to tackle in the darkness, but these Colonials are practical above all else, and went about it in a practical way. They stopped for a few minutes to pull themselves together, got rid of their packs and charged the magazines of their rifles. Then this race of athletes proceeded to scale the cliffs, without responding to the enemy's fire. They lost some men, but did not worry. In less than a quarter of an hour the Turks had been hurled out of their second position, all either bayoneted or fled.

As daylight came it was seen that a landing had been effected rather further north of Gaba Tepe than had originally been intended, and at a point where the cliffs rise very sheer. The error was a blessing in disguise, for there were no places down which the enemy could fire, and the broken ground afforded good cover once the Australians had passed the forty yards of the flat beach.

The country in the vicinity of the landing looked formidable and forbidding. To the sea it presents a steep front, broken into innumerable ridges, bluffs, valleys and sandspits, rising to a height of several hundred feet. The surface is bare, crumbly sandstone, covered with shrubbery about six feet in height. It is an ideal place for snipers, as the Australians and New Zealanders soon found to their cost. On the other hand, the Colonials proved themselves adept at this kind of warfare.

In the early part of the day heavy casualties were suffered in the boats conveying the troops from the torpedo-boat destroyers, tugs and transports. The enemy's sharpshooters, who were hidden everywhere, concentrated their fire on the boats. When close in, at least three boats broke away from their tow, and drifted down the coast without control, and were sniped at the whole way, and were steadily losing men.

The work of disembarking proceeded mechanically under point-blank fire, but the moment the boats touched the beach, the troops jumped ashore and doubled for cover. From hundreds of points this went on during the landing of troops, ammunition and stores.

When it was daylight the warships endeavoured to support the landing by heavy fire from their secondary armaments, but, not knowing the enemy's position, the support had more of a moral than a real effect.

When the sun had fully risen we could see that the Australians and New Zealanders had actually established themselves on the ridge, and were trying to work their way to the northward along it. The fighting was so confused, and occurred on such broken ground, that it was difficult to follow exactly what had happened on 25 April, but the task of the covering forces had been so splendidly carried out that the Turks allowed the disembarkation of the remainder to proceed uninterruptedly, except for the never-ceasing sniping. But then the Australians, whose blood was up, instead of entrenching, rushed to the northwards and to the eastwards searching for fresh enemies to bayonet. It was very difficult country in which to entrench, and they therefore preferred to advance.

The Turks only had a weak force actually holding the beach, and relied on the difficult ground and the snipers to delay the advance until reinforcement came. Some of the Australians and New Zealanders who pushed inland were counter-attacked and almost outflanked by oncoming reserves, and had to fall back after suffering heavy losses.

The Turks continued to counter-attack the whole of the afternoon, but the Colonials did not yield a foot on the main ridge. Reinforcements poured up from the beach, but the Turks enfiladed the beach with two field guns from Gaba Tepe. This shrapnel fire was incessant and deadly, and the warships vainly for some hours tried to silence it.

The majority of the heavy casualties received during the day were from shrapnel, which swept the beach and ridge where the Australians had established themselves. Later in the day the Turkish guns were silenced, or forced to withdraw, and a cruiser, moving close in shore, plastered Gaba Tepe with a hail of shell.

Towards dark the attacks became more vigorous. The enemy were supported by powerful artillery inland which the ships' guns were powerless to deal with. The pressure on the Australians became heavier, and their lines had been contracted.

General Birdwood and his staff landed in the afternoon, and devoted their energies to securing the position, so as to hold it firmly until the next morning when it was hoped to get the field guns into position.

Some idea of the difficulties in the way can be gathered when it is remembered that every round of ammunition and all the water and stores had to be landed on a narrow beach, and carried up pathless hills and valleys several hundred feet high to the firing line. The whole of the troops were concentrated upon a very small area, and were unable to reply, though exposed to a relentless and incessant shrapnel fire which swept every yard of ground. Fortunately, much of it was badly aimed or burst too high.

The most serious problem was the getting of the wounded to the shore, for all those unable to hobble had to be carried from the hills on stretchers; then their wounds were hastily dressed, and they were carried to the boats. The boat parties worked unceasingly the entire day and night.

The courage displayed by these wounded Australians and New Zealanders will never be forgotten. Hastily placed in trawlers, lighters or boats, they were towed to the ships, and, in spite of their sufferings, they cheered the ship from which they had set out in the morning.

In fact, I have never seen anything like these wounded Colonials in war before. Though many were shot to bits, and without hope of recovery, their cheers resounded throughout the night and you could see in the midst of a mass of suffering humanity arms waving in greeting to the crews of the warships. They were happy because they knew they had been tried for the first time, and had not been found wanting.

For fifteen mortal hours the Australians and New Zealanders occupied the heights under an incessant shell fire, and without the moral and material support of a single gun from the shore. They were subjected the whole time to violent counter-attacks from a brave enemy, skilfully led, and with snipers deliberately picking off every officer who endeavoured to give the command or to lead his men.

No finer feat has happened in this war than this sudden landing in the dark, and the storming of the heights, and, above all, the holding on whilst the reinforcements were landing. These raw colonial troops, in these desperate hours, proved worthy to fight side by side with the heroes of the battles of Mons, the Aisne, Ypres and Neuve-Chapelle.

Early on the morning of 26 April the Turks repeatedly tried to drive the Colonials from their position. The latter made local counter-attacks, and drove off the enemy with the bayonet, which the Turks will never face.

The Turks had been largely reinforced over night, and had prepared a big assault from the north-east, and the movement began at half-past nine. From the ships we could see the enemy creeping along the hill-tops, endeavouring to approach under cover. The enemy also brought up more guns, and plastered the position with shrapnel, while their rifle and machine-gun fire became unceasing.

Seven warships crept close in, with the *Queen Elizabeth* further out as a kind of chaperone. Each warship covered a section, and opened a terrific bombardment on the heights and valley beyond.

As the Turkish infantry advanced they were met by every kind of shell our warships carry from 'Lizzies' (eighteen-inch shrapnel) to twelve-pounders. Their shooting was excellent, yet, owing to the splendid cover they had, the Turks advanced gallantly, while their artillery not only shelled our positions, but tried to drive off the ships.

The scene at the heights of the engagement was sombre and magnificent. It was a unique day, and perfectly clear. We could see down the coast as far as Seddul Bahr. There the warships were blazing away, and on shore the rifle and machine-gun rattle was incessant. The hills before us were ablaze with shells, while masses of troops were on the beaches waiting their turn to take their places in the trenches.

The great attack lasted for two hours. We received messages that the fire of the ships was inflicting awful losses on the enemy, and then there came the flash of the bayonet in a sudden charge of the Colonials, before which the Turks broke and fled, amidst a perfect tornado of shells from the ships. They fell back sullen and checked, but they kept up an incessant fire throughout the day. The Colonials, however, were now dug in.

Some prisoners were captured, including officers, who said the Turks were becoming demoralised by the gunfire, and the Germans had had difficulty in getting them to attack.

Reprinted from the *Town and Country Journal* 12 May 1915

The Australians' splendid beginning

Mr Ashmead-Bartlett's graphic account of the glorious deeds of Australians in the Gallipoli Peninsula has sent a thrill of pride throughout the whole Commonwealth. It was a great achievement to land in the dark on a coast where the enemy's strength was unknown, and, having driven the Turks back, to hold the country firmly, while reinforcements followed. Every one of those who are taking part in the action against the Turks will appreciate the words of General Birdwood, who said he could not sufficiently praise their courage, endurance, and soldierly qualities. Though the list of casualties has brought grief to many homes, there is consolation in the thought that all our men at the front are fighting gloriously for the defence of the Empire. Many more thousands of young men are giving their services, and in course of time will join their comrades in the battle line. And in the coming years the memory of all those who fought in the greatest war the world has ever seen, and in the severest crisis through which the Empire has ever passed, will be handed down from generation to generation with pardonable pride.

THE GALLIPOLI LETTER

Keith Murdoch

1915

*Writing to Andrew Fisher, the Prime Minister
of Australia, on 23 September 1915.*

They cannot drive us from Anzac. Of that I am sure. Australasian ingenuity and endurance have made the place a fortress, and it is inhabited and guarded by determined and dauntless men. But Suvla is more precarious. I am not prepared to say that Suvla can be held during winter. There is a grave possibility of a German army appearing on the scene. In any case, the arrival of a number of heavy German guns might be quite sufficient to finish our expedition off. Big German howitzers could batter our trenches to pieces, and we would have no reply. And remember that several of our vital positions, such as Quinn's Post, are only a few small yards of land on the top of a cliff – mere footholds on the cliffs. Whether the Germans get their guns through or not, we must make up our minds that the Turkish activity will be much greater in winter than ever before. The enemy will be able to concentrate his artillery, when he knows that we are no longer threatening any of his positions. He will be able to drag across great guns from his forts, and give any position of ours a terrible mauling. He will have great reinforcements within reach, unless the published stories, and the tales of travellers, of his large new levies are quite untrue.

We have to face not only this menace, but the frightful weakening effect of sickness. Already the flies are spreading dysentery to an alarming extent, and the sick rate would astonish you. It cannot be less than 600 a day. We must be evacuating fully 1000 sick and wounded men every day. When the autumn rains come and unbury our dead, now lying under a light soil in our trenches, sickness must increase. Even now the stench in many of our trenches is sickening. Alas, the good human stuff that there lies buried, the brave hearts still, the sorrows in our hard-hit Australian households.

Supposing we lose only 30,000 during winter from sickness. That means that when spring comes we shall have about 60,000 men left. But they will not be an army. They will be a broken force, spent. A winter in Gallipoli will be a winter under severe strain, under shell fire, under the expectation of attack, and in the anguish which is inescapable on this shell-torn spot. The troops will in reality be on guard throughout the winter. They will stand to arms throughout long and bitter nights. Nothing can be expected from them when at last the normal fighting days come again. The new offensive must then be made with a huge army of new troops. Can we get them? Already the complaint in France is that we cannot fill the gaps, that after an advance our thinned ranks cannot be replenished.

But I am not a pessimist, and if there is really military necessity for this awful ordeal, then I am sure the Australian troops will face it. Indeed, anxious though they are to leave the dreary and sombre scene of their wreckage, the Australian divisions would strongly resent the confession of failure that a withdrawal would entail. They are dispirited, they have been through such warfare as no army has seen in any part of the world, but they are game to the end.

On the high political question of whether good is to be served by keeping the armies in Gallipoli, I can say little, for I am uninformed. Cabinet ministers here impress me with the fact that a failure in the Dardanelles would have most serious results in India. Persia is giving endless trouble, and there seems to be little doubt that India is ripe for trouble. Nor do I know whether the appalling outlay in money on the Dardanelles expedition, with its huge and costly line of communications, can be allowed to continue without endangering those financial resources on which we rely to so great an extent in the wearing down of Germany's strength. Nor do I know whether any offensive next year against Constantinople can succeed. On that point I can only say that the best military advice is that we can get through, that we would be through now if we had thrown in sufficient forces.

Whyte, whom we both admire as an able soldier and an inspiring Australian leader, assures me that another 150,000 men would do the job. I presume that would mean a landing on a large scale somewhere in Thrace, or north of Bulair. Certainly, any advance against the extraordinary strong trenches – narrow and deep, like all the Turks' wonderful trench work, and covered with heavy timber overhead protection against shell fire and bombs – from our present positions seems impracticable. You would have wept with Hughes and myself if you have gone with us over the ground where two of our finest Light Horse regiments were wiped out in ten minutes in a brave effort to advance a few yards to Dead Man's Ridge. We lost 500 men, squatter's sons and farmer's sons, on that terrible spot. Such is the cost of so much as looking out over the top of our trenches.

And now one word about the troops. No one who sees them at work in the trenches and on beaches and in saps can doubt that their morale is very severely shaken indeed. It is far worse at Suvla, although the men there are only two months from home, than anywhere else. The spirit at Suvla is simply deplorable. The men have no confidence in the staff, and to tell the truth they have little confidence in London. I shall always remember the stricken face of a young English lieutenant when I told him he must make up his mind for a winter campaign. We had had a month of physical and mental torture, and the prospect of a winter seemed more than he could bear. But his greatest dread was that the London authorities would not begin until too late to send winter provisions. All the new army is still clothed in tropical uniforms, and when I left, London was still sending out drafts in thin 'shorts'.

Everywhere one encountered the same fear that the armies would be left to their fate, and that the many shipments of materials, food and clothing required for winter would not be despatched until the weather made their landing impossible. This lack of confidence in the authorities arises principally from the fact that every man knows that the last operations were grossly bungled by the general staff, and that Hamilton has led a series of armies into a series of cul-de-sacs. You would hardly believe the evidence of your own eyes at Suvla. You would refuse to believe that these men were really British soldiers. So badly shaken are they by their miserable defeats and by their surroundings, so physically affected are they by the lack of water and the monotony of a salt beef and rice diet, that they show an atrophy of mind and body that is appalling.

I must confess that in our own trenches, where our men have been kept on guard for abnormally long periods, I saw the same terrible atrophy. You can understand how it arises. It is like the look of a tortured dumb animal. Men living in trenches with no movement except when they are digging, and with nothing to look at except a narrow strip of sky and the blank walls of their prisons, cannot remain cheerful or even thoughtful. Perhaps some efforts could have been made by the War Office to provide them with cinemas, or entertainments, but of course Gallipoli is at the end of a long and costly, not to say dangerous, line of communications. This fact is the only excuse for the excess of bully-beef feeding.

The physique of those at Suvla is not to be compared with that of the Australians. Nor is their intelligence. I fear also that the British physique is very much below that of the Turks. Indeed, it is quite obviously so. Our men have found it impossible to form a high opinion of the British K. men and territorials. They are merely a lot of childlike youths without strength to endure or brains to improve their conditions. I do not like to dictate this sentence, even for your eyes, but the fact is that after the first days at Suvla an order had to be issued to officers to shoot without mercy any soldiers who lagged behind or loitered in an advance. The Kitchener army showed perfection in manoeuvre training – they kept a good line on the Suvla plain – but that is not the kind of training required at the Dardanelles, and it is a question really of whether the training has been of the right kind. All this is very dismal, and they are of course only my impressions. But every Australian officer and man agrees with what I say.

At Anzac the morale is good. The men are thoroughly dispirited, except the new arrivals. They are weakened sadly by dysentery and illness. They have been overworked, through lack of reinforcements. And as an army of offence they are done. Not one step can be made with the first Australian division until it has been completely rested and refitted. But it is having only one month's rest at Mudros. The New Zealand and Australian Division (Godley's) also is reduced to only a few thousand men and has shot its bolt. But the men of Anzac would never retreat. And the one way to cheer them up is to pass the word that the Turks are going to attack, or that an assault by our forces is being planned. The great fighting spirit of the race is still burning in these men; but it does not burn amongst the toy soldiers of Suvla. You could imagine nothing finer than the spirit of some Australian boys – all of good parentage – who were stowed away on a troopship I was on in the Aegean, having deserted their posts in Alexandria out of mere shame of the thought of returning to Australia without having taken part in the fighting on Anzac's sacred soil. These fine country lads, magnificent men, knew that the desertion would cost them their stripes, but that and the loss of pay did not worry them. How wonderfully generous is the Australian soldier's view of life! These lads discussed quite fearlessly the prospects of their deaths, and their view was, 'It is no disgrace for an Australian to die beside good pals in Anzac, where his best pals are under the dust.'

But I could pour into your ears so much truth about the grandeur of our Australian army, and the wonderful affection of those fine young soldiers for each other and their homeland, that your Australianism would become a more powerful sentiment than before. It is stirring to see them, magnificent manhood, swinging their fine limbs as they walk about Anzac. They have the noble faces of men who have endured. Oh, if you could picture Anzac as I have seen it, you would find that to be an Australian is the greatest privilege the world has to offer.

WOMEN IN AUSTRALIA

Maybanke Anderson

1920

Women and immigration

During the early years of settlement in Australia, the colony, of necessity, contained very few women. The government made some attempt to alter the balance by importing women from 'the islands', as the many archipelagos in the Pacific were then called, but except for the wives of the few officials, there were for many years hardly any free white women in Australia. Assisted immigration began very early in the century, for labour was greatly needed, but the excess of males was not relieved. Women and children were troublesome passengers, the voyage was long, and contractors often refused to carry them. The difficulty seemed almost insuperable, but at length a woman found a remedy. No account of the work of women for Australia would be complete without mention of Caroline Chisholm.

She was the wife of Major Chisholm, who came to Sydney on leave from India in 1846, and she was, as one of her intimate friends has recorded, 'a woman whose chief characteristics were commonsense and energy'. She found in her new home ample need for both. The immigrants being brought to the little colony by the government were supposed to be single men, but many were so only because they had been obliged to leave wife and children behind. Besides these, there were, all over the settled portions of the colony, ticket-of-leave men, as they were called – men released because their crimes had been more the result of misfortune than vice, and because their behaviour under sentence had been consistently good. Many of these had also left wives and families 'somewhere' in the United Kingdom, whom they longed to see. It was a time of illiteracy, and Caroline Chisholm began her work by writing to authorities in villages, in workhouses, in asylums, to try to help the men who could not help themselves, and at the same time to bring to the struggling little settlement the population it so greatly needed.

Without rank, without influence, and with an income barely a decent competence, she began a correspondence to try to reach thousands of the poorest women and children 'somewhere at home'. She has left on record that in one year she wrote and received over three thousand letters. She was exceedingly methodical, arranging, docketing, dating and sending proofs of identity, and at length the Commissioner for Emigration in London, worn out by her pertinacity, began to discuss her cases, and the first two shiploads of wives and children came to Sydney.

In the course of her labours she felt obliged to expose the abominable conditions under which emigrants were sent out of English ports, and she did it so fearlessly that her life was threatened in Liverpool. But she knew no fear. She came back to Australia in charge of a great shipload of women, and visited the goldfields with them in order to see that the wives were safely placed in the homes of their husbands, and that the single were happily married at once. She addressed meetings of the roughest men to tell them of their social duties and their responsibilities as husbands and fathers. In many cases she united husband and wife after many years of separation.

The street in Islington where she lived was often crowded on the day of her meeting, and fine ladies, who came in carriages, and gentlemen in broadcloth waited while she talked to scavengers and cooks. Robert Lowe wrote an ode to her, *Punch* published a poem about her, in which he said – 'Instead of making here and there a convert of a Turk / She made the idle multitude turn fruitfully to work.'

Domestic and industrial

Australia has always had a domestic problem. In the beginning, 'the assigned servant', often a martyr to harsh custom rather than a criminal, was naturally distrusted, and she often repaid suspicion with ill deeds. She passed, and now lives only in the tales of our great-grandmothers, but her influence remains in our domestic architecture. When there was no choice but to take servants from among well-behaved criminals, the kitchens and servants' quarters were built far from the main dwelling. In all old Australian houses, now fast disappearing, this is a noticeable feature. The practice thus begun remains to this day; perhaps also because it is sanitary, and suitable for a climate where there is very little unpleasant weather.

With increase of population and harder times, the Australian girl began to 'go to service'. There is no better domestic worker anywhere. She can do anything, unlike the English girl, who always wants her work to be defined, and she will do it with a smile, if you treat her well and refrain from displaying your superiority. But she must be allowed her freedom, and she must be well paid, and have ample consideration. The old retainer, who stayed on for years, because she loved the family, never existed, except in isolated instances, in Australia.

Despite high wages, this service is not popular, and work in a private house is even less so. Many women who were brought up in homes where two or more servants were kept thirty or more years ago, now live in a small house, and do their own work, because they find it almost impossible to get help. There are many reasons for the widespread dislike of domestic service, and in a community where there is equal opportunity for all, or nearly so, they must carry more weight than in older lands, where there is a tradition of subservience. Despite continual and strong protest, the Australian girl still believes that if she does housework for wages, she must lose social status, and she prefers factory work, though with it she gets no board and no lodging, and is therefore not so well paid.

Factory work is well paid in all the states, and highest in NSW, though, in the opinion of many able to judge, it is not yet sufficiently remunerated even here. Among factory workers, the tailoress stands highest socially, and receives the highest pay. In New South Wales the last award gives the coat maker over twenty-one years of age 38/- per week. The award is, of course, the minimum. Many expert women who undertake order work receive from £2 to £3 per week. Other workers are paid less, but none are low. The last award gives the dressmaker's assistant, who may be a schoolgirl, unable, despite excellent public school teaching, to use a needle properly, 15/- per week. This award, which will probably have the effect of putting many little dressmakers out of business, is condemned even by those who are in favour of high wages, and may lead to a demand that women should be allowed to sit on boards which consider the awards in women's trades.

Higher education and professions

Australian women were late in stepping into the ranks of advance. Communication with the homeland was slow and expensive in mid-Victorian days, and in 1848, when in London, Queen's College was opened for the better instruction of teachers in girls' schools. Australian women were content to accept the little that was offered to them as education. They knew of nothing better. In wide spaces, under clear skies, far from the turmoil of cities, they bore large families, and developed in themselves and their children that freedom from convention, that practical deftness and resource which still distinguishes the Australian – a habit and a manner which make us different from those who spend their childhood within the encompassing narrowness of walls.

The English woman who 'had seen better days', and the poor gentleman whose education had taught him everything except how to earn a living, were much in demand in those days. As governess and tutor, they carried an example of delicacy and refinement into country homes which otherwise might have known only roughness, and their influence remains to this day in many a country town.

The first step towards the higher education of women was actually taken by those far-seeing men who, in 1851, founded the University of Sydney and declared in the Act of Incorporation that its education was to be offered to all classes of Her Majesty's subjects 'without any distinction whatsoever'. The general attitude towards the subject of the education of the woman of that time may be estimated by the fact that in the opinion of the Senate of the university this comprehensive declaration did not apply to women, and that no woman attempted to question the opinion.

When classes at Sydney University were declared open to women, they did not enter in large numbers. Every teacher in the public schools of the colony had then to begin as a pupil teacher; a degree was, therefore, impossible for them, and private schools did not desire teachers so qualified. All this was changed many years ago, and hundreds of women now attend classes and take degrees. This year – 1919 – there are 699 women students at the Sydney University.

In each of the states, university women are at work as inspectors, heads of scientific experimental work, lecturers, teachers and coaches. A few are lawyers, and three have been appointed judges' associates; but the woman lawyer cannot generally command an assured position in Australia, and despite occasional assertions and demands, it cannot be said that the majority of women desire at present to employ a lawyer of their own sex.

The case for Medicine is very different. Medical women practise in each of the capitals, and many of them enjoy a position equal with their brothers. Hospital arrangements in Melbourne and Adelaide have encouraged medical women. In Sydney no woman could, until very lately, hope to obtain an appointment in a general hospital, though in the opinion of our most experienced nurses provision should be made, so that a woman patient might be attended by one of her own sex if she so preferred. The war, in taking from us many of our best men, is helping to modify prejudice; but it dies hard.

Woman suffrage in Australia

What has been the result of the woman's vote? There are men who would weigh thought in ounces and count inspiration by pennies, as though life were a child's state. They say that we have simply doubled the number of voters and done nothing. And there are women who look on the vote as if it were a magic wand, which in their hands might solve every problem and right every wrong. They think that we do not value our possession and do not know how to use it. It is a possession they covet. Both are mistaken.

The possession of the vote by Australian women has done exactly what those who sanely demanded it expected it to do. When it gave us the right to express our opinions at the ballot box, it gave that opinion an importance it never had before, and we therefore offer it more freely, and with more consideration and more effect, than in a land where women are by law silent. The result may be seen in laws relating to the drink traffic, in those relating to women and children, and in the altered status of the woman, an alteration hard to define, but everywhere perceptible. To the woman the vote has been an education. It is enlarging her outlook, and it tempers her judgement. To be somebody where before you were nobody, increases responsibility and develops character. Women sit on boards and

31

committees, no longer as a concession, but equal with men, and while they learn at first in the wisdom of silence – the business of dealing with intricate affairs, men learn from their instinctive knowledge of humanity, and from their domestic habit of looking for causes, rather than at effects, much which formerly they missed. The Australian woman who takes part in public affairs is more sure of her position as an individual and less conscious of sex than her unenfranchised sisters. This result of the vote is visible everywhere to those who choose to observe.

There were enthusiasts who thought and hoped that when we were enfranchised a woman's party would be formed, which would vote as one for great reforms. A similar hope probably inspires unenfranchised women all over the world. They suppose that all women will think alike in politics, although they know from easy experience that they differ widely on every other subject, and they ignore the fact that in the practical conduct of political life under party government, such a course would be almost impossible. In Sydney a few women, led by Miss Rose Scott, who, as secretary of the Suffrage League during the whole term of its existence, had done an immense work, did form an association to obtain reform and to ignore party differences. For some time they worked with energy, and undoubtedly succeeded in influencing politicians and in introducing reforms in matters relating to women and children. But the great majority of women who were interested in politics divided, and the more keenly they were interested the more quickly they divided and joined the party whose theories and methods they favoured. Women's Labour Leagues and Women's Liberal Leagues were quickly formed, and women generally proved themselves capable of being partisans quite as unreasoning as their husbands and brothers.

In every state of the Commonwealth there are a few active political women who bestir themselves occasionally, and before an election call political meetings for women alone. But many – probably the larger portion of women voters – are content to consider politics by their own firesides and to vote as conscience, or the influence of a friend, may direct. In this, as in other respects, they resemble their husbands and fathers.

None of the dire results foretold by gloomy prophets have been fulfilled since Australian women began to vote. Domestic quarrelling has not increased. There have been no disgraceful scenes at the polling booths. Election day is more than ever like a Sunday – to which effect the closing of all public-houses contributes, perhaps, more than the women. Our homes are no more neglected than before, perhaps because, in small towns and in suburbs, many women of leisure go to visit the busier housewives and mind the baby while its mother votes. The woman finds no difficulty in recording her vote, and probably makes no more mistakes than her fellow man, and despite the foreboding most horrible of all, we are still womanly women.

Visitors from other countries always notice, and some times bitterly resent the fact, that our women workers are less deferential in their manner than those of older countries. These strangers cling to the belief that there must be, perforce, an inferior class, and they like to feel that they themselves are superior. It is sometimes a pleasant feeling. The independence of our workers is the result of many causes, and the vote must be accorded its share. It has imperceptibly acted as a social leveller, and has helped to increase the pay of female labour. High wages encourage independence. Because of these effects, many young Australian women, born in homes which in England or Scotland would feel disgraced by their labour, here work as a matter of course, and think labour honourable. The daughter of a professional man may be a typiste in an office where the daughter of the grocer in the little back street is a forewoman. In the office each will, nay, must, esteem the other according to her merit, and outside will not disdain her acquaintance. There will be bounds beyond which neither will pass, but they will not be as rigid as the bounds in older countries. It is not then surprising that the grocer's daughter should sometimes assume equality. She judges from the standpoint of labour and salary; she knows that it is quite possible that she may marry a rich man, perhaps become Lady Mayoress some day, if the Fates are kind, and, like the housemaid who is paid as highly as the accomplished teacher, she behaves as if she were an equal.

They are young, these girls, like their country. They have never felt the influence of an hereditary aristocracy, and though they might be willing to 'behave lowly and reverently to all their betters', they are as yet hardly able to recognise their betters when they see them.

These differences in conduct, like the alterations in our laws, may not be entirely the result of our enfranchisement. They may be in part the result of the many causes which led up to it, and to other reforms. But they are now characteristic of young Australian womanhood, and to those who can look back they seem to have had their beginning about the same time as the demand for the vote.

The North

One part of our great island – the North – has in its scanty population a very small proportion of women. Two, who both lived there for a time, have written charming books about it, but neither Mrs Gunn, who describes her life on a station in the Never Never, or Miss Masson, who lived at Darwin for a year, succeeds in making our tropical North attractive as place of residence. The climate may be endured by men, who live an outdoor life, but women, tied to domestic duties, suffer much. They cannot, as in other tropical countries, have abundant help. The blackfellow, with his lubra, inefficient at best, and often when most needed, filled with an irresistible longing for 'the bush', is dying out. The Chinaman, an excellent servant generally, is going home, for Australia insists on being 'white'. Few women of any white race will stay there to do housework, while high wages offer in a temperate climate, and the housekeeper's burden becomes heavy.

An American expert says of life in the Northern Territory – 'The white man individually may exist; racially, he cannot persist.' To this critics reply 'Not proven,' but the idea remains, and since few mothers at present stay there for long, proof for one side or the other is difficult. A few women go north as nurses for the Australian Inland Mission, a few officials try to make homes there, and a settler or two, with their wives, may be found in favoured spots, but on the whole we tacitly agree that for the present, while wide spaces in a cooler climate are waiting for settlers, women need not attempt to conquer the heat of North Australia. Some time ago a commissioner, sent by the Welsh settlers in Patagonia, made investigations, and, after a visit, reported favourably on the prospects of Patagonians who might decide to make a change from the cold South to the warm North. But we have had no more visitors from there, and we conclude that the commissioner's clients were not so easily convinced as he was.

Class

'Society', as it is in Europe, does not exist in Australia. With no queen, no court, no hereditary nobility, we know nothing of aristocracy, except what we glean from the few admirable isolated specimens who come to us as governors. Nor have we, as in the United States, an exclusive 'Four

Hundred', or an association of self-satisfied first families. Here are no railway magnates, no multimillionaires, and we display no grandiose mansions, and are dazzled by no 'diamond horse shoes'. There are among us, it is true, a few knights whose wives assume the title of lady, but as they have been, in many instances, lifted to the little pinnacle by the frothy swirl of party politics, the title is not very highly esteemed. The woman who was estimable as the wife of a tradesman, remains estimable, though she call herself 'Lady'; but the title does not increase our regard for the vain and self-seeking. Society there is, in every city and country town – society of a sort, where like attracts like, and where the wealthy and those who live in expensive suburbs meet their fellows, and perchance consider themselves somewhat above the common herd. But even there the one-time toiler may dwell in affluence, and his wife, in early days, a cook or dressmaker, may learn the manners of the better nurtured, and hold her own among them.

Education in our public schools, where the child of the rich man shares the free education which is given equally to all, tends to lessen differences of social position, and we may hope to see some day an Australia in whose clear sunshine the only aristocracy will be one of education and high worth.

KANGAROO

D.H. Lawrence

1923

Somers sighed and shivered and went down to the house. It was chilly. Why had he come? Why, oh, why? What was he looking for? Reflecting for a moment, he imagined he knew what he had come for. But he wished he had not come to Australia, for all that.

He was a man with an income of four hundred a year, a writer of poems and essays. In Europe, he had made up his mind that everything was done for, played out, finished, and he must go to a new country. The newest country: young Australia! Now he had tried Western Australia, and had looked at Adelaide and Melbourne. And the vast, uninhabited land frightened him. It seemed so hoary and lost, so unapproachable. The sky was pure, crystal pure and blue, of a lovely pale blue colour: the air was wonderful, new and unbreathed: and there were great distances. But the bush, the grey, charred bush. It scared him. As a poet, he felt himself entitled to all kinds of emotions and sensations which an ordinary man would have repudiated. Therefore he let himself feel all sorts of things about the bush. It was so phantom-like, so ghostly, with its tall pale trees and many dead trees, like corpses, partly charred by bush fires: and then the foliage so dark, like grey-green iron. And then it was so deathly still. Even the few birds seem to be swamped in silence. Waiting, waiting – the bush seemed to be hoarily waiting. And he could not penetrate into its secret. He couldn't get at it. Nobody could get at it. What was it waiting for?

And then one night at the time of the full moon he walked alone into the bush. A huge electric moon, huge, and the tree-trunks like naked pale Aborigines among the dark-soaked foliage, in the moon-light. And not a sign of life – not a vestige.

Yet something. Something big and aware and hidden! He walked on, had walked a mile or so into the bush, and had just come to a clump of tall, nude, dead trees, shining almost phosphorescent with the moon, when the terror of the bush overcame him. He had looked so long at the vivid moon, without thinking. And now, there was something among the trees, and his hair began to stir with terror on his head. There was a presence. He looked at the weird, white, dead trees, and into the hollow distances of the bush. Nothing! Nothing at all. He turned to go home. And then immediately the hair on his scalp stirred and went icy cold with terror. What of? He knew quite well it was nothing. He knew quite well. But with his spine cold like ice, and the roots of his hair seeming to freeze, he walked on home, walking firmly and without haste. For he told himself he refused to be afraid, though he admitted the icy sensation of terror. But then to experience terror is not the same thing as to admit fear into the conscious soul. Therefore he refused to be afraid.

But the horrid thing in the bush! He laboured as to what it would be. It must be the spirit of the place. Something fully evoked tonight, per-haps provoked, by that unnatural West Australian moon. Provoked by the moon, the roused spirit of the bush. He felt it was watching, and waiting. Following with certainty, just behind his back. It might have reached a long black arm and gripped him. But no, it wanted to wait. It was not tired of watching its victim. An alien people – a victim. It was biding its time with a terrible ageless watchfulness, waiting for a far-off end, watching the myriad intruding white men.

This was how Richard Lovatt Somers figured it out to himself, when he got back into safety in the scattered township in the clearing on the hill-crest, and could see far off the fume of Perth and Fremantle on the seashore, and the tiny sparking of a farther-off lighthouse on an island. A marvellous night, raving the moonlight – and somebody burning off the bush in a ring of sultry red fire under the moon in the distance, a slow ring of creeping red fire, like some ring of fireflies, upon the far-off darkness of the land's body, under the white blaze of the moon above.

It was always a question, whether there is any sense in taking notice of a poet's fine feelings. The poet himself has misgivings about them. Yet a man ought to feel something, at night under such a moon.

Richard S. had never quite got over that glimpse of terror in the West Australian bush. Pure foolishness, of course, but there's no telling where a foolishness may nip you. And now that night had settled over Sydney, and the town and the harbour were sparkling unevenly below, with reddish-seeming sparkles, whilst overheard the marvellous Southern Milky Way was tilting uncomfortably to the South, instead of crossing the zenith; the vast myriads of swarming stars that cluster all along the Milky Way, in the Southern sky, and the Milky Way itself leaning heavily to the south, so that you feel all on one side if you look at it; the Southern sky at night, with that swarming Milky Way all bushy with stars, and yet with black gaps, holes in the white star-road, while misty blotches of star-mist float detached, like cloud-vapours, in the side darkness, away from the road; the wonderful Southern night-sky, that makes a man feel so lonely, alien: with Orion standing on his head in the west, and his sword-belt upside down, and his dog-star prancing in mid-heaven, high above him; and with the Southern Cross insignificantly mixed in with the other stars, democratically inconspicuous; well then now that night had settled down over Sydney, and all this was happening overhead, for R.L. Somers and a few other people, our poet once more felt scared and anxious. Things seemed so different. Perhaps everything *was* different from all he had known. Perhaps if St Paul and Hildebrand and Darwin had lived south of the equator, we might have known the world all different, quite different. But it is useless 'iffing'. Sufficient that Somers went indoors into his little bungalow, and found his wife setting the table for supper, with cold meat and salad.

'The only thing that's really cheap,' said Harriett, 'is meat. That huge piece cost two shillings. There's nothing to do but to become savage and carnivorous – if you can.'

'The kangaroo and the dingo are the largest fauna in Australia,' said Somers. 'And the dingo is probably introduced.'

'But it's very good meat,' said Harriett.

'I know that,' said he.

✳

The Somerses now had neighbours: somewhat to the chagrin of Richard Lovatt. He had come to this new country, the youngest country on the globe, to start a new life and flutter with a new hope. And he started with a rabid desire not to see anything and not to speak one single word to any single body – except Harriett, whom he snapped at hard enough. To be sure, the mornings sometimes won him over. They were so blue and pure: the blue harbour like a lake among the land, so pale blue and heavenly, with its hidden and half-hidden lobes intruding among the low, dark-brown cliffs, and among the dark-looking tree-covered shores, and up to the bright red suburbs. But the land, the ever-dark bush that was allowed to come to the shores of the harbour! It was strange that, with the finest of new air dimming to a lovely pale blue in the distance, and with the loveliest stretches of pale blue water, the tree-covered land should be so gloomy and lightless. It is the sun-refusing leaves of the gum-trees, that are like dark, hardened flakes of rubber.

He was not happy, there was no pretending he was. He longed for Europe with hungry longing: Florence, with Giotto's pale tower: or the Pincio at Rome: or the words in Berkshire, heavens! the English spring with primroses under the bare hazel bushes, and thatched cottages among plum blossom. He felt he would have given anything on earth to be in England. It was May – end of May – almost bluebell time, and the green leaves coming out on the hedges. Or the tall corn under the olives in Sicily. Or London Bridge, with all the traffic on the river. Or Bavaria with gentian and yellow globe flowers, and the Alps still icy. Oh, God, to be in Europe, lovely, lovely Europe that he had hated so thoroughly and abused so vehemently, saying it was moribund and stale and finished. The fool was himself. He had got out of temper and so had called Europe moribund: assuming that he himself, of course, was not moribund, but sprightly and chirpy and too vital, as the Americans would say, for Europe. Well, if a man wants to make a fool of himself it is as well to let him.

Somers wandered disconsolate through the streets of Sydney, forced to admit that there were fine streets, like Birmingham, for example, that the parks and the Botanical Gardens were handsome and well-kept, that the harbour with all the two-decker brown ferryboats sliding continuously from the Circular Quay was an extraordinary place. But, oh, what did he care about it all! In Martin Place he longed for Westminster, in Sussex Street he almost wept for Covent Garden and St Martin's Lane, at the Circular Quay he pined for London Bridge. It was all London without being London. Without any of the lovely old glamour that invests London. This London of the Southern Hemisphere was all, as it were, made in five minutes, a substitute for the real thing. Just a substitute – as margarine is a substitute for butter. And he went home to his little bungalow bitterer than ever, pining for England.

But if he hated the town so much, why did he stay? Oh, he had a fanciful notion that if he was really to get to know anything at all about a country, he must live there for a time in the principal city. So he had condemned himself to three months at least. He told himself to comfort himself, that at the end of three months he would take the steamer across the Pacific, homewards, towards Europe. He felt a long navel string fastening him to Europe, and he wanted to go back, to go home. He would stay for three months. Three months' penalty for having forsworn Europe. Three months in which to get used to this Land of the Southern Cross. Cross indeed! A new crucifixion. And then away, homewards!

The only time he felt at all happy was when he had reassured himself that by August, by August he would be taking his luggage on to a steamer. That soothed him.

He understood now that the Romans had preferred death to exile. He could sympathise now with Ovid on the Danube, hungering for Rome and blind to the land around him, blind to the savages. So Somers felt blind to Australia, and blind to the uncouth Australians. To him they were barbarians. The most loutish Neapolitan loafer was nearer to him in pulse than these British Australians with their aggressive familiarity. He surveyed them from an immense distance, with a kind of horror.

Of course he was bound to admit that they ran their city very well, as far as he could see. Everything was very easy, and there was no fuss. Amazing how little fuss and bother there was – on the whole. Nobody seemed to bother, there seemed to be no policemen and no authority, the whole thing went by itself, loose and easy, without any bossing. No real authority – no superior classes – hardly even any boss. And everything rolling along as easily as a full river, to all appearances.

That's where it was. Like a full river of life, made up of drops of water all alike. Europe is really established upon the aristocratic principle. Remove the sense of class distinction, of higher and lower, and you have anarchy in Europe. Only nihilists aim at the removal of all class distinction, in Europe.

But in Australia, it seemed to Somers, the distinction was already gone. There was really no class distinction. There was a difference of money and of 'smartness'. But nobody felt *better* than anybody else, or higher; only better-off. And there is all the difference in the world between feeling *better* than your fellow-man, and merely feeling *better-off*.

Now Somers was English by book and education, and though he had no antecedents whatsoever, yet he felt himself to be one of the *responsible* members of society, as contrasted with the innumerable *irresponsible* members. In old, cultured, ethical England this distinction is radical, between the responsible members of society, and the irresponsible. It is even a categorical distinction. It is a caste distinction, a distinction in the very being. It is the distinction between the proletariat and the ruling classes.

But in Australia nobody is supposed to rule, and nobody does rule, so the distinction falls to the ground. The proletariat appoints men to administer the law, not to rule. These ministers are not really responsible, any more than the housemaid is responsible. The proletariat is all the time responsible, the only source of authority. The will of the people. The ministers are merest instruments.

Somers for the first time felt himself immersed in real democracy – in spite of all disparity in wealth. The instinct of the place was absolutely and flatly democratic, *à terre* democratic. Demos was here his own master, undisputed, and therefore quite calm about it. No need to get the wind up at all over it; it was a granted condition of Australia, that Demos was his own master.

And this was what Richard Lovatt Somers could not stand. You may be the most liberal liberal Englishman, and yet you cannot fail to see the categorical difference between the responsible and the irresponsible classes. You cannot fail to admit the necessity for *rule*. Either you admit yourself an anarchist, or you admit the necessity for *rule* – in England. The working classes in England feel just the same about it as do the upper classes. Any working man who sincerely feels himself a responsible member of society feels it his duty to exercise authority in some way or other. And the irresponsible workingman likes to feel there is a strong boss at the head, if only so that he can grumble at him satisfactorily. Europe is established on the instinct of authority: 'thou shalt'. – The only alternative is anarchy.

Somers was a true Englishman, with an Englishman's hatred of anarchy, and an Englishman's instinct for authority. So he felt himself at a discount in Australia. In Australia authority was a dead letter. There was no giving of orders here; or, if orders were given, they would not be received as such. A man in one position might make a suggestion to a man in another position, and this latter might or might not accept the suggestion, according to his disposition. Australia was not yet in a state of anarchy. England had as yet at least nominal authority. But let the authority be removed, and then – ! For it is notorious, when it comes to constitutions, how much there is in a name.

Was all that stood between Australia and anarchy just a name? – the name of England, Britain, Empire, Viceroy, or Governor General, or Governor? The shadow of the old sceptre, the mere sounding of a name? Was it just the hollow word 'Authority', sounding across seven thousand miles of sea, that kept Australia from Anarchy? Australia – Authority – Anarchy: a multiplication of the alpha.

So Richard Lovatt cogitated as he roamed about uneasily. Not that he knew all about it. Nobody knows all about it. And those that fancy they know *almost* all about it are usually most wrong. A man must have *some* ideas about the thing he's up against, otherwise he's a simple wash-out.

But Richard *was* wrong. Given a good temper and a genuinely tolerant nature – both of which the Australians seem to have in a high degree – you can get on for quite a long time, without 'rule'. For quite a long time the thing just goes by itself.

Is it merely running down, however, like a machine running on but gradually running down?

Ah, questions!

THE AUSTRALIAN DEMOCRACY

W.K. Hancock

1930

The Australian soldier has frequently been admired for his personal independence and individual initiative. The Australian voter has been continually blamed for his lack of initiative and for his excessive dependence upon the State. Unless we are to assume that the fighters have not voted and the voters have not fought, we must seek some explanation of these contradictory reputations.

We shall exaggerate the importance of the inquiry if we imagine that the Australians have made very original discoveries in the science and art of government. The last few generations have witnessed in many countries noteworthy extensions of the functions of the State; and the differences in Australian practice are differences, not of principle, but of degree. They are the product, not of theory, but of circumstances. New countries, observed Wakefield, demand 'ample government'. Consider the predicament of the pioneers: they are separated from each other by unheard-of distances which, somehow or other, must be bridged; they are strangers to each other, and have broken every familiar association by their voyage across the sea; no one of them is sufficient to himself, yet each is so isolated from his fellows and so engrossed in his struggles that effective local co-operation is impossible; or, if co-operation is achieved in some favoured locality, there still remain the great gaps which separate this happy community from its neighbours. Collective action is indispensable if an obstinate environment is to be mastered. But how can this scattered and shifting aggregate of uprooted units act collectively except through the State? They look to the Government to help them because they have nowhere else to look.

It may be objected that these general arguments are refuted by the experience of the United States of America; but the geographical conditions of the two countries are so different that any comparisons between them must be misleading. 'Uncle Sam is rich enough to give us all a farm,' sang the Americans, and their song calls up a picture of family holdings and the comfort of neighbourliness. From the time when the subsistence farmers of New England established themselves around their townships and worked so steadily outwards that the spreading fields of one community were checked by the spreading fields of another, until the time when trans-continental railways opened western lands to the small homesteader, America (although it may seem absurd to say so) has not been seriously troubled by the problem of distance. At least, not as Australians understand that problem. At the present time there is no doctor between Hawker and Port Darwin, a distance of 1300 miles, and until the aeroplane came it might have taken an injured man a month of agonised travelling to reach an operating theatre. The greater part of Australia can only be opened for settlement (which, according to European standards, must be sparse settlement) by heavy initial expenditure. Who is to undertake it? About the middle of the nineteenth century there were some experiments in railway construction by private companies, but the conditions of Australia's economic geography made the land-grant railway, save in exceptional cases, an impossibility. English investors themselves insisted upon having the guarantee of the State. So Government remains responsible for communications. But, in Australia, drought is an enemy no less formidable than distance. Government interests itself in the storage and circulation of water. Perhaps it should have been content with this. But growing bureaucracies do not readily submit themselves to self-denying ordinances, and debtors, in their anxiety to push the income from their assets up to the level of the interest on their liabilities, sometimes incur new debts. Government, therefore, begins to place settlers on the lands which it has 'developed'. And the settlers, remembering that the Government has put them there, not infrequently imagine that it has in some way or other accepted an obligation to keep them there.

This sketch ignores or confuses the differences between pastoral and agricultural occupation of the land, and does no more than suggest the circumstances and the spirit of Government activity in pioneering. What of that majority of Australians who are not pioneers, who have tried and failed, or who have never tried? The dominant theme in Australian political history is the lament of an unsatisfied land-hunger. This theme swells angrily in the decades which follow the gold rushes, when men who have been their own masters on the diggings fight for a farmer's independence and are driven back – partly by vested interests and bad laws, chiefly by forces of economics and geography, which have created the interests and which cannot be altered by the laws. Yet the defeated landless ones are not altogether inconsolable. They have, at any rate, possessed themselves of the State. Within ten years of the discovery of gold, practically the whole political programme of the Chartists is realised in the Australian colonies. What class, what tradition is there in Australia which can hold the State against the assault of numbers? Numbers *are* the State, and thankfully accept those traditions of its omni-competence which were built up by the military autocrats of early days. Circumstances would not in any case permit a complete break with these traditions; to attempt such a break is the last thing which the landless majority desires. For if, as a judge of the Commonwealth Arbitration Court once suggested, the machinery of the State exists for the sake of the 'divine average', then the majority, controlling this machinery, becomes, after all, a master class.

Thus Australian democracy has come to look upon the State as a vast public utility, whose duty it is to provide the greatest happiness for the greatest number. The results of this attitude have been defined as *le socialisme sans doctrines*. Its origins, however, are individualistic, deriving from the levelling tendency of migrations which have destroyed old ranks and relationships and scattered over wide lands a confused aggregate of individuals bound together by nothing save their powerful collectivity. Each of these individuals is a citizen, a fragment of the sovereign people; each of them is a subject who claims his rights – the right to work, the right to fair and reasonable conditions of living, the right to be happy – from the State and through the State. Some day, when Australian universities have assembled the dismal paraphernalia of sociological research, an energetic young graduate will produce a learned thesis in three volumes (with appendices) tracing the theory of rights from the first settlers, whose 'democratical tendencies' were so obnoxious to autocratic Governors, through England's emigrant

Chartists and Ireland's emigrant Liberators, to the fathers of the Australian Labour movement, who showed how the right of association might be used to capture the State and transform all rights into powers. This will be one of those interesting yet irritating inquiries to which the answer is already known before the search for it has begun. The whole of Australian history lies within the period which succeeded the French Revolution and the Industrial Revolution, a period filled with a deafening clamour for rights and a few shrill protests about duties. In Australia the assertion of rights has been less a matter of theory than of instinct; nor has this instinct been peculiar to any one class.

To the Australian, the State means collective power at the service of individualist 'rights'. Therefore, he sees no opposition between his individualism and his reliance upon Government. Whether or not the two tendencies will exist together so comfortably when the frontiers are finally drawn, when occupation has slackened into settlement and the Australian begins to feel himself cramped for elbow-room, is another question. At the time when Australian democracy was elaborating its characteristic social policies, Australians still thought of their country as 'an unlimited out-of-doors', as 'the land of lots o' time'. They wished to justify their peculiar freedom by demonstrating to the world that individual wretchedness was not a necessary feature of human society, that justice, which they understood as the recognition and satisfaction of the rightful claims of every individual, might be made the cornerstone of the State. Men more easily take in vain the name of justice than the name of God; yet the Australians who a generation ago appealed so frequently to justice did so in all sincerity. Interwoven with the egotistical assertion of rights was a disinterested enthusiasm, the aspiration of young men and poets who preached as 'The Golden Rule of Young Democracy' –

That culture, joy, and goodliness
Be th' equal right of all;
That Greed no more shall those oppress
Who by the wayside fall.

Thus the angers of class struggle were softened by the mediation of those 'tolerants' and enthusiasts of the middle classes who voted for Labor or the Deakin Liberals, and applauded when the State intervened to protect the weak, to annex industry as 'a new province for law and order', to recognise rights. Intolerance of oppression and sympathy with the underdog are among the most attractive features of the Australian character. And yet, is it not possible to exaggerate even these virtues? A dull fellow cannot really assert a right to culture; nor can the State satisfy a grumpy fellow's claim to joy. The passion for equal justice can so easily sour into a grudge against those who enjoy extraordinary gifts, and the aspiration for fraternity can so easily express itself by pulling down those lonely persons who are unable to fraternise with the crowd. The ideal of 'mateship', which appeals very strongly to the ordinary good-hearted Australian, springs, not only from his eagerness to exalt the humble and meek, but also from his zeal to put down the mighty from their seat. If ever the ship of Australian democracy enters the calm waters of its millennium, it will carry a fraternal but rather drab company of one-class passengers –

> *But the curse of class distinctions from our shoulders shall be hurled*
> *An' the sense of Human Kinship revolutionise the world;*
> *There'll be higher education for the toilin', starvin' clown,*
> *An' the rich an' educated shall be educated down;*
> *Then we all will meet amidships on this stout old earthly craft;*
> *We'll be brothers, fore-'n'-aft!*
> *Yes, an' sisters, fore-'n'aft!*
> *When the people work together, and there ain't no fore-'n'aft.*

This, then, is the prevailing ideology of Australian democracy – the sentiment of justice, the claim of right, the conception of equality, and the appeal to Government as the instrument of self-realisation. The ideology is simple; but the instrument is not. The fact that the Australians live in a federation complicated their politics, which in idea are extremely straightforward and unsophisticated. Australia frequently impresses the outside observer as being the most uniformly monotonous of continents, and the Australians impress him as being the most monotonously uniform of peoples. There may be no alligators in the Derwent and no platypuses in the Roper, no pineapples on the Tasmanian plateaux and no deciduous beeches on the plains of Queensland, yet everywhere the visiting geographer remarks a relative uniformity in 'topography, climate, vegetation, animals, and people'. He is astonished at a racial homogeneity unparalleled in the New World, and impressed by a continent-wide sameness of the social structure. The price-index numbers of total household expenditure show no provincial variation greater than 5 per cent from the Commonwealth average, and this striking standardisation of material circumstances is emphasised by an equally striking standardisation of habits. The housewife, whether her iron-roofed kitchen is situated on the 'polar front' of Southern Victoria or in the steaming coastal plains of Queensland, observes the same hours of labour, cooks the same stews and puddings, and goes shopping in the same fashion of hat. Despite all this, provincial sentiment is still strong in Australia. The colonies whose pre-Federation rivalries scattered Customs houses along their land frontiers and broke the unity of Australia's one great river system by competitive railway building, still hold obstinately to the 'sovereignty' proper to them as States. Western Australia is the only State which might without serious danger withdraw from the national economic system, but majorities in all the States are keenly conscious of their economic difficulties and sensitive to their economic grievances. The conservative classes, whose tactics are to divide and defend, cling to the States (the majority of which still retain bi-cameral Legislatures) as bulwarks of the producer's interest. The average citizen looks more frequently to the Government which sits in Melbourne or Adelaide than to the Government which sits in Canberra. It is this closer, more intimate Government which protects him from the wicked, educates him, watches over his health, develops roads and railways and water supplies so that he may find permanent employment as a farmer or temporary employment as a navvy, regulates his local trade conditions, inspects his factory – performs, in short, all those functions which seem to affect most nearly his economic and social well-being. Canberra itself is less a national capital than the monument of a compromise between jealous provincialisms. Even the radicals must accept and turn to the best advantage these facts which give meaning to Australian federalism. They hope, it is true, that federal sentiment is but a temporary stage in national growth. They preach unification. They would, if they could, stake everything on the issue of one struggle for the control of one Government. But, in the meantime, they exploit to the full the resources of six provincial Governments. Within the States is to be found one very important expression of the Australian ideology. State Government is the instrument with which Australian democracy has fashioned its experimental socialism.

Control of the Federal Government is, nevertheless, the great prize of political struggle. Even in the first decade of the present century, when unification seemed utterly remote from practical possibilities, the radical forces of Australian democracy instinctively understood that the newly formed Federal Parliament must occupy the dominant position in Australian politics. It alone could guarantee the isolation necessary for those experiments which were to demonstrate to the world the possibility of social justice. It could restrict the entry of aliens; it could tax the entry of goods. Some day, perhaps, it might make itself the chief experimenter. In the meantime, every experiment which the Australians had initiated and every experiment which they hoped to begin depended upon something which only the Commonwealth could supply – a *cordon sanitaire*. Australian democracy already knew that it could survive only behind a ring-fence of immigration restriction. Gradually it came to believe that it needed a second ring-fence of fiscal protection.

The policy of White Australia is the indispensable condition of every other Australian policy. Embodied in the Immigration Restriction Act, 1901–25, its intention and significance are exceedingly easy to understand once they have been freed from the rhetoric and special pleading in which they have been enveloped. During the debates of 1902, the rhetoricians declared that it would be unfair for 'a nation of yesterday' (China) to interfere with the destiny of the 'noblest race upon this sphere' (the Australians). They even doubted whether some European nations, such as the Italians, were 'civilised in the ordinary Australian sense'. However, their immediate concern was with black men and yellow men – 'the servile nations of the world'. In legislating against the entry of such people, they knew themselves obedient to the will of God, who had set aside Australia 'exclusively for a Southern empire – for a Southern nation'. They knew also that they had the approval of science, whose laws, no less immutable than those of God, warned the races of this world that they might intermix only at their own dire peril. So convinced were these good legislators that the Most High spoke through them, that they would have engraved His laws – their laws – on tables of stone. Chamberlain had requested, at the Colonial Conference of

1897, that the colonies should clothe their legislation in 'a form of words which will avoid hurting the feelings of any of Her Majesty's subjects'. He had commended to them the method adopted by Natal, which had dissimulated a resolution to discriminate against Asiatics on the ground of race, by pretending to test their educational attainments. The rhetoricians denounced such diplomacy as 'a hypocritical measure', 'a backdoor method', 'a crooked and dishonest evasion'.

Fortunately, the majority of Australians were not rhetoricians, but practical people. The miners who had assailed Chinese fossickers on the diggings in the late 50s and early 60s of the nineteenth century had not pondered deeply over the teachings of God and science. And the responsible leaders of the Parliament of 1901 understood that, in this imperfect world, it is necessary to make concessions to expediency and common sense. By insisting upon the expedient of the dictation test they read their people a lesson in international good manners, and achieved Australia's purpose without recklessly wounding the self-respect of other nations. Moreover, they had sufficient honesty and courage to understand and to confess that their legislation was founded, not on the special nobility of the Australian people, but on the obvious fact of its individuality, which was compounded not only of good qualities, but of bad. 'I contend,' declared Deakin, 'that the Japanese need to be excluded because of their high abilities.' Their very virtues would make them dangerous competitors. This is one aspect of the economic argument. But Deakin took his stand on higher ground: 'The unity of Australia means nothing if it does not imply a united race. A united race means not only that its members can intermarry and associate without degradation on either side but implies ... a people possessing the same general cast of character, tone of thought, the same constitutional training and traditions.'

Every honest exposition of the White Australia policy must start from this double argument of economic and racial necessity. Every justification of it is hypocrisy and cant if it does not admit that its basis is *salus populi suprema lex*. An influx of the labouring classes of Asia would inevitably disorganise Australia's economic and political life. The experience of Natal, of North America, of the Australian colonies themselves in pre-Federation days, proves that labourers of different colours are seldom sufficiently meek to live side by side in human brotherhood. Always there is danger of a threefold demoralisation; demoralisation of the coolie over-driven by white capital, demoralisation of the poor white overwhelmed by coolie competition, demoralisation of the half-breed children of coolie and poor white who can find no firm place in either of the competing civilisations. Reasonable Australians are determined that their country shall not know these evils. It is not a matter of pride, for they remember Australia's Aborigines, and confess that they cannot trust themselves to be merciful and just in their dealings with a weaker people on their own soil. It is not merely a question of primitive fear, for they understand that racial war within a State is none the less hateful if one race does all the lynching. What they fear is not physical conquest by another race, but rather the internal decomposition and degradation of their own civilisation. They have gloried in their inheritance of free institutions, in their right to govern themselves and freely make their own destiny. But self-government, they know, becomes impossible when the inhabitants of a country do not agree upon essentials. No community can without great danger give a share of political power to aliens unable or unwilling to accept and defend what most it values. Every State must maintain its own *ethos*, and Australians understand that even a successful tyranny over Orientals would destroy the character of their own democracy.

It is unreasonable for Australians to pretend that their policy is grounded upon loftier motives than these. The best that can be hoped from communities in issues which touch them most nearly is that their self-interest will be reasonably enlightened. Nations do not habitually sell all that they have and give to the poor, and White Australia is not (as the rhetoricians seem sometimes to suggest) a self-denial offering made to Asiatic and African brothers and to a world hungry for beef and mutton. Australians feel so intensely about this matter that they would willingly inflict grievous harm on other peoples in their effort to protect themselves. But, in fact, one is genuinely puzzled to discover any material harm which their action had inflicted on any community outside Australia. Polynesians in their wild state never clamoured for admission to the Queensland sugar-fields; they were pursued and rounded up and shipped to Australia by enterprising gentlemen called blackbirders. The great Eastern nations have never shown any inflexible determination to export coolies; they seem generally to have been more interested in protecting their emigrant labourers from the oppressions of white capital. The Government of India has fought a strenuous battle within the Empire to win justice, not for subjects excluded from Australia, but for subjects attracted to Natal. It would indeed be folly to imagine that Australia's comparative immunity from external pressure must be eternal; the contrast between her empty north and the crowded Orient which faces it is too striking to be ignored. It is, nevertheless, certain that the policy of White Australia (which, after all, has depended for its practical validity upon the guarantee of the British Empire) has been more readily reconcilable than any other alternative policy which it is possible to imagine, with goodwill among the members of the Empire, and friendly relations between the Empire and foreign Powers.

The Australians have always asserted that immigration restriction is but the negative condition of a positive policy; that White Australia – to use Deakin's phrase – means an Australia peopled by white citizens, and not white 'merely because of the blank, unoccupied spaces on the map'. These blank, unoccupied spaces on the map seem both to accuse the policy of exclusion and to endanger it. In their eagerness to stake their claim to a continent the Australians have made strenuous and sometimes very crude efforts to increase the quantity of their population. But, it must be confessed, they are more concerned with its quality. They would rather have a small and prosperous community than one which would be 'a prey to all the abuses of industry'. Outside observers have sometimes noted this preference and criticised it as an expression of 'the parochial spirit extended to a continent'. Yet it has its roots, not merely in self-interest, but in idealism. It is the natural fruit of Australia's mid-nineteenth century radicalism. Protesting Chartism became on Australian soil a protesting nationalism, fired with the passion to fashion a new community free from the hereditary oppressions of the Old World.

> Last sea-thing dredged by sailor Time from Space
> Are you a drift Sargasso, where the West
> In halcyon calm rebuilds her fatal nest?

Australian democracy pictured itself as a vine brought out of Europe and dreamed of a time when its boughs would be like the goodly cedar tree. But the vine was still young and tender and must be encompassed with a hedge, lest the wild boar out of the woods (the capitalistic boar of Europe's industrial woods) should root it up.

The present chapter is concerned, not with the economics of Australian protectionism, but with its emotional and ideological flavour. When the Australian colonies federated in 1900, Victoria had for several decades been Protectionist, while New South Wales remained obstinately loyal to Free Trade. The partisans of Protection and of Free Trade pointed warning fingers at one or other of the rival colonies as exemplifying the horrible results of one or other of the rival policies. But economic disruption did not decide Australia policy. Protection triumphed in Australia because it appealed irresistibly to the most ardent sentiments of Australian democracy and to the interests which lurked behind the sentiments. The history of Labor's conversion illustrates this. In the early days of the Commonwealth, the Labor Party, playing the profitable game of 'support in return for concessions', held the balance between the two older parties and refused to make up its mind upon the fiscal issue which divided them. But gradually it drifted towards the Protectionist side. Free Trade Labor men must have become uneasy during the debates on the Immigration Restriction Bill, which focused their eyes upon the competitive strength of frugal Orientals. An outcry against trusts and dumping made them look for danger in another quarter. Finally, Deakin's invention of a device which seemed to give direct protection to wages turned them from hesitating converts into ardent testifiers and missionaries. 'The "old" Protection,' explained Deakin, 'contented itself with making good wages possible. The "new" Protection seeks to make them actual … Having put the manufacturer into a position to pay good wages, it goes on to assure the public that he does pay them.' In this way the economic doctrine of Protection adapted itself to the favourite ideas of Australian democracy. It offered a weapon of defence against that dangerous outside world which struggled for profit and cared nothing for Australia's adventurous quest of justice.

Deakin's New-Protectionist legislation asserted the principle that protection was due to those employers only who offered wages and conditions of labour which agreed with a standard of 'fair and reasonable'. The phrase has become the popular refrain of Australian democracy, repeated incessantly in pleas and judicial decisions, in statutes, Parliamentary debates, trade union conferences, and platform orations.

But how is it to be defined? What is fair for Hottentots may not be fair for Australians, and what is reasonable in 1907 may not be reasonable in 1927. The deduction of practical rules from so relative a principle must obviously depend upon special conditions of time and place. It is against the peculiar background of Australia's emptiness and isolation – emphasised by immigration restriction and a protective tariff – that the Australian experiment must be viewed. In addition, there are the peculiar complications resulting from Australian federalism. At the very beginning the neat fiscal devices designed by Deakin for the enforcing of New-Protection proved to be unconstitutional. Since then the Commonwealth Court of Conciliation and Arbitration, which has been entrusted with the task of defining 'fair and reasonable', has pursued its arduous labours amidst the never-ending din of legal and political argument.

All this makes it harder for politicians and lawyers to achieve results, and for historians to judge them. It does not, however, make it harder to perceive purposes. Amidst all the complications of Australian machinery, the guiding Australian ideas remain simple and clear. The Commonwealth Court of Conciliation and Arbitration wasted no time in giving a practical meaning to Deakin's 'fair and reasonable'. Mr Justice Higgins, a man of outstanding character, whose work as President of the Court counts for a good deal in Australian history, interpreted 'fair and reasonable' as 'the normal needs of an average employee regarded as a human being in a civilised country'. In a series of judgements he catalogued those needs. They included food, shelter, clothing, 'frugal comfort', 'provision for evil days', a reasonable amount of leisure, security to marry and to rear a family of about three children – altogether a by no means niggardly extension of the rights of man. With the aid of figures, which roughly indicate the cost of living, the Court declared a wage adequate to satisfy these needs. Thus was created the Australian standard of a living wage, or basic wage, which is 'the bedrock below which the Court cannot go', and serves as the basis from which are determined the economic variations of wages, such as the minimum wage in a particular industry or the margins allotted to skilled labour. The criterion of needs has been adopted throughout the whole continent. In South Australia, for example, the State Industrial Court is forbidden by statute to award less than a living wage, 'whatever the consequences may be'. Obviously, ethics have once again got entangled with economics. The Australian conception of 'fair and reasonable' is ethical, like the medieval idea of the just price. To those who object that such a standard may conflict with economic possibilities, the courts reply that Australia is 'not quite so bankrupt in resources of material or of mind or of will' as to be unable to provide for workers 'the bare necessities of life in a supposedly civilised community'. The medieval idea of concrete externalist justice here joins hands with modern optimism, which insists that man is in control of nature, and that he can make his life tolerable if he chooses to do so. Manufacturers must learn to seek economy through efficiency, rather than efficiency through parsimony; they must make economic facts conform to the idea of justice. If an industry is unable to achieve this, it must die – unless the State chooses to intervene in order to prolong its existence. With this saving clause the argument completes its circle; it has led back to Protection. Does this mean that the distinctive ethics of Australian democracy are dependent, after all, upon its distinctive economics?

The Australians have always disliked scientific economics and (still more) scientific economists. They are fond of ideals and impatient of technique. Their sentiments quickly find phrases, and their phrases find prompt expression in policies. What the economists call 'law' they call anarchy. The law which they understand is the positive law of the State – the democratic State which seeks social justice by the path of individual rights. The mechanism of international prices, which signals the world's need from one country to another and invites the nations to produce more of this commodity and less of that, belongs to an entirely different order. It knows no rights, but only necessities. The Australians have never felt disposed to submit to these necessities. They have insisted that their Governments must struggle to soften them or elude them or master them. In this way they have created an interesting system of political economy.

THE FOUNDATIONS OF CULTURE IN AUSTRALIA

P.R. Stephensen

1936

Genius of the place

Australia is a unique country. All countries are unique, but this one is particularly so. Visitors such as D.H. Lawrence have discerned a spiritual quality of ancient loveliness in our land itself. The flora and fauna are primitive, and for the most part harmless to man, but to the visitor there is another element, of terror, in the Spirit of the Place. The blossoming of the waratah, the song of the lyrebird, typify the spirit of primitive loveliness in our continent; but the wail of the dingo, the gauntness of our tall trees by silent moonlight, can provide a shiver of terror to a newcomer. Against a background of strangeness, of strange beasts and birds and plants, in a human emptiness of three million square miles, our six million white people, of immigrant stock, mainly from Europe, are becoming acclimatised to this environment new to them but geologically so old that Time seems to have stood still here for a million years.

A new nation, a new human type, is being formed in Australia.

For the first hundred and fifty years of colonising, the immigrants have merely raped the land, or 'settled' it, as we say, with unconscious irony in our choice of a word to describe the process of destroying its primitiveness. Now there are cities, half the people live in cities, huddled there, it may be, for mutual protection against the loneliness of the bush. Ships come and go, from Europe, America, Asia and Africa. Ideas and people also come and go – we Australians ourselves come and go. All is in flux, a nation is being formed. Can it be a cultured nation?

Australia, throughout its brief whiteman's history, has been primarily a colony of Britain, as Britain was once a colony of Rome, a place to be exploited commercially. For a hundred and fifty years all our vast production of gold, most of our wheat, wool, meat and butter have been sent 'home' to Britain. In trade exchange we have received manufactured goods, and many loans. Britain, it may be, has had the best of the deal financially. We have sent our troops, too, to fight in British wars. We accept British exploitation of Australia as a natural fact, and scarcely protest. The price has been worth it, for has not Britain sent us, as makeweight and compensation for economic exploitation, the great heritage of her laws, her customs, her language and literature and philosophy, her *culture*?

Culture in Australia, if it ever develops indigenously, begins not from the Aborigines, who have been suppressed and exterminated, but from British culture, brought hither by Englishmen, Irishmen and Scotsmen throughout the nineteenth century. In a new and quite different environment from that of those damp British Islands we are here developing the culture which evolved there. We spring fully armed from the head of Jove, or fully cultured from the head of John Bull. Australian culture begins with a general background of Chaucer, Shakespeare, Herrick, Byron, Charles Dickens; and more specifically with a background of Samuel Smiles, Mr Gladstone and Queen Victoria. We inherit all that Britain has inherited, and from that point we go on – to what?

As the culture of every nation is an intellectual and emotional expression of the *genius loci*, our Australian culture will diverge from the purely local colour of the British Islands to the precise extent that our environment differs from that of Britain. A hemisphere separates us from 'home' – we are Antipodeans; a gum tree is not a branch of an oak; our Australian culture will evolve distinctively.

Colony or nation

What then of culture in Australia? Here is not a mere vicinity, but a whole continent, unique in its natural features, and unique in the fact of its continental homogeneity of race and language. Australia is the only continent on the earth inhabited by one race, under one government, speaking one language. The population at present is not much greater than was that of Britain in Shakespeare's time, but by the end of the twentieth century we may expect that the population will expand to at least twenty millions, remaining of European parent-stock, but with locally developed characteristics, and with a locally created culture. Australia will then become indubitably recognised as a nation, and will lose all trace of colonial status.

As a colony, we exported raw material and imported manufactured goods and loans. The trade traffic was two-ways. *We imported also the imponderables, culture, by a system of one-way traffic.* As a nation we shall continue to import culture, but we shall export it also, as our contribution to world-ideas – there will then be a two-ways traffic in the imponderables.

At this present time (1935) we are no longer a colony pure and simple, nor yet are we a Nation fully-fledged. We are something betwixt and between a colony and a nation, something vaguely called a 'Dominion', or a 'Commonwealth' with 'Dominion status'. We are loosely tied to other Dominions in the British Empire by law, strongly tied by sentiment and an idea of mutual protection. Inasmuch as we are politically autonomous, we have entered into virtual alliances (political, military, commercial and sentimental) with other Dominions or Colonies in the Empire, including Canada, the Irish Free State, South Africa, New Zealand, Great Britain and Jamaica. Where it will all lead to we do not know; but the virtual alliance gives us a sense of security in international affairs for the time being. The political and legal ties that bind us to the other 'Dominions' are loose enough, but the sentimental and financial ties are strong, particularly with the 'Dominion' called Great Britain. And the cultural tie is strong.

Is it sedition or blasphemy to the idea of the British Empire to suggest that each Dominion in this loose alliance will tend to become autonomous politically, commercially and *culturally*? A military alliance between the various component 'nations' of the Empire may perhaps survive long after the other ties have, in fact, been weakened – though this would be contrary to the lessons of history. Such a prognostication has nothing to do with aesthetics. What matters for present purposes is that Australia has nowadays an acknowledged right to become one of the nations of the world. Australian nationalism, with or without the idea of the British Empire, has a right to exist; and there can be no nation without a national place-idea; a national culture.

An Englishman's view

An Englishman resident in Australia, Professor G.H. Cowling, who is professor of English literature at the University of Melbourne, recently ventured from his own field to criticise Australian literature. In an article published in the *Age* newspaper of 16 February 1935, the learned professor made several statements expressing doubt concerning the possibilities of Australian literature. Catalogued, his more provocative remarks were as follows:

1. 'Australia is not yet in the centre of the globe, and it has no London.'
2. 'The rewards of literature in Australia are not good enough to make it attract the best minds.'
3. 'Book production (in Australia) is, on the average, poor.'
4. 'In spite of what the native-born say about gum trees, I cannot help feeling that our countryside is "thin" and lacking in tradition.'
5. 'There are no ancient churches, castles, ruins – the memorials of generations departed. You need no Baedeker in Australia. From the point of view of literature this means that we can never hope to have a Scott, a Balzac, a Dumas ... nor a poetry which reflects past glories.'
6. 'What scope is there for Australian biography? Little, I should say.'
7. 'What scope is there for Australian books on travel? Little, I think.'
8. 'Good Australian novels which are entirely Australian are bound to be few ... Australian life is too lacking in tradition, and too confused, to make many first-class novels.'
9. 'We might have one Australian Sinclair Lewis but not many more.'
10. 'Literary culture is not indigenous, like the gum tree, but is from a European source.'

A certain amount of indignant controversy followed the well-meaning professor's pessimistic analysis of the situation. Nobody thanked him, as he ought to have been thanked, for putting the Unteachable Englishman's point of view so succinctly on record. There is as yet no chair of Australian Literature at Melbourne University, nor at any other Australian university, and the professor is to that extent quite correct in saying that literary culture is not indigenous, but is from a European source. With his unteachability we cannot here argue; it is of the same brand as that which lost England the American colonies. Substitute the word 'America' for the word 'Australia' in each of Professor Cowling's remarks, and you have the kind of 'criticism' which Americans had to put up with from generations of learned Englishmen; even while American literature was developing so strongly that today – despite a lack of ancient churches, castles and ruins – American literature is at least as strong as contemporary English literature, and some think it is stronger.

The Empire is in greater danger from patronising Englishmen than from insurgent colonials. Professor Cowling's critique is a wet blanket applied to the fire of Australian literary creativeness. It can be read in no other way than as an attempt to throw cold water on our nationalistic literary ardour. His attitude is precisely that of the Latinists who, perceiving Wycliffe and Chaucer writing books in the English vernacular, sniffed (no doubt) at the very idea of literature in Australia. Here we are on the threshold of Australian self-consciousness, at the point of developing Australian nationality, and with it Australian culture, we are in our Chaucerian phase, and this professor cannot begin to perceive the excitement of it, overlooks his grand opportunity of studying and recording for posterity this birth-phase of a new literature in formation under his very nose – and directs our vision, if he could, towards old churches, castles and ruins in Europe!

The academic mind, by timorous instinct, rarely concerns itself with the present or future; the past is safer.

Some day there will be learned professors to write textbooks on the developments of literature in Australia during the nineteen-twenties and nineteen-thirties. They will soak themselves in the period, and attempt to reconstruct it for their students. They will find Cowling's article and quote it to show some of the difficulties which literature in Australia had to contend against at that time – the discouragements, the gratuitous insults of the learned, the Unteachability of the already-too-well-taught. They may go on record that, as a result of Professor Cowling's demonstration of hostility towards Australian culture, a Chair of Australian Literature was ultimately endowed at Melbourne University and at six other Australian

Universities (including Canberra), to supplement the traditional teaching in English, French, German and other European literatures; and that thus Professor Cowling's excursus into journalism indirectly helped to establish Australian literature in a way which he did not intend.

Is this all too fanciful? I, at any rate, have to thank Professor Cowling for his venture into controversy. He provides me with a contemporary example to illustrate my present thesis. Instead of blaming him for blanketing the flame, I at least can thank him for inadvertently fanning it. His arguments are all cogent, *from his point of view.* From an Australian point of view they are, by provocation, equally cogent.

No place like home

The culture of a country is the essence of nationality, the permanent element in a nation. A nation is nothing but an extension of the individuals comprising it, generation after generation of them. When I am proud of my nationality, I am proud of myself. My personal shortcomings, of which I am only too painfully aware, are eliminated to some extent by my nationality, in which I may justly take pride – such is the reason for nations and nationalities, and also for tribes, mobs and herds. In numbers there is a strength and permanence not found in individuals.

The nation as an extension of the ego, as a permanent idea which lives when the individual dies, is essential to an individual's well-being. One's nationality is something to boast of.

This does not mean, or should not mean, sabre-rattling, challenges to fight other nations to prove superiority, except in the case of Huns like Hitler, who are intrinsically lacking in culture, mentally equipped like a school bully. It is possible to be proud of one's nationality without wishing to prove it by slaughter. In what, at present, can an Australian take pride? In our cricketers, merino sheep, soldiers, vast open spaces – and what then?

Until we have a culture, a quiet strength of intellectual achievement, we have really nothing except our soldiers to be proud of!

Birth of a new idea

Banjo Paterson and Henry Lawson may be regarded as typical pioneers of indigenous culture in Australia. Whatever their faults, their work has an outstanding quality of being drawn direct from Australian life, and not from a bookish or 'literary' idea, in imitation of English poets. Lawson and Paterson were both Australian-born, and wrote for Australian readers primarily. Their work is crude enough in parts; it is the raw material of an Australian culture, but it is of high national significance, as being truly indigenous. The poet Kendall, who immediately preceded them, was also Australian-born, but his mind had an 'English' cast. His first poems were sent to England to be published; he wanted to please the English. Kendall wrote of Australia, but in a prim English way, not in a robust Australian way.

Adam Lindsay Gordon was English-born, an immigrant to Australia, and never saw Australia except through his English fox-hunting squire's eyes. He is, therefore, acclaimed, *in England*, as the typical Australian poet. In Westminster Abbey his bust is placed with the absurd, indeed impertinent description, 'Australia's National Poet'.

From Gordon, the *Englishman* writing about Australia in an English way, to Kendall, the *Australian* writing about Australia in an English way; thence to Lawson and Paterson, *the Australians writing about Australia in an Australian way*, is the evolution of our indigenous culture. This evolution, in a general way, went on, in the works of Australian writers, or writers in Australia, throughout the whole of the nineteenth century, the process of Australian self-definition gradually becoming more clarified, until, with Paterson's and Lawson's work, it could be seen plainly that Australian literature proper was beginning to stand on its own feet.

Lawson (or Larsen) was of Scandinavian extraction, and to such a man, born in Australia, the European time is irrevocably severed. Such a man will fight passionately for his Australian nationality. He has no direct sentimental tie with England. Australia is his only motherland and home. Even though his ancestors, of a thousand years ago, may have raped, raided, plundered, colonised and settled England, Ireland and Scotland, and put the red-headed spirit of adventure into the British race – even though he be a direct descendant of the Angles, Saxons and Jutes – he has no lively interest in his present-day collateral cousins, no vicarious 'home' and 'motherland' in the British Islands. Australia is home to him, the only motherland. If Australia is not a nation, then he belongs to no nation. This same feeling arises in *the second and third generation of Australian-born*, no matter what their ancestry, whether it be English, Irish, Scots or Chinese. England is 'home' to the first-generation English immigrants to Australia, and sometimes by legend to their children. But to their grandchildren and great-grandchildren, Australia is the only convincing homeland.

The pretty legend that England is 'home' to all Australians arises from a figure of speech, or a habit of speech, rather than from any reality of thought.

In denying that England is, in contemporary reality, 'home' to the Australian-born, I insist and reiterate that I am not arguing politics, imperial or otherwise. I am seeking a basis for indigenous culture in Australia, for a state of mind from which Australian culture can emerge. One of my model Australians, Banjo Paterson, is, I believe, a convinced imperialist in politics. There is no reason why a good Australian should not consider it expedient for Australia to remain forever in the political-economic-military alliance called the British Empire. England would not try to keep us in by force if we ever wished to secede. This question does not, at the moment, arise. The point is that, on the basis of nationality, of theoretical equality in nationhood with all the other nations of the earth, within or without the British Empire, we must find our own culture and define it; we cannot suck pap forever from the teats of London.

Democratic morale

In the absence of facilities for publishing sophisticated or even moderately intelligent books; in the absence of any critical magazines or reviews comparable with the *New Statesman,* the *Spectator,* or with any of the English monthlies; in the absence of any great newspapers with traditions of fair reporting and fair play such as the *Manchester Guardian* or the *Times*; and in the overwhelming presence of our dreadful, venal, sycophantic, partisan, or screaming and stunting Australian daily press (edited by promoted cadet reporters and office boys), there has been no opportunity for our Australian intellectuals to do anything else except lurk in isolation, withdrawn from the life about them.

I say this in extenuation, for I have called them cowardly. I meant lazy. No means of expression existing, *they should have brought the means of expression into existence.* Lazy is the word, or dazed – by the fantasy of Europe. Isolated, and without a forum of any kind, they have daydreamed themselves into futility, and often enough allowed their intellects to rust. Long bouts of laziness, inertia, frustration, seem to have demoralised them. They want others to save them, themselves they cannot save. Through sheer inertia, arising from persistent discouragement but none the less inertia, they would allow the smug, the second-rate (the editors and publishers who 'give the public what it wants'), to define the name of Australia.

By some means or other Australia's lazy intellectuals, cowardly intellectuals, inert intellectuals, must now be cajoled and wheedled, galvanised or shocked, into playing their full part in the national life. Without matured book-publishing facilities and conventions, without sophisticated journals of information and of opinion, our pathetic intellectuals are in a pitiable, as well as a deplorable, fix. We must provide those facilities, those rallying points. Without them our poor isolated thinkers are scattered and deployed, an army without a plan – 'each man his own General'. Some kind of plan or objective must be formulated.

At Mont St Quentin, in September 1918 (one of the most remarkable Australian feats of the war), there was a stated objective – the top of the hill. There was also an order, probably the strangest order ever issued to troops (*each man to act on his own, and as many as possible to reach the top*), emanating from General Monash, who, from the point of view of British Brass Hats, was three times an outsider – a civilian, an Australian, a Jew – but was nevertheless a man inspired when he issued that command which was a negation of all army ideas. Monash knew his Australians, who, deployed and scattered (each man his own General), casually and in broad daylight scaled the plateau bristling with German machine-guns, and promptly put vastly superior numbers of conscript goose-steppers into retreat. The attack was so audacious in plan, so unprecedented in method of execution, that the Germans could not believe in it – until it had happened.

If our Australian intellectual forces of today are similarly deployed and scattered, I believe that, recalling Mont St Quentin, they will nevertheless reach the top – once they realise that there *is* an objective, and that a thousand others (or even a hundred) are also 'hopping over' into this intellectual fight.

Soldiers

The men of the AIF were worthy of note, not as mere soldiers, as cogs in a military machine, but as *men*, as civilians who went willingly into war from a conviction that their cause was just. That they may have been proved wrong in this conviction by subsequent events does not alter the fact that they *volunteered*, and were never conscripted, to fight in a cause which they believed to be right. Neither does it alter the fact that, having become thus organised for a purpose into an army, *these average Australian civilians made history* – as their late enemy, and all their allies, well know and admit.

Made history – not jingo death-and-glory history, flag-flapping history, chauvinistic history – but a new kind of history, our history, of special significance to us, a history founded on individual initiative which became an outstanding collective *morale*. Peeling all chauvinism off the history of the AIF (which is not difficult), we need with the utmost care to study that turning-point in our national life, 1914 to 1918, in its moral, its psychological, its national aspects.

The story of the Australian soldiers on Gallipoli, in Palestine and in France, should be told, in precise detail, to all oncoming Australians, not in glorification of militarism, but as the reverse: as a lesson in *self-imposed* individual discipline, comradeship, *the superior value of the individual man*, of individual initiative and self-respect. And also it should be taught as a warning to the nation never to be fooled again into participation in a war of European conquest, to keep out of other people's brawls; to be prepared, if necessary, to defend our own soil against any invasion of any kind; to be prepared (as W.M. Hughes told them at Versailles) to 'defy the opinion of the whole civilised world', if need be, in defence of our own soil and our right to develop our own new civilisation here.

If we never had a history before 1914, let the imported professors observe, the AIF gave us one, from which we suddenly perceived that we are indeed a Nation, with our own permanent quality.

With the spirit of the AIF still in the land, what need is there for an Australian to fear proclaiming his Australianism? The 'Diggers' were never ashamed of being known as Australians: they found their nationality during the ordeal of war. Let our intellectual defeatists remember this. There is no need to be ashamed of Australia: we have qualities. There is no need to ape English 'culture' any more than there was need for the AIF to imitate English army parade-ground spit and polish. We can establish our own culture, our own discipline, our own *morale*. We shall not be respected until we do so.

Let our lurking intellectuals have no fear in resisting fascism, tyranny, commercial hegemony, the Rule of the Smug and imperialist permeation, wherever they find it. The common man, the typical Australian, is a democrat, a free-thinker, an individualist to his core, a believer in Australia. The common man, the public, the allegedly rough and crude 'Diggers' and their sons and daughters, will defend Australian freedom whenever they are called upon to do so, and will follow the intellectuals whenever these decide to give a strong and unwavering lead in the matter of proclaiming 'Australia First' as the only constructive national idea.

No need for a protector

Defence is also a prime national question. On the practical need of defending Australia against the possibility of a Japanese invasion, all Australian parties (including the communists) are in agreement. The only doubt which may arise is whether the Japanese imperialists are really so stupid as to wish to conquer and colonise Australia. These deep thinkers may have realised that, even if they were to conquer Australia and people it, Australia would then become the home of a new kind of Japanese person, a *Japanese-Australian*, who would be as different from the original parent Japanese as the present-day British-Australian is becoming different from the original parent British! Australia colonised by the Japanese would nevertheless become a great nation – one of the leading nations of the earth – and thus eventually would be a serious rival to the Mother Japan of the northern hemisphere.

Concretely, however, I perceive that Australian national *morale*, which alone can establish a culture here, has been undermined to a greater extent by the 'protection' offered by Britain and the British Navy than by any foreign threat of aggression.

If the Japanese intend to assault and invade Australia, they will of course wait until there is war or revolution or some such distraction in Europe to keep the British Navy in its 'Home' waters. When Germany or Italy, or both of these dictator-ruled countries simultaneously, go berserk in Europe, the British Navy will, very properly, stay in the North Sea or the Mediterranean, to defend England: and will not be available for the defence of Australia should Japan choose that moment for its onslaught on this continent. That is not only plain truth and common sense but also a completely justifiable fact.

The British Navy has been built to defend, in any emergency, England first. *In any such contingency, Australians will be in the*

exhilarating position of having to defend their own country, unaided.
Such a responsibility, I say, brings with it a sense of exhilaration, the
feelings of a young eagle leaving the nest, or of a young man who, leaving his parents' home, occupies a house which he himself has built.

The Englishman's view of Australia's destiny, and the Australian patriot's
view, do not in this respect coincide. One must give way to the other:
both cannot prevail. The industrialisation of Australia means that the
population will substantially increase; and with that increase will
come an increase of Australian national self-consciousness: in other
words, a distinctive Australian culture. The industrialisation of
Australia means that Australians will manufacture wool, *and books*,
and almost every other civilised necessity, here. This is a view directly
in conflict with the view of Australia as a solely primary producing
country: the 'narrow' Englishman's view of the destiny of this portion
of the Empire.

The development of Australian industry, and its accompanying
growth of population, is the only means of holding Australia as a home
for the white race.

And what a home! An entire continent, diversified from the snowy
peaks of Kosciuszko to the 'sunlit plains extended' of the west; from the
sub-arctic islands of Bass Strait to the palm-clad tropic islets of the
Barrier Reef; a continent with enormous deposits of coal and iron, and
with every mineral that industry requires; a continent capable of producing
every kind of fruit and grain; with coastal waters that teem with fish –
herring and pilchard in shoals greater than any that visit the cold North
Sea: a continent capable of sustaining, at a high standard of living, a population of forty million yeomen and industrial workers, with ease.

The true Australian creed

In his New Year message to his fellow-Australians, speaking at fifty-nine
minutes to 1 a.m., on the first day of January 1936, the respected
Governor-General of the Commonwealth, Sir Isaac Isaacs, uttered these
historic words:

Whatever the future may have in store, one thing is certain – no inferiority complex ever found a place in the true Australian creed of life.

Those who heard this message realised that the words were spoken with a peculiar intensity, and almost a passion of sincerity: the well-loved Australian-born governor-general could not, on such an occasion, speak in cold official terms.

It was more than a New Year Greeting. The message was Sir Isaac's valedictory to the high office which he had filled with such distinction: having proved thereby that Australian birth is no barrier to the highest achievement.

His name will go down in history as one of those who helped to remove the 'inferiority complex' from the Australian mind.

His words were carefully chosen, and will bear the closest scrutiny. He does not say that the inferiority complex is absent from Australians. He says that it never found a place in the *true* Australian creed of life.

This presupposes a vast difference between true creeds and false creeds.

The inferiority complex finds a very big place indeed in the Australian creed of life.

But not in the *true* Australian creed.

WHAT IS SIGNIFICANT
IN US WILL SURVIVE

Vance Palmer

1942

T he next few months may decide not only whether we are to survive as a nation, but whether we deserve to survive. As yet none of our achievements prove it, at any rate in the sight of the outer world. We have no monuments to speak of, no dreams in stone, no Guernicas, no sacred places. We could vanish and leave singularly few signs that, for some generations, there had lived a people who had made a homeland of this Australian earth. A homeland? To how many people was it primarily that? How many penetrated the soil with their love and imagination? We have had no peasant population to cling passionately to their few acres, throw down tenacious roots, and weave a natural poetry into their lives by invoking the little gods of creek and mountain. The land has been something to exploit, to tear out a living from and then sell at a profit. Our settlements have always had a fugitive look, with their tin roofs and rubbish-heaps. Even our towns ... the main street cluttered with shops, the million-dollar town hall, the droves of men and women intent on nothing but buying or selling, the suburban retreats of rich drapers! Very little to show the presence of a people with a common purpose or a rich sense of life.

If Australia had no more character than could be seen on its surface, it would be annihilated as surely and swiftly as those colonial outposts white men built for their commercial profit in the East – pretentious facades of stucco that looked imposing as long as the wind kept from blowing. But there is an Australia of the spirit, submerged and not very articulate, that is quite different from these bubbles of old-world imperialism. Born of the lean loins of the country itself, of the dreams of men who came here to form a new society, of hard conflicts in many fields, it has developed a toughness all its own. Sardonic, idealist, tongue-tied perhaps, it is the Australia of all who truly belong here. When you are away, it takes on a human image, an image that emerges, brown and steady-eyed from the background of dun cliffs, treed bushlands and tawny plains. More than a generation ago, it found voice in the writings of Lawson, O'Dowd, Bedford and Tom Collins: it has become even more aware of itself since. And it has something to contribute to the world. Not emphatically in the arts as yet, but in arenas of action, and in ideas for the creation of that egalitarian democracy that will have to be the basis of all civilised societies in the future.

This is the Australia we are called upon to save. Not merely the mills and mines, and the higgledy-piggledy towns that have grown up along the coast: not the assets we hold or the debts we owe. For even if we were conquered by the Japanese, some sort of normal life would still go on. You cannot wipe out a nation of seven million people, or turn them all into wood-and-water joeys. Sheep would continue to be bred, wheat raised, there would be work for the shopkeeper, the clerk, the baker, the butcher. Not everyone could be employed pulling Japanese gentlemen about in rickshaws.

Some sort of comfort might even be achieved by the average man under Japanese dominance; but if anyone believes life would be worth living under the terms offered, he is not worth saving. There is no hope for him unless a breath of the heroic will around him stirs him to come out of the body of this death. Undoubtedly we have a share of the decadent elements that have proved weakness in other countries – whisperers, faint-hearts, near-fascists, people who have grown rotten through easy living; and these are often people who have had power in the past and now feel it falling away from them. We will survive according to our swiftness in pushing them into the background and liberating the people of will, purpose and intensity; those who are at one with Australia's spirit and are capable of moulding the future.

I believe we will survive; that what is significant in us will survive; that we will come out of this struggle battered, stripped to the bone, but spiritually sounder than we went in, surer of our essential character, adults in a wider world than the one we lived in hitherto.

These are great, tragic days. Let us accept them stoically, and make every yard of Australian earth a battle-station.

THE FORGOTTEN PEOPLE

Robert Menzies

1942

Quite recently, a bishop wrote a letter to a great daily newspaper. His theme was the importance of doing justice to the workers. His belief apparently was that the workers are those who work with their hands. He sought to divide the people of Australia into classes. He was obviously suffering from what has for years seemed to me to be our greatest political disease; the disease of thinking that the community is divided into the rich and relatively idle, and the laborious poor, and that every social and political controversy can be resolved into the question: what side are you on?

Now, the last thing that I want to do is to commence or take part in a false war of this kind. In a country like Australia the class war must always be a false war.

But if we are to talk of classes, then the time has come to say something of the forgotten class – *the middle class* – those people who are constantly in danger of being ground between the upper and the nether millstones of the false class war; the middle class who, properly regarded, represent the backbone of this country.

We don't have classes here as in England, and therefore the terms don't mean the same. It is necessary, therefore, that I should define what I mean when I use the expression 'the middle class'.

Let me first define it by exclusion: I exclude at one end of the scale the rich and powerful; those who control great funds and enterprises, and are as a rule able to protect themselves – though it must be said that in a political sense they have as a rule shown neither comprehension nor competence. But I exclude them because in most material difficulties the rich can look after themselves.

I exclude at the other end of the scale the mass of unskilled people, almost invariably well-organised, and with their wages and conditions safeguarded by popular law. What I am excluding them from is my definition of the middle class. We cannot exclude them from the problem of social progress, for one of the prime objects of modern social and political policy is to give to them a proper measure of security, and provide the conditions which will enable them to acquire skill and knowledge and individuality.

These exclusions being made, I include the intervening range, the kind of people I myself represent in parliament – salary-earners, shop-keepers, skilled artisans, professional men and women, farmers and so on. These are, in the political and economic sense, the middle class. They are for the most part unorganised and unselfconscious. They are envied by those whose social benefits are largely obtained by taxing them. They are not rich enough to have individual power. They are taken for granted by each political party in turn. They are not sufficiently lacking in individualism to be organised for what in these days we call 'pressure politics'. And yet, as I have said, they are the backbone of the nation.

The communist has always hated what he calls 'the bourgeoisie' because he sees clearly that the existence of one has kept British countries from revolution, while the substantial absence of one in feudal France at the end of the eighteenth century and in tsarist Russia at the end of the last war made revolution easy and indeed inevitable.

You may say to me: 'Why bring this matter up at this stage when we are fighting a war, in the result of which we are all equally concerned?'

My answer is that I am bringing it up because under the pressures of war we may, if we are not careful, if we are not as thoughtful as the times will permit us to be, inflict a fatal injury upon our own backbone.

In point of political, industrial and social theory and practice there are great delays in time of war. But there are also great accelerations. We must watch each, remembering always that whether we know it or not, and whether we like it or not, the foundations of whatever new order is to come after the war are inevitably being laid down now. We cannot go wrong right up to the peace treaty and expect suddenly thereafter to go right.

Now, what is the value of this middle class, so defined and described?

First: It has 'a stake in the country'. It has responsibility for homes – homes material, homes human, homes spiritual.

I do not believe that the real life of this nation is to be found either in great luxury hotels and the petty gossip of so-called fashionable suburbs, or in the officialdom of organised masses.

It is to be found in the homes of people who are nameless and unadvertised, and who, whatever their individual religious conviction or dogma, see in their children their greatest contribution to the immortality of their race. The home is the foundation of sanity and sobriety; it is the indispensable condition of continuity; its health determines the health of society as a whole.

I have mentioned homes material, homes human and homes spiritual.

Let me take them in their order: what do I mean by 'homes material'?

The 'material home' represents the concrete expression of the habits of frugality and saving 'for a home of our own'. Your advanced socialist may rage against private property even whilst he acquires it; but one of the best instincts in us is that which induces us to have one little piece of earth with a house and a garden which is ours, to which we can withdraw, in which we can be among our friends, into which no stranger can come against our will.

If you consider it, you will see that if, as in the old saying, 'The Englishman's home is his castle,' it is this very fact that leads on to the conclusion that he who seeks to violate that law by violating the soil of England must be repelled and defeated.

National patriotism, in other words, inevitably springs from the instinct to defend and preserve our own homes.

Then we have 'homes human': A great house, full of loneliness, is not a home. 'Stone walls do not a prison make' nor do they make a house; they may equally make a stable or a piggery. Brick walls, dormer windows and central heating need not make more than a hotel.

My home is where my wife and children are; the instinct to be with them is the great instinct of civilised man; the instinct to give them a chance in life is a noble instinct, not to make them leaners but lifters.

If Scotland has made a great contribution to the theory and practice of education, it is because of the tradition of Scottish homes. The Scottish ploughman, walking behind his team, cons ways and means of making his son a farmer, and so he sends him to the village school.

The Scottish farmer ponders upon the future of his son, and sees it most assured not by the inheritance of money but by the acquisition of that knowledge which will give him power, and so the sons of many Scottish farmers find their way to Edinburgh and a university degree.

The great question is: 'How can I qualify my son to help society?' and not, as we have so frequently thought: 'How can I qualify society to help my son?' If human homes are to fulfil their destiny, then we must have frugality and saving for education and progress.

And, finally, we have 'homes spiritual': this is a notion which finds its simplest and most moving expression in 'The Cotter's Saturday Night' of Burns. Human nature is at its greatest when it combines dependence upon God with independence of man.

We offer no affront, on the contrary we have nothing but the warmest human compassion, for those whom fate has compelled to live upon the bounty of the state, when we say that the greatest element in a strong people is a fierce independence of spirit.

This is the only *real* freedom and it has as its corollary a brave acceptance of unclouded individual responsibility.

The moment a man seeks moral and intellectual refuge in the emotions of a crowd, he ceases to be a human being and becomes a cypher.

The home spiritual so understood is not produced by lassitude or by dependence; it is produced by self-sacrifice, by frugality and saving.

In a war, as indeed at most times, we become the ready victims of phrases. We speak glibly of many things without pausing to consider what they signify. We speak of 'financial power', forgetting that the financial power of 1942 is based upon the savings of generations which have preceded it.

We speak of 'morale' as if it were a quality induced from without, created by others for our benefit, when in truth there can be no national morale which is not based upon the individual courage of men and women. We speak of 'man power' as if it were a mere matter of arithmetic, as if it were made up of a multiplication of men and muscles without spirit.

Second: The middle class, more than any other, provides the intelligent ambition which is the motive power of human progress. The idea entertained by many people that in a well-constituted world we shall all live on the state is the quintessence of madness, for what is the state but *us* – we collectively must provide what we individually receive.

The great vice of democracy, a vice which is exacting a bitter retribution from it at this moment, is that for a generation we have been busy getting ourselves onto the list of beneficiaries and removing ourselves from the list of contributors, as if somewhere there was somebody else's effort on which we could thrive.

To discourage ambition, to envy success, to hate achieved superiority, to distrust independent thought, to sneer at and impute false motives to public service, these are the maladies of modern democracy, and of Australian democracy in particular. Yet ambition, effort, thinking and readiness to serve are not only the design and objectives of self-government but are the essential conditions of its success.

If this is not so, then we had better put back the clock and search for a benevolent autocracy once more.

Where do we find these great elements most commonly?

Among the defensive and comfortable rich?

Among the unthinking and unskilled mass?

Or among what I have called 'the middle class'?

Third: The middle class provides more than perhaps any other the intellectual life which marks us off from the beast; the life which finds room for literature, for the arts, for science, for medicine and the law.

Consider the case of literature and art. Could these survive as a department of state? Are we to publish our poets according to their political colour? Is the state to decree surrealism because surrealism gets a heavy vote in a key electorate? The truth is that no great book was ever written and no great picture ever painted by the clock or according to civil service rules. These things are done by *man*, not men. You cannot regiment them. They require opportunity, and sometimes leisure. The artist, if he is to live, must have a buyer; the writer, an audience. He finds them among frugal people to whom the margin above bare living means a chance to reach out a little towards that heaven which is just beyond our grasp.

It has always seemed to me, for example, that an artist is better helped by the man who sacrifices something to buy a picture he loves than by a rich patron who follows the fashion.

Fourth: This middle class maintains and fills the higher schools and universities and so feeds the lamp of learning.

What are schools for?

To train people for examinations?

To enable people to comply with the law?

Or to produce developed men and women?

Are the universities mere technical schools, or have they, as one of their functions, the preservation of pure learning, bringing in its train not merely riches for the imagination but a comparative sense for the mind, and leading to what we need so badly – the recognition of values which are other than pecuniary?

One of the great blots on our modern living is the cult of false values, a repeated application of the test of money, of notoriety, of applause.

A world in which a comedian or a beautiful half-wit on the screen can be paid fabulous sums, whilst scientific researchers and discoverers can suffer neglect and starvation, is a world which needs to have its sense of values violently set right.

Now, have we realised and recognised these things, or is most of our policy designed to discourage or penalise thrift, to encourage dependence on the state, to bring about a dull equality on the fantastic idea that all men are equal in mind and needs and desires, to level down by taking the mountains out of the landscape; to weigh men according to their political organisations and power, as votes and not as human beings?

These are formidable questions and we cannot escape from answering them if there is really to be a new order for the world.

I have been actively engaged in politics for fourteen years in the State of Victoria and in the Commonwealth of Australia. In that period I cannot readily recall many occasions upon which any policy was pursued which was designed to help the thrifty, to encourage independence, to recognise the divine and valuable variations of men's minds. On the contrary, there have been many instances in which the votes of the thriftless have been used to defeat the thrifty. On occasions of emergency, as in the Depression and during the present war, we have hastened to make it clear that the provision made by a man for his own retirement and old age is not half as sacrosanct as the provision which the state would have made for him had he never saved at all.

We have talked of income from savings as if it possessed a somewhat discreditable character. We have taxed it more and more heavily. We have spoken slightingly of the earnings of interest at the very moment when we have advocated new pensions and social schemes. I have myself heard a minister of power and influence declare that no deprivation is suffered by a man if he still has the means to fill his stomach, to clothe his body and to keep a roof over his head!

And yet the truth is, as I have endeavoured to show, that frugal people who strive for and obtain the margin above these materially necessary things are the whole foundation of a really active and developing national life.

The case for the middle class is the case for a dynamic democracy as against a stagnant one. Stagnant waters are level and in them the scum rises. Active waters are never level; they toss and tumble and have crests and troughs, but the scientists tell us that they purify themselves in a few hundred yards.

That we are all, as human souls, of like value cannot be denied; that each of us should have his chance is and must be the great objective of political and social policy.

But to say that the industrious and intelligent son of self-sacrificing and saving and forward-looking parents has the same social desires and even material needs as the dull offspring of stupid and improvident parents is absurd.

If the motto is to be: 'Eat, drink and be merry for tomorrow you will die, and if it chances you don't die, the state will look after you; but if you don't eat, drink and be merry, and save, we shall take your savings from you' – then the whole business of life will become foundationless.

Are you looking forward to a breed of men after the war who will have become boneless wonders? Leaners grow flabby; lifters grow muscles. Men without ambition readily become slaves. Indeed there is much more slavery in Australia than most people imagine.

How many hundreds of thousands of us are slaves to greed, to fear, to newspapers, to public opinion – represented by the accumulated views of our neighbours? Landless men smell the vapours of the street corner. Landed men smell the brown earth and plant their feet upon it and know that it is good.

To all of this many of my friends will retort: 'Ah, that's all very well, but when this war is over the levellers will have won the day.'

My answer is that, on the contrary, men will come out of this war as gloriously unequal in many things as when they entered it. Much wealth will have been destroyed; inherited riches will be suspect; a fellowship of suffering, if we really experience it, will have opened many hearts and perhaps closed many mouths. Many great edifices will have fallen, and we will be able to study foundations as never before, because war will have exposed them.

But I don't believe that we shall come out into the overlordship of an all-powerful state on whose benevolence we shall live, spineless and effortless; a state which will dole out bread and ideas with neatly regulated accuracy; where we shall all have our dividend without subscribing our capital; where the government – that almost deity – will nurse us and pension us and bury us; where we shall all be civil servants, and all presumably, since we are equal, head of departments!

If the new world is to be a world of men we must be not pallid and bloodless ghosts, but a community of people whose motto shall be '*to strive, to seek, to find and not to yield*'.

Individual enterprise must drive us forward. That doesn't mean that we are to return to the old and selfish notions of laissez faire. The functions of the state will be much more than merely keeping the ring within which the competitors will fight. Our social and industrial obligations will be increased. There will be more law, not less; more control, not less.

But what really happens to us will depend on how many people we have who are of the great and sober and dynamic middle class – the strivers, the planners, the ambitious ones.

We shall destroy them at our peril.

THE CULTURAL CRINGE

A.A. Phillips

1950

Once upon a time (and not very long ago), the Australian Broadcasting Commission used to present a Sunday programme, designed to cajole a mild Sabbatarian bestirment of the wits. Paired musical performances were broadcast, one by an Australian, one by an overseas executant, but with the names and nationalities withheld until the end of the programme. The listener was supposed to guess which was the Australian and which the alien performer. The idea was that quite often he guessed wrong, or gave it up, because, strange to say, the local lad proved no worse than the foreigner. This unexpected discovery was intended to inspire a nice glow of patriotic satisfaction.

I am not jeering at the ABC for its quaint idea. The programme's designer had rightly diagnosed a disease of the Australian mind, and was applying a sensible curative treatment. The dismaying circumstance is that such a treatment should be necessary, or even possible; that, in any nation, there should be an assumption that the domestic cultural product will be worse than the imported article.

The devil of it is that the assumption will often be correct. The numbers are against us, and an inevitable quantitative inferiority easily looks like a qualitative weakness, under the most favourable circumstances – and our circumstances are not favourable. We cannot shelter from invidious comparisons behind the barrier of a separate language; we have no long-established or interestingly different cultural tradition to give security and distinction to its interpreters; and the centrifugal pull of the great cultural metropolises works against us. Above our writers – and other artists – looms the intimidating mass of Anglo-Saxon achievement. Such a situation almost inevitably produces the characteristic Australian Cultural Cringe – appearing either as the Cringe Direct, or as the Cringe Inverted, in the attitude of the Blatant Blatherskite, the God's-Own-country-and-I'm-a-better-man-than-you-are Australian Bore.

The Cringe mainly appears in a tendency to make needless comparisons. The Australian reader, more or less consciously, hedges and hesitates, asking himself, 'Yes, but what would a cultivated Englishman think of this?' No writer can communicate confidently to a reader with the 'Yes, but' habit; and this particular demand is curiously crippling to critical judgement. Confronted by Joseph Furphy, we grow uncertain. We fail to recognise the extraordinary original structure of his novel because we are wondering whether an Englishman would not find it too complex and self-conscious. No one worries about the structural deficiencies of *Moby Dick*. We do not fully savour the meaty individualism of Furphy's style because we are wondering whether perhaps his egotistic verbosity is not too Australianly crude; but we accept the egotistic verbosity of George Borrow as part of his quality.

The Australian writer normally frames his communication for the Australian reader. He assumes certain mutual pre-knowledge, a responsiveness to certain symbols, even the ability to hear the cadence of a phrase in a certain way. Once the reader's mind begins to be nagged by the thought of how an Englishman might think about this, he loses the fine edge of his Australian responsiveness. It is absurd to feel apologetic about *Such is Life* or *Coonardoo* or *Melbourne Odes* because they would not seem quite right to an English reader; it is part of their distinctive virtue that no Englishman can fully understand them.

I once read a criticism which began from the question, 'What would a French classicist think of *Macbeth*?' The analysis was discerningly conducted and had a certain paradoxical interest; but it could not escape an effect of comic irrelevance.

A second effect of the Cringe has been the estrangement of the Australian intellectual. Australian life, let us agree, has an atmosphere of often dismaying crudity. I do not know if our cultural crust is proportionately thinner than that of any other Anglo-Saxon community – such evidence as the number of books we buy and the proportion of subscribers commanded by our more intelligent papers would suggest that in fact our cultural attainments are rather above the average Anglo-Saxon level. To the intellectual, however, the crust *feels* thinner, because, in a small community, there is not enough of it to provide the individual with a protective insulation. Hence, more than most intellectuals, he feels a sense of exposure. This is made much worse by that deadly habit of English comparison. There is a certain type of Australian intellectual who is forever sidling up to the cultivated Englishman, insinuating 'I, of course, am not like these other crude Australians. I understand how you must feel about them; I should be more at home in Oxford or Bloomsbury' (the use of Bloomsbury as a symbol of intellectuality is badly out of date; but, then, so as a rule is the Australian Cringer).

This tendency is deepened by the nature of the Englishman – at least of the upper-class Englishman. It is not simply that he is sure of his superiority. The Frenchman and the German are no less firmly convinced that they are the crowning achievements of history. The trouble is that the Englishman is so quietly convincing about his superiority. The beautiful sheen of his self-assurance exercises an hypnotic influence on its victims.

Let us pause here for a moment to observe the Cringe in action. A visiting Englishman was lecturing to a Melbourne audience on a literary theme. Wishing to define a certain character in a drama, he said, 'He's the sort of chap you might meet on a Melbourne tram – rather a crude sort of chap but ...' At that point his audience laughed. No independent auditor, I believe, could have resisted an impulse of disgust at the sycophancy of that laugh.

In fact, of course, the lecturer did not intend the criticism which his audience read into that remark – their readiness to misinterpret it is itself significant. He was repeating a lecture which he had often given in England. Probably at this point he was accustomed to say, 'He's the sort of person you might meet on a London bus – rather a crude sort of chap but ...' He had simply made a transposition into a setting better known to his audience, since the point about the setting was to emphasise the familiarity of the character. Had he really intended to make a criticism of the specifically Australian Common Man, it would have been, in a guest, a piece of gratuitously discourteous irrelevance. The natural response to it would have been shocked and mildly annoyed surprise. Yet his audience – highly selected for Cringe by the nature of the occasion – laughed. They were, in fact, hastening to assert 'Yes, yes, *I* know that Australians are crude; I'm on your side of the fence.'

A similar tendency is revealed in the Australian intellectual's habit of hurling denigratory criticisms at the Australian community without any attempt to check their accuracy. Thus it was long his morose pleasure to repeat that 'the Australian' did not read, that his home was a bookless monument to Philistinism – until the figures which the Cringer ignored got into the press, and established the fact that the Australian *per capita* purchase of books was higher than in any other Anglo-Saxon community. It is still a favourite Cringer's parrot-cry that the Australian is jealous of outstanding ability, that he demands a dead-level of mediocrity. I have never found a shred of evidence to support this accusation – its chanters have certainly never supplied me with any. It is not, of course, the sort of statement that can be objectively tested with any precision, but one obvious check of its accuracy might be applied. If it were true, it would surely appear in the choice of political leaders, since that is a field acutely sensitive to popular prejudice. Yet a comparative observation of political leadership in England and Australia suggests an opposite conclusion. Here is a list of the English party leaders since 1919: Lloyd George (appointed at a moment of acute crisis in war, and falling not long after the attainment of victory), Bonar Law, Baldwin, Neville Chamberlain, Churchill (again appointed when the country was on the brink of war-time disaster, after a decade in the political wilderness), Eden, Macmillan; and on the other side of the House, MacDonald, Lansbury, Attlee and Gaitskell.

If we ignore the special case of the war-time leaders, this list does suggest a popular preference for safe mediocrity. Almost all the peace-time premiers were served by subordinates of solider mind and more forceful personality than their leaders. A Curzon, a Cripps, an Austen Chamberlain, does not become an English prime minister.

The comparable Australian list reads: Hughes (paralleling Lloyd George in his appointment and fall), Bruce, Latham, Lyons and Menzies; and on the Labor side, Charlton, Scullin, Curtin, Chifley and Evatt. The highest common factor of choice is simply that the accepted leader was the ablest man available – there are at most two exceptions to this rule. The genially mediocre extrovert is conspicuously absent from the list; a surprising proportion of the men comprising it were distinguished either by a cool austerity or by an arrogant assertiveness of their own superiority; yet surely these are the types which would be most firmly slapped down, if the community were really afflicted by a jealousy of outstanding ability.

The critical attitude of the intellectual towards the community is, of course, not in itself harmful; on the contrary, it could be a healthy, even a creative influence, if the criticism were felt to come from within, if the critic had a sense of identification with his subject, if his irritation came from a sense of shared shame rather than from a disdainful separation. It is his refusal to participate, the arch of his indifferent eyebrows, which exerts the chilling and stultifying influence.

Thinking of this type of Australian intellectual, I am a little uneasy about my phrase 'cultural cringe'; it is so much the kind of missile which he delights to throw at the Australian mob. I hope I have made it clear that my use of the phrase is not essentially unsympathetic, and that I regard the denaturalised intellectual as the Cringe's unhappiest victim. If any of the breed use my phrase for his own contemptuous purposes, my curse be upon him. May crudely-Dinkum Aussies spit in his beer, and gremlins split his ever-to-be-precisely-agglutinated infinitives.

The Australian writer is affected by the Cringe, because it mists the responsiveness of his audience, and because its influence on the intellectual deprives him of a sympathetically critical audience. Nor can he entirely escape its direct impact. The core of the difficulty is the fact that, in the back of the Australian mind, there sits a minatory Englishman. He is not even the most suitable type of Englishman – not the rare pukka sahib with his deep still pool of imaginativeness, and his fine urbanity; not the common man with his blending of solidity and tenderness: but that Public School Englishman with his detection of a bad smell permanently engraved on his features, who has left a trail of exasperation through Europe and of smouldering hatred through the East, and whose indifference to the Commonwealth is not even studied.

Subconsciously the educated Australian feels a guilty need to placate this shadowy figure (Freud has a name for it). His ghost sits in on the tête-à-tête between Australian reader and writer, interrupting in the wrong accent.

It may be said – it often is – that this is a healthy influence, ensuring that we shall measure our cultural achievements by universal standards, protecting us from the dangers of parochialism. This is only a little of the truth. Finely responsive reading is primarily an act of surrender, only secondarily an act of judgement. That minatory ghost prevents the unqualified readiness to meet the writer on his own terms which should precede a critical appraisement. The Australian writer has almost conquered the problems of colonialism; they still sit as heavily on the Australian reader as the plum pudding of an Australian Christmas.

What is the cure for our disease? There is no short-cut to circumvent the gradual processes of national growth – which are already having their effect. As I have already suggested, the most important development made in Australian writing over the last twenty years has been the progress in the art of being self-consciously ourselves. In the same period there has also been a similar, though slower, development in the response of the Australian reader. That response will develop more rapidly in discrimination and maturity of judgement, as the present increasing interest in Australian studies within the universities takes its effect. Meanwhile the pace of those developments can be quickened if we articulately recognise two facts: that the Cringe is a worse enemy to our cultural development than our isolation, and that the opposite of the Cringe is not the Strut, but a relaxed erectness of carriage.

RE-WRITING AUSTRALIAN HISTORY

Manning Clark

1955

I t would be appropriate to begin an essay on such a young subject as the writing of Australian history by quoting a powerful passage from one of the oldest faiths in the world. This is from the first book of Samuel: 'And it came to pass, when the *evil* spirit from God was upon Saul, that David took an harp, and played with his hand; so Saul was refreshed, and was well, and the evil spirit departed from him.'

True, in comparison with religion and music, history has not been one of the great comforters of mankind. But our ideas of the past are part of that great enormous attic of the mind which devours everything which looks as though it might help us to achieve what we are all after – 'to be there when everyone suddenly understands what it has all been for'. And of course these ideas have a big influence on the way we think and even the way we behave. One of the convictions of the majority of educated people in, say, England or Australia, is that British political institutions and the Protestant religion were the creators of political liberty and material progress.

It was because Macaulay persuaded teachers that the seventeenth century was the decisive period in the moulding of both British political institutions and the Protestant religion that the study of the seventeenth century became the centre of courses of history in the English-speaking world and all those areas which came under British influence in the nineteenth century. So men and women studied that era not as a discipline or diversion for the mind, but because such a study would reveal to them the secrets of political liberty and material progress. Men then are refreshed, comforted and instructed by their ideas of the past.

But, this study of British political institutions and the Protestant religion seemed worthwhile only so long as people believed strongly in political liberty and material progress. When such beliefs perish people still involved in the old mental habits seem to be 'Darling Dodoes'. This is the situation we are now in in Australia. Our ideas of the past are those of preceding generations. They are not a response to the problems and aspirations of this generation. I believe that the task of the historians for this generation is twofold – to show why the comforters of the past should be dropped, and to put forward new ideas for this generation.

First, let us drop the idea that our past has irrevocably condemned us to the role of cultural barbarians. The past, it is said, has made us resourceful, good improvisers, but not made possible the cultivation of the things of the mind – it has left us coarse and vulgar, forced us to accept the second-rate; more, given us a taste for the second-rate, and a rather perverse pleasure in taking down the mighty and talented from their seats, what Sir Howard Florey called 'the apparently endless nagging at anyone who pokes his head slightly above the ruck'. So we can never become cultivated, graceful Europeans; must remain well-fed barbarians forever.

Our ancestors took a terrible drubbing on this score. As early as November 1835 a writer in the *Van Diemen's Land Monthly Magazine* was chiding the locals for their 'too engrossing pursuit of riches', a habit which he said was 'prejudicial to the cultivation of science and literature'. The English historian Froude was still harping on the same theme in 1880 – reminding Sydneysiders of their lack of 'severe intellectual interests'. 'They aim,' he wrote, 'at little except what money will buy; and to make money and buy enjoyment with it is the be-all and end-all of their existence.' In January 1921 Sir Arthur Conan Doyle, who, of course, could claim to speak with peculiar authority on the things of the spirit, made this terse comment to an *Age* reporter: 'It is the unliveliness and spiritual deadness of the place which gets on my nerves.' But it was left to D.H. Lawrence to go the whole hog. After a quick look at Perth, Sydney and the south coast of New South Wales, he dashed off this account to his sister-in-law in 1922:

This is the most democratic place I have *ever* been in. And the more I see of democracy the more I dislike it. It just brings everything down to the mere vulgar level of wages and prices, electric light and water-closets, and nothing else. You *never* knew anything so nothing, Nichts, nullus, niente, as the life here. They have good wages, they wear smart boots, and the girls all have silk stockings ... That's what the life in a new country does to you: makes you so material, so *outward*, that your real inner life and your inner self dies out and you clatter around like so many mechanical animals.

Although a few of our ancestors made rude replies such as that of the bullock driver in *Such is Life*: 'But what — good does that do to the likes of us?' the majority were all too willing to confess their unworthiness. Oddly enough, at the same time as Lawrence was fulminating against our lack of an inner life, Henry Handel Richardson in *The Fortunes of Richard Mahony* was pouring out on paper how her father had been tortured by this lack of refinement and things of the spirit in Australia. With more urbanity, Martin Boyd raised the same sort of problem in *The Montforts*, but it was left to Keith Hancock to borrow this idea from the creative writers and circulate it amongst the historians. 'This middling standard,' he wrote in his *Australia* in 1930, 'is characteristic of democracy in Australia ... they [i.e. the Australians] have accepted the 'middling standard'. They have been willing to water good wine so that there may be enough for everybody. Their democratic theory asserts that the divine average has, potentially, a cultivated palate.'

We now no longer need to use cheek and ridicule, or to clutch convulsively on that broken reed that history explains everything, or to pitch our tents in the camp of the Philistines. Europe is no longer the creative centre, the teacher of the world. Today the English send their observers to China. Is it not time for our historians to abandon their preoccupation with the causes and effects of the Australian Cultural Desert?

For one thing, this harping on our pursuit of material gain, and our indifference to the things of the mind, and satisfaction with the middling standard creates the idea that there were no differences in the past – that there is, as it were, a dull and depressing sameness in our history – no great issues, no difference of principle, but always the same pursuit of filthy material gain and only a sordid struggle for power between various groups believing they can show us how to achieve it.

The trouble is that this view encouraged the historians to look in the wrong places for differences – i.e. in politics. There you saw none, and complained about sameness, middling standards and mediocrity. Actually there have been big differences. Take, for example, the differences in values between these two statements. The first is from the *Hummer*, a newspaper published in Wagga, on 16 January 1892:

> Socialism … is the desire to be mates, is the ideal of living together in harmony and brotherhood and loving kindness … if things were once fixed right we should no more need laws to make healthy men good mates than we need laws to make healthy women good mothers. It is diseased, vicious, evil conditions that breed infanticide and competition, which to me are each about as bad as the other – no better, no worse. Neither of them are being MATES!

That was the faith of one socialist in 1891.

In the same community there were people with quite different opinions on human behaviour and human destiny. Here is an extract from the sermon preached by Cardinal Moran in St Mary's Cathedral at a mass for the repose of the soul of Cardinal Newman:

> In many respects it is an age of ruins, and amid these ruins false scientists will set before us a phantom temple of socialistic atheism, or infidelity, or pantheism, in which selfishness and pride, the idols of a corrupt heart, demand our homage and worship. It is otherwise within the domain of the Catholic Church. She gathers her children around the altar of God to impart to them a divine life, to instruct them in heavenly wisdom, to unfold to them the secret of true happiness, and to lead them to their eternal destiny.

Today there are only two great beliefs in Australia – two tremendous Utopias. There are those who believe in that tremendous dream sketched in the Communist Manifesto. Then there are those who believe in the last paragraph of the Apostles' Creed. Earlier generations worried themselves sick trying to explain why in Australia there was what Professor Hope has called an 'Arabian desert of the human mind'. This generation was to worry out this question of fundamental faith. That is one of the great differences today – and I suggest that one of the great tasks of our historians is to explain how it came about.

Another significant difference they missed was and is the difference between the Catholic and the Protestant view of the world. I will illustrate this with an example from the history of political liberty – a subject highly coloured in our history books by the Protestant and secular view of liberty. To these historians liberty was a frail but precious bark nosing its way between the Scylla of economic privilege and the Charybdis of the tyranny of the majority. The attitude of the Church was severely snubbed by this school – that is, they did not even deign to mention it.

Yet in fact the attitude of the Catholic Church to liberty illuminates two of the great events in the last 100 years – the education controversy and the conscription crisis. They really were big differences. Here is an example of a pronouncement by the bishops of the Roman Church on liberty. This is from a pastoral to their priests commanding them to forbid their parishioners to read a Church of England periodical:

> These roaring lions [they are referring to the Church of England writers] in their audaciousness, usurp everything to themselves; everything must be examined; everything must be weighed by minds, perhaps but lightly imbued with Catholic truth and discipline; and nothing at all reserved for episcopal authority and the loving obedience of the faithful and confiding soul. Wherefore, most beloved brethren, we, whom the Holy Ghost has appointed to rule the Church of God, cannot in so great a corruption and blindness, do otherwise than arouse, as far as in us lies, the spirit of your devotion ... to unite with us ... for the same end. You having been made dispensers of the mysteries of God, be careful that the sheep entrusted to your care, and redeemed with the blood of Christ, be kept from such poisoned pasturage as just alluded to.

That pastoral was issued in Melbourne on the occasion of the feast of St Barnabas in 1858 – one year, by the way, before the publication of Mill's essay on Liberty.

This was not the Protestant conception of liberty. As an all too brief example of their view, we have the brilliant judgement of Mr Justice Windeyer in 1888:

The time is surely past when countenance can be given to the argument that knowledge of the truth either in physics or in the domain of thought is to be stifled because its abuse might be dangerous to society ... Ignorance is no more the mother of chastity than of true religion.

It was partly because they were not prepared to run the risk of exposing the children of the faithful to teachers with such a conception of liberty that the Catholic Church used extreme measures to force its members into the Catholic Schools. This meant, of course, that one set of values was taught to the Catholics and another to the Protestants. For the former, education was a preparation for eternity: for the latter, the aim was more mundane. It meant, as well, two different views of history. The minds of the Catholic children were steeped in the wrongs of Ireland, and the injustices of English domination: the minds of the Protestant with such works as 'Deeds that won the Empire'. Compare, for example, the attitude to the war of 1914: 'At the beginning of the war,' said Archbishop Mannix, 'I had made up my mind that the recruiting platform was not the place for a Catholic priest or a Catholic bishop.' By contrast, in September 1916 Dr Leeper told the Anglican synod in Melbourne that the war was a religious war. The synod then carried without opposition a resolution in favour of conscription. The *Age* account ends: 'The National anthem was then sung.'

By 1919 the *Argus* was warning the Protestants that the real grievance of the Irish Catholics was that the Empire was a Protestant Empire with a Protestant monarch (the *Argus*, 4 November 1919). And in November of 1919 an elector wrote to the *Argus* urging every returned digger and every Protestant to vote for the Nationalist Party, because the Labor Party would increase the power and the prominence of the Roman Catholic Church (the *Argus*, 8 November 1919). Surely, by now, it has become urgent for the historians to explain why there is a close association between the Catholic Church and the Labor Party – and to remind us that there are two traditions in the community with different conceptions of liberty, of equality and of democracy. So let us drop the talk about middling standards, mediocrity and sameness, and have a look at these differences.

The next comforter I want us to drop is the one about our convict origins. This was created to heal the wounds about the 'birth stain'. Let me remind you of the picture of transportation designed to comfort such diverse groups as the humanitarians, the Australian nationalists, the radicals, and the old Australian families with a skeleton in the cupboard from the convict era. First we are told that economic changes in England in the eighteenth century forced large numbers of respectable breadwinners and their dependants to choose between starvation, the humiliation of poor relief or theft. Then we are given a harrowing account of peasants crushed by cruel landlords and a monstrous criminal law, transported to Australia for minor offences against property, and there forced to associate with the dregs of humanity from the underworld of the towns. The heroes of this melodrama, the middle-class politicians, then enter on the scene to rescue the victims of such a vicious system by making the criminal law more humane and abolishing transportation. The extreme view was put by the late Professor Wood: '… the atrocious criminals remained in England, while their victims, innocent and many, founded the Australian democracy'. There is only one trouble with this opinion. It is just not true. You will notice one thing about this approach – you are never shown a convict. Instead you are reassured with generalisations such as 'innocent and manly' or 'village Hampdens' or some other high-flying phrase. Yet the facts were there, if they had wanted to see them. The great majority of the convicts were professional criminals. So instead of stirring up pity for the victims of enclosure, the rise in prices, the inadequate system of poor relief, and instead of castigating the savagery of the English criminal law, let us rather examine the habits and values of the criminals.

That, I can assure you, is far more illuminating, for there you will find the germ of some of the great themes in our history – the attitude to work, the curious paradox of the warm embrace for members of the same group but a snarl for the rest of the world. It is just as illuminating to examine the habits and values of the Irish thieves – partly because their contempt for all the laws of the Anglo-Saxon gave, as it were, a flying start to building up a tradition of lawlessness in Australia, but mainly because they were the cause of the coming of the Roman Catholic Church to Australia. This meant not only the Irish brand of Catholicism, but also the close association between that church and one section of the working classes in Australia. In fact, if one dropped the habit of dismissing the whole convict question after due censure of the English governing classes, and some quivers of horror on the vices of convicts, one would have time to acknowledge their contribution. I am thinking not only of their contribution to the wealth of individuals or of society in general. I am thinking also of our extreme good fortune that they did the pioneer work without leaving an ugly social problem for after generations – as, for example, did the Negro in the United States and the Kaffir in South Africa.

My next suggestion is that we should drop the idea of the past created and used to support the political and cultural movements at the turn of the century – say, to be safe, 1880–1920. First let me show you how this idea came to birth. There were three movements which were sometimes identical, sometimes separate. First, there were the nationalists. What they were after was put simply by W.J. Sowden:

It had become the fashion to belittle everything Australian. Our wealthier men boasted, when they gave a dinner to their friends, that there was nothing 'Colonial' upon their tables. Colonial wine was sour, Colonial ale was watery, Colonial cheese was rancid … Colonial writers were clumsy; the Colonial sun had a sickly glare; the Colonial firmament was an exceedingly poor and shockingly burlesqued copy of the dear old original heavens canopying the dear old original Mother Country!

Like most nationalist movements they were quite impressive when putting their claim for recognition, but often ludicrous when they talked about what they would put in place of the habits of the 'dear old mother country'. For instance, this same Sowden suggested that the old world 'three cheers' be replaced by an Australian 'three cooees'. Then there was the movement for political democracy, supported by the Liberals and the new political labour movement. I imagine some of the Liberals, and even the prosaic labour leaders, must have been embarrassed by the language used to describe their creed. Take this piece of doggerel from the *Bulletin* of 8 November 1890:

Down with old world race dissensions,
Truth and Justice leads the van.
Creed and hate are hell's inventions,
Trust the brotherhood of man.

This was put more soberly in the labour paper the Brisbane *Worker* on 5 January 1901, but you can see the idea developing:

> Australia has ever been an exemplar to the old lands ... By a happy fortune it sprang up free of most of the superstitions, traditions, class distinctions and sanctified fables and fallacies of the older nations.

Notice how this writer is beginning to sketch an idea of the past to fit in with his political aims – to justify and sanctify them. The mundane journalists had their eyes on the present, and were prepared to use the past. The poets went on with astonishing pictures of the future. Do you remember the coy question in Bernard O'Dowd's 'Australia'? 'Or lurks the millennial Eden 'neath thy breast?'

That is a hackneyed line. I should like, by courtesy of the work of Mr Vance Palmer, to resurrect from the past O'Dowd's *Lyceum Tutor*. The prophet is asked: 'Peer into the future and tell me what you see there.' He replies: 'The spectacle of a United Australia! Free from all connections with old world tyrannies, rich in possession of a glorious race, free from religious tyranny as from political.'

In a moment I will show you how the poets built up an idea of the past to persuade people that history too was on the side of democracy. But first a word on the third strand in this movement – the creed of the bushman. '[A] gambler and a nomad' the *Times* correspondent in Australia called him in an article in the *Times* for 31 August 1903. And he went on:

> ... in such surroundings he remains perpetually a child ... And he is especially like a child in this, that his code of social ethics is based on the family. The bush folk are of his family, every one of them *ipso facto* a mate of his, to be welcomed and treated as such unless some meanness demands expulsion; outsiders are for that very reason to be suspected – people to whom he owes few or no duties except that of hospitality – though the best of them may, after due trial made, be admitted among his comrades. Within that family it is the cardinal virtue to be 'straight', and property is shared to an extent that might almost be called communism.

And he went on to point out shrewdly that the bushman's politics were those of a child – that he felt misunderstood, and was therefore inclined to accept the advice and friendship of anyone who was sympathetic.

Now notice that all three trends are anti-English: the last two believe in brotherhood, in being mates, and in equality. Gradually the men holding these opinions built up their own idea of the past. You can see this beginning during their campaign for more political democracy. Remember those words of the Brisbane *Worker*: 'Australia has *ever* been an exemplar to the old lands.' The poets were not slow to take up the hint given by these working journalists. So Victor Daley in 'A Ballad of Eureka', written in 1901, went further and began to create a pantheon of democratic victories in the past. He settled on the Eureka rebellion in 1854:

> *Yet 'ere the year was over,*
> *Freedom rolled in like a flood:*
> *They gave us all we asked for –*
> *When we asked for it in blood.*

By 1904 the prose publicists were popularising the idea – e.g. Robert Ross' pamphlet *Eureka: Freedom's Fight of '54*. The historians were late into the field – but quickly filled in the details left blank by the poets, and industriously dug up an array of evidence to support their view. So 1850–54 became the great watershed in Australian history – the start of a crusade for the victory of political democracy and equality in the constitutions of the colonies, the ownership of land, education and social conventions.

In fact, by 1948 the idea became so safe, so respectable that the Labor Party, with great daring, climbed on the bandwagon and decided to name a Commonwealth electorate after the diggers' leader – Lalor – and a Labor minister justified this by showing that he too accepted this idea of the past: 'Democracy in this country,' he said, 'began at Eureka.'

That is the great Australian illusion – the idea that we were pioneers of democracy – that while Europe reverted to the blackest reaction after the abortive revolutions of 1848–51, Australia was the political and social laboratory of the world – with her experiments in democracy, equality of opportunity and *material progress*. And, it is argued, we owe this distinction to the diggers, to Eureka and to a delightfully vague movement called 'Chartism'. It is time to prick the bubble of this conceit.

First, it ignores the contribution of the period before gold, a great pity, because there, rather than on the goldfields, is the germ of the belief in equality. It was the labour shortage in country districts, rather than imported social and political ideals, which eroded the centuries-old belief in inequality. Second, it over-emphasises the degree of political democracy introduced after the gold rushes. Third, it concentrates attention on the political achievements in the period of gold and thus loses sight of two of the central facts of the period. This was the great period of the squatters – up to 1890. It was also the great period of bourgeois civilisation in our cities – the period in which cathedrals, town halls, universities, schools, banks and pastoral company buildings were put up as symbols of their faith. There has been nothing like it since. That is the sort of picture one begins to build up, once one drops the idea that the past is a mirror of Australia's radical tradition – and that if one looks very closely one can find reasons for believing that Australians, unlike Europeans, can build a heaven on earth.

Perhaps the most striking example of the way in which this belief in a radical tradition distorts and warps our writing of Australian history is in the interpretation of the labour movement. The two most illuminating writers on the subject – Mr V. Gordon Childe and Mr Brian Fitzpatrick – were (at the time they wrote their works) disappointed radicals. That is to say, they thought of the past as a vast manure heap to fertilise the soil for some future harmony – a harmony which Labor would complete. But Labor, as they knew it, was not worthy of such a high calling, and showed no intention of working for the regeneration of mankind. It was corrupt, opportunist, riddled with bourgeois prejudices. Why? This illustration of the radical past had a disastrous effect on the way in which they answered the question. It gave both of them the illusion that there was a time when labour was pure, untainted by the world, the flesh and the devil. That was in the 1890s. So Childe said that the history of political Labor was a story of 'how a band of inspired socialists degenerated into a vast machine for the capture of political power'. Fitzpatrick followed suit. So did all the people who have borrowed so heavily from their work – Portus, Sir Keith Hancock, and others. This makes most of the histories of labour read rather like the stories of fallen women – with the personality of the writer dictating the final twist: Childe on the iron law of oligarchy, Fitzpatrick's infectious optimism, and G.W. Campbell's belief that the communists can rescue labour in very much the same way as Dr Arnold rescued Rugby. Then again, people who believed that labour was once a menace assumed that all 'fusions' of non-labour parties were dictated by this need to keep labour at bay – hence the label of 'parties of resistance' – which, incidentally, is grossly unfair to the non-labour parties.

One final example of the insidious influence of the past as evidence of a radical tradition: The past, we are assured, weighs on the brain of the living. If you give great prestige to the past, or a section of the past, it can have a stultifying effect on the present; that is the effect of a belief in a golden age in the past. This idea of the past not only weighs on the brains of our radicals, but threatens to stop them thinking altogether.

So much for the way in which this illusion of a radical tradition distorts and warps our idea of the past. I doubt, however, whether one would have much success in persuading people to drop it just because it is not true. The truth about the past excites a tiny minority – it is their spiritual pleasure and their bread and butter. There are, however, more compelling reasons for dropping it. Take, for example, one of the strands in the creed: the ideal of mateship. This was the great comforter of the bushman:

> *They tramp in mateship side by side*
> *The Protestant and the Roman*
> *They call no biped Lord or Sir*
> *And touch their hats to no man.*

So Lawson. It was their holy of holies – the last disgrace was to be proved unworthy of 'mateship'.

I doubt whether it is wise for us to treat this ideal with such awe and veneration. Like most groups living in conditions of material hardship, they built up a code of love and fellowship for each other and damnation for the rest of the world. This is an all too frequent feature in schemes of brotherhood. You will remember the Jews made this sharp distinction in their version of harmony: 'The wolf,' wrote the prophet Isaiah, 'shall also dwell with the lamb; and the leopard shall lie down with the kid … They shall not hurt nor destroy in all my holy mountain.' That was, however, reserved for the Jews. As for their neighbours:

'Their children … shall be dashed to pieces before their eyes; their houses shall be spoiled and their wives ravished.'

You will find it too in a less exalted form in the ideals of the coster-mongers of London. The members of society outside their own circle were described with one term of contempt – they were all 'bloody aris-tocrats'. The Australian ideal had this same taint of xenophobia – they were contemptuous of Englishmen and savage on money-lenders and Jews – that was bad enough. But they reserved their bitterest bile for the one group we can ill afford to offend. So the high priest of mateship, William Lane, warned his fellow mates and 'dinkum Aussies' about the 'piebald brats'. And the bushman's staple reading matter – the *Bulletin* – sneered at Edward VII's stupendous nigger empire – 'the greatest nig-ger empire in the world' (22 February 1902) and reminded mates of the blessings of a White Australia: 'A White Australia will never have to fry a nigger at the stake' (25 November 1906). Instead of worshipping at the altar of mateship, we may find ourselves making expiation and atone-ment for such arrogance – for are we not that third and fourth generation on whom the sins of the fathers are to be visited?

Nor is that the only reason for jibbing at their ideal. Mateship was the product of a way of life – a mate was a bulwark against loneliness, a help in time of sickness and accident. There was no attempt to make mateship universal in application – to extend it from the people they knew to all people – nor was there any attempt to find universal reasons for believing in it. You do not find them putting forward any metaphys-ical or religious reasons for their belief. In fact, in comparison with the questions raised by another group of semi-nomads, their questions seem shallow and trivial: 'If a man die, shall he live again? all the days of my appointed time will I wait, till my change come.' And this one: 'What is man that he should be clean? and be which is born of a woman, that he should be righteous?'

Beside such questions, the Lawsonian precept 'to call no biped Lord or Sir, and touch your hat to no man' is rather small beer.

Finally a point which should not need underlining. The conditions to which belief in mateship was a response have almost entirely disap-peared. This was beginning to happen almost when the ideal was first taking shape:

Those golden days are vanished
And altered is the scene;
The diggings are deserted,
The camping-grounds are green;
The flaunting flag of progress
Is in the West unfurled,
The mighty Bush with iron rails
Is tethered to the world.

So Lawson in a nostalgic mood at the turn of the century. In less than a decade, Japan showed at Mukden and Tsushima that the material superiority of European civilisation was not unassailable. World war, revolution, and the revival of persecution were soon to sow doubts about its spiritual supremacy. This had gradually caused a change in the subjects chosen by our poets. They, at least, have moved on to other subjects, and other comforters than those of earlier generations. Where the nationalists wrote of happiness founded on material well-being for all, Douglas Stewart writes of a much older theme in the lot of mankind:

... a man must learn
To endure agony, to endure and endure again
Until agony itself is beaten out into joy.

Where the nationalists preached democracy as the panacea for the ills of society, James McAuley has some doubts:

The great Unculture that you feared might be
'Drawn to the dregs of a democracy'
Is full upon us; here it sours and thickens
Till every work of art and honour sickens.

Where they had the sort of confidence of a Rugby blue in the here and now, and a corresponding enthusiasm for life, Kenneth Slessor raises questions about Time and Death. In this extract from 'Five Bells', he is putting some questions to a dead friend:

Why do I think of you, dead man, why thieve
These profitless lodgings from the flukes of thought

Anchored in Time? You have gone from earth,
Gone even from the meaning of a name;
Yet something's there, yet something forms its lips
And hits and cries against the ports of space,
Beating their sides to make its fury heard.

Are you shouting at me, dead man, squeezing your face
In agonies of speech on speechless panes?
Cry louder, beat the windows, bawl your name!

But I hear nothing, nothing ... only bells,
Five bells, the bumpkin calculus of Time.

So the first move to be made in the re-writing of Australian history is to drop the ideas of the past which have comforted and instructed earlier generations. What then shall we put in their place? To that question I have only given snatches of an answer for the simple reason that the whole answer has so far eluded me. But I do believe that it is a great and noble task to answer that question, and that what I have discussed is a necessary preparation for it.

I do not believe that this re-writing will come from the universities, though they will greatly assist the work of the creative writer. It will not come from the universities because they, instead of being the fiercest critics of the bankrupt liberal ideal, are its most persistent defenders. Then too they have been made afraid by the angry men of today with their talk about 'corrupters of youth'. It will not come from the measurers, for they hold the terrible belief that measuring will show there is no mystery. It will not come from the radicals of this generation because they are either tethered to an erstwhile great but now excessively rigid creed, or they are frightened by the self-appointed inquisitors of our morals and political opinions.

History, to be great as history, must have a point of view on the direction of society. It must also have something to say, some great theme to lighten our darkness – that, for example, the era of bourgeois liberalism, of democracy, and belief in material progress is over, and that those who defend such a creed are the reactionaries of today. To be great as literature – the aim of all historians – it must be written by someone who has something to say about human nature, but, above all, it must be written by someone who has pondered deeply over the problems of life and death. Like the fox in the Greek fragment, the historian must know many things, but like the hedgehog, he must know one big thing – and feel it deeply.

While I believe that Australians should drop the comforters of the days of their youth and innocence, I believe even more strongly that the historians should come back to the great themes they abandoned when they joined in the vain search for a science of society.

THE AUSTRALIAN LEGEND

Russel Ward

1958

For I'm a ramble-eer, a rollicking ramble-eer,
I'm a roving rake of poverty, and a son of a gun for beer.

In the last seventy-odd years millions of words have been written about Australian nationalism and the 'Australian character'. Most writers seem to have felt strongly that the 'Australian spirit' is somehow intimately connected with the bush and that it derives rather from the common folk than from the more respectable and cultivated sections of society. This book seeks, not to give yet another cosily impressionistic sketch of what wild boys we Australians are – or like to consider ourselves – but rather to trace and explain the development of this national *mystique*.

Nearly all legends have some basis in historical fact. We shall find that the Australian legend has, perhaps, a more solid substratum of fact than most, but this does not mean that it comprises all, or even most, of what we need to know to understand Australia and Australian history. It may be, however, a very important means to this end, if only because we shall certainly be wrong if we either romanticise its influence or deny it.

National character is not, as was once held, something inherited; nor is it, on the other hand, entirely a figment of the imagination of poets, publicists and other feckless dreamers. It is rather a people's idea of itself and this stereotype, though often absurdly romanticised and exaggerated, is always connected with reality in two ways. It springs largely from a people's past experiences, and it often modifies current events by colouring men's ideas of how they ought 'typically' to behave.

According to the myth the 'typical Australian' is a practical man, rough and ready in his manners and quick to decry any appearance of affectation in others. He is a great improviser, ever willing 'to have a go' at anything, but willing too to be content with a task done in a way that is 'near enough'. Though capable of great exertion in an emergency, he normally feels no impulse to work hard without good cause. He swears hard and consistently, gambles heavily and often, and drinks deeply on occasion. Though he is 'the world's best confidence man', he is usually taciturn rather than talkative, one who endures stoically rather than one who acts busily. He is a 'hard case', sceptical about the value of religion and of intellectual and cultural pursuits generally. He believes that Jack is not only as good as his master but, at least in principle, probably a good deal better, and so he is a great 'knocker' of prominent people unless, as in the case of his sporting heroes, they are distinguished by physical prowess. He is a fiercely independent person who hates officiousness and authority, especially when these qualities are embodied in military officers and policemen. Yet he is very hospitable and, above all, will stick to his mates through thick and thin, even if he thinks they may be in the wrong. No epithet in his vocabulary is more completely damning than 'scab', unless it be 'pimp' used in its peculiarly Australasian slang meaning of 'informer'. He tends to be a rolling stone, highly suspect if he should chance to gather much moss.

In the following pages we shall find that all these characteristics were widely attributed to the bushmen of the last century, not, primarily, to Australians in general or even to country people in general, so much as to the outback employees, the semi-nomadic drovers, shepherds, shearers, bullock-drivers, stockmen, boundary-riders, station-hands and others of the pastoral industry.

This was so partly because the material conditions of outback life were such as to evoke these qualities in pastoral workers, but partly too because the first and most influential bush-workers were convicts or ex-convicts, the conditions of whose lives were such that they brought with them to the bush the same, or very similar, attitudes.

In nineteenth-century Australia, this particular social group developed a surprisingly high degree of cohesion and self-consciousness but, in isolating it for the purposes of study, some distortion may be inevitable. In fact, of course, pastoral workers were constantly influencing, and being influenced by, other sections of colonial society. A convict often spent months or years on government constructional work in the city before being assigned to the service of a country settler, or he might be returned to the city after some years 'up the country'. Small farmers and selectors often sought work as shearers on the western runs to supplement their incomes, and many a city wage-earner did the same for a few seasons, especially during bad times when work was scarce on the sea-board. Bullock-drivers, especially before railways began to creep farther and farther into the interior after about 1870, regularly flogged their teams from the colonial capitals and coastal ports to outback stations and back again. They carried news, gossip, manners and songs, as well as stores, wool and hides. One of them, Charles Macalister, wrote of Sydney in the 1840s:

> A chief house of call for us country folk then was the old Blackboy Hotel, at the corner of George and King Streets. A kind of theatre or people's music-hall was kept in connection with this Hotel, where the leading comedians and singers were Jim Brown and 'Micky' Drew; but, as the platform of the Blackboy 'theatre' was somewhat free and easy, sometimes a strong sailorman, just off a six months cruise, would favour us with 'Nancy Lee' or other jolly sea-song; or an ambitious carrier or drover would 'rouse the possum' by giving some long-winded ditty of the time.

Drovers brought not only cattle and sheep to the city markets but also exotic styles of dress, speech and behaviour, wherewith to impress respectable citizens and newly arrived immigrants. And many a bushman from the interior settled down in the agricultural areas or the city, after a happy marriage or old age had terminated his roving habits. As Alan Marshall wrote, in 1955, of his father:

> After he started work he drifted round from station to station horse-breaking or droving. His youth and early manhood were spent in the outback areas of New South Wales and Queensland, and it was these areas that furnished the material for all his yarns. Because of his tales, the saltbush plains and the red sand-hills of the

outback were closer to me than the green country where I was born and grew to manhood.

Up to about 1900 the prestige of the bushman seems to have been greater than that of the townsman. In life as in folklore the man from 'up the country' was usually regarded as a romantic and admirable figure. The attitude towards him was reminiscent, in some interesting ways, of that towards the 'noble savage' in the eighteenth century. We shall see that, in general, he had more influence on the manners and *mores* of the city-dweller than the latter had on his. The tide turned somewhere between 1900 and 1918. Even today the tradition of the 'noble bushman' is still very strong in both literature and folklore, but, at least since the publication in 1899 of *On Our Selection*, it has been counterpoised by the opposing tradition of 'Dad and Mum, Dave and Mabel'. True, Dad and Dave were not pastoral workers, bushmen proper, but poor selectors, 'stringybark cockatoos', who were sneered at by the men from farther out long before it became fashionable for townsmen to regard them as figures of fun. It is also true that the original creators of A.H. Davis ('Steele Rudd') were real comic characters and not the semi-moronic, burlesque puppets which they have since become in popular imagination. Nevertheless their appearance in literature fifty years ago was symptomatic of a real change in Australian attitudes towards the 'bush'. Since the early days of Federation the capital cities have grown rapidly both in prestige and in their relative share of state populations, and bushmen are now usually willing to be taken for city-dwellers where formerly the reverse was the case.

In making generalisations about the bush-worker, a difficulty springs from the fact of separate origins of the colonies which later became the federated states of the Commonwealth. There have always been, and still are, differences between them in speech, manners, tradition and outlook. But compared with similar differences in, say, Canada or the USA, they are slight indeed, tending to be differences of degree and emphasis rather than of substance. They are more noticeable among middle-class than among working-class people, and in and near the state capitals than in the back country. We shall see that the convict-derived bush ethos grew first and flourished in its most unadulterated form in the mother colony of New South Wales, but that it early spread thence, by osmosis as it were, to become the most important basic component of the national *mystique*.

Two recent newspaper reports will indicate how strong the tradition still is today, and also the extent to which it has been regionally modified. A semi-editorial article in the *Sydney Morning Herald* of 19 July 1953 declared:

> One of the ugly features of Australian city life is the refusal of bystanders to help, in fact their inclination to hinder, a policeman in trouble. There have been some bad cases in Sydney, Melbourne is no better, judging by an incident last week. A man who turned out to be an escaped mental patient had kicked one policeman unconscious and was struggling with another. A gathering crowd yelled, 'Why don't you give him a go, you big mug?'
>
> Only onlooker to intervene was a New Australian, Steve Ovcar, who secured the escapee's hands with a tie. Said Ovcar afterwards, 'People are terrible here. They just watched. They were all against the policemen.'

A report in the Adelaide *Advertiser* on 12 December 1953 modified the picture slightly:

> The attitude of the police to the public in such matters as traffic control did much to establish the regard in which the Police Department was held in the community, Mr John Bonython, a director of the *Advertiser*, said yesterday ... Mr Bonython said that the public's attitude to the police in S.A. was such that he was sure a recent incident in Sydney where members of the public failed to assist two constables who were being attacked, could not happen here ...

Many South Australians may feel that Mr Bonython was over-stating his case. Inter-colonial and inter-state population movements have gone far towards establishing a general Australian outlook which, in this as in other ways, naturally derives mainly from traditions which early struck root in New South Wales, the oldest colony and, except during the last half of the nineteenth century, the most heavily populated. As R.W. Dale wrote in 1889:

The development of the typical Australian character has at no time been subjected to any violent disturbance. Among the people of New South Wales I thought that I found those qualities of life and temperament which distinguish all the colonies from the mother country; and I did not observe those secondary characteristics which belong to the special types exhibited in Victoria and South Australia.

The fact that no convicts and relatively few Irishmen emigrated directly to South Australia explains some real differences in outlook which are still discernible, especially in Adelaide and the thickly-settled agricultural districts near it. But the dry, pastoral interior of the state is separated from the station country of New South Wales and Queensland by nothing but a line on the map. Since occupation of the interior began a hundred and fifty years ago almost every observer of outback life has been forcibly struck by the extreme mobility of the pastoral population, and especially of the wage-earning part of it in which we are interested. This mobility has naturally resulted in a diffusing of attitudes and values throughout the interior regardless of state boundaries.

Nineteenth-century observers were no less struck by the essential mobility of the outback pastoral workers than they were by their unity. Anthony Trollope travelled extensively in the outback and spent some months in 1871 and again in 1875 staying on sheep stations, including that of his son Frederick, in western New South Wales. To him it seemed that:

> … the nomad tribe of pastoral labourer – of men who profess to be shepherds, boundary-riders, sheep-washers, shearers and the like – form altogether one of the strangest institutions ever known in a land, and one which to my eyes is more degrading and more injurious even than that other institution of sheep-stealing. It is common to all the Australian colonies …

Trollope thought that these itinerant workmen were degraded by their customary right to receive free rations and shelter for the night in station 'huts', but he was not blind to their virtues. As Harris had noted of them half a century earlier when the convict element still predominated among them, though they might cheat and rob respectable people, they were honest and loyal to each other. Also they were still, as in the time of Harris, very capable at performing practical bush tasks, and very prone to vary long periods of hard work by short bouts of tremendous drunkenness. As Trollope further wrote:

The bulk of the labour is performed by a nomad tribe, who wander in quest of their work, and are hired only for a time. This is of course the case in regard to washing sheep and shearing them. It is equally so when fences are to be made, or ground to be cleared, or trees to be 'rung' ... For all these operations temporary work is of course required, and the squatter seldom knows whether the man he employs be married or single. They come and go, and are known by queer nicknames or are known by no names at all. They probably have their wives elsewhere, and return to them for a season. They are rough to look at, dirty in appearance, shaggy, with long hair, men who, when they are in the bush, live in huts, and hardly know what a bed is. But they work hard, and are both honest and civil. Theft among them is almost unknown. Men are constantly hired without any character but that which they give themselves; and the squatters find from experience that the men are able to do that which they declare themselves capable of performing. There will be exceptions, but such is the rule. Their one great fault is drunkenness – and yet they are sober to a marvel. As I have said before, they will work for months without touching spirits, but their very abstinence creates a craving desire which, when it is satisfied, will satisfy itself with nothing short of brutal excess.

A just understanding of the distinctive ethos of the 'nomad tribesmen' is of cardinal importance for the understanding of many aspects of Australian history, both in the last century and subsequently.

Among the influences which shaped the life of the outback community, the brute facts of Australian geography were probably most important. Scanty rainfall and great distances ensured that most of the habitable land could be occupied only sparsely and by pastoralists. In combination with nineteenth-century economic conditions, climatic factors ensured too that the typical station should be a very large unit employing many casual 'hands', but owned by a single man or company of substantial capital. If Australia had been occupied by the French or any other Western European people, it is likely that somewhat the same kind of pastoral proletariat would have been shaped by the geographical and economic conditions. Still, there would have been important differences.

As it happened, the interior was occupied by British people who naturally brought with them much cultural luggage. Moreover, in the early period of the 'squatting rush', when the nomad tribe was forming, the vast majority of its members were British people of a certain type. At first convicts and ex-convicts tended the flocks of the advancing 'shepherd-kings', and at least until 1851 these pioneers predominated in influence and prestige, if not in numbers. But the germ of the distinctive 'outback' ethos was not simply the result of climatic and economic conditions, nor of national and social traditions brought with them by the 'government men' who first opened up the 'new country' beyond the Great Divide. It sprang rather from their struggle to assimilate themselves and their *mores* to the strange environment. We shall find much evidence to suggest that the main features of the new tradition were already fixed before 1851. A considerable number of the gold-seekers and of the later immigrants who found their way to the western plains differed from most of their predecessors in having a middle-class background. They influenced the 'bush' outlook in certain ways, but in the upshot its main features were strengthened, modified in certain directions perhaps, but not fundamentally changed.

From the beginning, then, outback manners and *mores*, working upwards from the lowest strata of society and outwards from the interior, subtly influences those of the whole population. Yet for long this was largely an unconscious process recorded in folklore and to some extent in popular speech, but largely unreflected in formal literature. Towards the end of the nineteenth century, when the occupation of the interior had been virtually completed, it was possible to look back and sense what had been happening. Australians generally became actively conscious, not to say self-conscious, of the distinctive 'bush' ethos, and of its value as an expression and symbol of nationalism. Through the trade union movement, through such periodicals as the Sydney *Bulletin*, the *Lone Hand*, or the Queensland *Worker*, and through the work of literary men like Furphy, Lawson or Paterson, the attitudes and values of the nomad tribe were made the principal ingredient of a national *mystique*. Just when the results of public education acts, improved communications, and innumerable other factors were administering the *coup de grace* to the actual bushman of the nineteenth century, his idealised shade became the national culture-hero of the twentieth. Though some shearers are now said to drive to work in wireless-equipped motor-cars, the influence of the 'noble bushman' on Australian life and literature is still strong.

A NICE NIGHT'S ENTERTAINMENT

Barry Humphries

1958

S ANDY, *in pyjamas and dressing gown, is discovered seated in a shabby armchair. He addresses the audience.*

I went to the RSL the other night and had a very nice night's entertainment. Beryl, that's the wife, came along too. Beryl's not a drinker but she had a shandy. She put in quite a reasonable quantity of time yarning with Norm Purvis' good lady and I had a beer with old Norm and some of the other chappies there. I don't say no to the occasional odd glass and Ian Preston, an old friend of mine, got up and sang a few humorous numbers – not too blue, on account of the womenfolk – so that altogether it was a really nice type of night's entertainment for us both. We called it a day round about ten-ish; didn't want to make it too late a night as Beryl had a big wash on her hands on the Monday morning and I had to be in town pretty early, stocktaking and one thing and another.

Well, we got back to Gallipoli Crescent about twenty past and Beryl and I went to bed.

We were very glad we hadn't made it too late a night on the Sunday because the Chapmans were expecting us over on the Monday night for a couple of hours to look at some slides of their trip. They're a very nice type of person and some of the coloured pictures he'd taken up north were a real ... picture. Vi Chapman had gone to a lot of trouble with the savouries and altogether it was a really lovely nights' entertainment for the two of us. Educational too. Well, round about ten I said we'd have to be toddling. You see, we didn't want to make it too late a night because

Tuesday was the Tennis Club picture night and Beryl had a couple of tickets.

Well, there's not much I can say about the Tuesday, except that it was a really lovely night's entertainment. We're not ones for the pictures as a rule but when we do go we like to see a good bright show. After all, there's enough unhappiness and sadness in the world without going to see it in the theatre. Had a bit of strife parking the vehicle – you know what it's like up around that intersection near the Civic. Anyway, we found a possie in the long run just when we were beginning to think we might miss the blessed newsreel. The newsreel had a few shots of some of the poorer type of Italian housing conditions on the Continent and it made Beryl and I realise just how fortunate we were to have the comfort of our own home and all the little amenities round the home that make life easier for the womenfolk, and the menfolk generally, in the home. We left soon after interval as the next show wasn't the best and I was feeling a bit on the tired side. Besides, Beryl was expecting her sister and her husband over for five hundred on the Wednesday and we didn't want to make it too late a night.

So, Beryl and I went to bed.

Had to slip out of the office on the Wednesday lunch hour to get a few cashews to put around the card table. Beryl was running up a batch of sponge fingers with the passionfruit icing. There's no doubt about it, Beryl makes a lovely sponge finger.

Well, the card night went off very nicely indeed, except that Beryl's sister Lorna got a bit excited during the five hundred and knocked over a cup of tea and a curried egg sandwich on the new carpet. Oh, she was very apologetic, but as I said to Beryl later, being sorry won't buy you a new wall-to-wall. And you know what curried egg does to a burgundy Axminster.

By and large though, all things considered, and taking everything into account, it was a pretty nice night's entertainment.

They left early-ish. And Beryl and I went to bed ...

Thursday was a bit quiet at the office and I was just as glad because I'd been feeling a bit more on the tired side than usual. Beryl had another fitting that night. She's having a new frock made for Geoff and Janice's wedding at Holy Trinity on the twenty-first and she wants to wear something a bit special – you know what the womenfolk are like. Anyway, I dropped her off at the dressmaker's on the way to the Lodge.

It was a bit on the latish side when I got home and I went straight to bed and we had a very nice night's ... rest.

Always glad when Friday comes. Beryl and I usually have a nice quiet night in the home. It's the only chance I get to view the TV. There's usually a good story on of a Friday night – or else an education quiz. Beryl had been down to the Town Hall library and got herself a good mystery so that, between the two of us, we had a nice night's home entertainment. We'd had a run of late nights and we were both pretty fagged so round about ten I filled the hottie and Beryl and I went to bed.

I was glad we hadn't made it too late a night as we had to be down the junction pretty early on the Saturday morning for the weekend shopping. Had a bit of strife parking the vehicle though. You know what it's like at the junction of a Saturday morning. However, I found a nice possie in the long run just when we were beginning to think we might miss the blessed butcher. I had a few minutes' worry, though. I lost Beryl in the Foodorama but she had the good sense to go back to the car.

I got home in time for a bite of lunch and then I had to whiz out again to the football. Beryl stayed at home to do the weekend baking.

Had the usual trouble parking the vehicle. You know what it's like at Memorial Park on a Saturday arvo. However, found a possie in the long run just when I was thinking I'd be late for the bounce. Oh, you wouldn't catch me missing an important semi. Beryl had packed me a nice Thermos of Milo and I was pretty glad of it. It's very cold and blowy in the outer.

Had a bit of trouble shifting the vehicle. You know what it's like at Memorial Park after a big match – utility wedged right there in front of me. However I got out in the long run, just when I was beginning to think Beryl would have to wait tea. By the time I got home it was *that* blowy, the *Herald* was all over the front lawn.

Next door had invited us in to hear their *My Fair Lady* record but I'd had a very nice afternoon's entertainment and Beryl wasn't that keen, so we made an early night of it and went to bed.

I always clean the car of a Sunday morning and do a bit of pottering in the garden. Bit worried about those rhodies.

Had the roast midday as we only like a light tea if we're going out of a Sunday night. Saves a big wash-up.

I'm really looking forward to the RSL tonight because – if you can go by experience – it ought to be a very nice night's entertainment.

THE AUSTRALIAN UGLINESS

Robin Boyd

1960

U nlike most countries, this red backland of Australia looks from the air satisfyingly like its own maps. Most of the trees cling to the wildly vermiculated creek beds and mark them as firm dark crayon lines. Near the rare settlements a white road darts zigzagging in long straight draftsmanly lines. Every element stands out clearly: a tiny black square of water, a spidery track, twenty or so buildings at a station headquarters, their iron roofs dazzling white.

This is the Australian Never Never, the back of beyond; hard, raw, barren and blazing. Yet it is not malevolent in appearance. There is something deceptively soft about its watercolour tints of pinks and umbers. And it is a subtle desert, insinuating itself into the background of Australian life, even to the life of the factory worker in a southern city or the sports-car enthusiast who never leaves the bitumen. Its presence cannot be forgotten for long by the inhabitants of its fertile fringe. It colours all folklore and the borrowed Aboriginal mythology, and in a more direct and entirely unmystical way, two or three times every summer, it starts a wind of oven intensity which stirs the net curtains of the most elegant drawing-rooms in the most secluded Georgian retreats of Vaucluse or Toorak.

On the northern edge of this great red heart, on the far side of this back country of Australia, the white man has scrabbled on the surface and made a foothold at Darwin, an outpost of southern Australian culture. This the visitor who arrives by air sees first in a reception lounge inserted into a hangar at the airport. He sees numerous primary colours in paintwork and brilliant plastic chair coverings, richly polished wood trimmings, spun light fittings of bright copper preserved in lacquer, black wrought-iron vases shaped like birds screwed to the wall at eye-level and holding bright little bunches of pink and orange flower-heads.

The springs are deep beneath the washable plastic upholstery. The air is cool, conditioned. After his quick but sticky leap across the equator the visitor finds crisp white tablecloths again, and marmalade in sturdy plated dishes, and showers, hot water, piles of snowy towels surrounded by square yards of glazed ceramic tiles. Here is a good introduction to Australian ways, and it is a cheerful and compact example of the visual style which rules everywhere that man has made his mark on this continent: the style of Featurism.

Featurism is not simply a decorative technique; it starts in concepts and extends upwards through the parts to the numerous trimmings. It may be defined as the subordination of the essential whole and the accentuation of selected separate features. Featurism is by no means confined to Australia or to the twentieth century, but it flourishes more than ever at this time and place. Perhaps the explanation is that man, sensing that the vastness of the landscape will mock any object that his handful of fellows can make here, avoids anything that might be considered a challenge to nature. The greater and fiercer the natural background, the prettier and pettier the artificial foreground: this way there are no unflattering comparisons, no loss of face.

Featurism is not directly related to taste, style or fashion. The features selected for prominence may be elegant, in good taste according to the current arbiters, or they may be coarse and vulgar. Featurism may be practised in Classical or Contemporary style, in the most up-to-date or the dowdiest of old-fashioned manners. It may be found in architecture or in the planning of cities or the design of magazines, espresso bars, neon signs, motorcars, gardens, crockery, kitchenware, and everywhere between. It is the evasion of the bold, realistic, self-evident, straightforward, honest answer to all questions of design and appearance in man's artificial environment. Voluntarily or involuntarily, Featurism dogs Australia even when she sets out with good intentions of avoiding it.

Many sensitive Australians are uncomfortably aware of the rootless nature of their artificial environment. Nevertheless Featurism is frequently perpetrated as much by the artistic section of the community as by the commercialisers, as much by sentimentalists as by the crass and uncaring. As the suburbs grow outwards, as the holiday resorts round the beaches and on the hills fill with campers and weekenders, the continuous process of denudation accelerates. It is the same non-pattern of unrelated snippets of blight whether the countryside which is being overtaken happens to be beautiful or barren. Nature's features of beauty – the waterways, glades, hills, headlands – are not so familiar in the neighbourhood of Australian cities that one would expect them to be treated with contempt, yet the process of their development is this:

Long before civilisation reaches out to the beautiful region a few non-conformists find it, love it, and make sympathetic, uncomfortable homes among, and possibly of, the trees. Often these pioneers are artists, some complete with canvas and some content to talk about it. Then comes the first wave of domestication. The people are still comparatively non-conformist, artistic and sympathetic, but they have families and want a house and garden of reasonable conventional form. Like the pioneers, they were attracted to the area by its natural beauty, but unlike the pioneers they do not realise – simply because they never analyse it – what makes the beauty. They are not wanton, but in the course of solving the practical problems of making a comfortable shelter, several trees may have to go. This minimises the danger of roots in the drains. Then the wandering creek may have to be filled in to reduce the mosquito menace. The newcomers are not without artistic soul, and please do not think they are without taste or aesthetic education. They are as sophisticated in these ways as most readers of Herbert Read or the *Ladies' Home Journal.* Frequently they commission one of the more imaginative architects, even if his fees mean abandoning the idea of an extra bedroom and some clever architectural device means postponing the acquisition of a dishwasher and central heating. Each newcomer builds an attractive house, an original house, a nice feature on the landscape. After several of these have been built, each tugging at nature in a different direction, the earlier settlers look about in dismay and pronounce the area spoiled. About this time the subdividers arrive, and behind them the main wave of suburbia. Then all the remaining native trees come crashing down before the bulldozers, and soon rows of cottages and raw paling fences create a new landscape. The time required for this metamorphosis varies from place to place, but once any man sets his eyes on any pretty place in Australia the inexorable process of uglification begins. It is inevitable because, even while the intentions of the early settlers towards the landscape are honourable, every one of them has different intentions. They condemn one another for spoiling the landscape, but in fact none is to blame individually while all are to blame collectively. It is not lack of imagination or sensitivity or originality which causes the spoliation, but an over-abundance of these qualities without the coordinating discipline of traditional craft technique and, more important of course, without a common artistic aim. Behind the tidy gardens of English annuals and feature shrubs in the vanquished beauty-spot each house is a little cluster of Featurist elements. Many of the occupants know that their neighbours have spoiled the area, and hate them and Australia for their Featurism. Yet when they themselves build again, even when they redecorate, they will be drawn back to Featurism as to a drug, hating themselves for it and knowing inside, even as they apply the Peony Blush paint to the wrought iron, how terrible it will all look tomorrow morning.

Sydney is the unconstituted capital of Australian popular culture. It is larger than Melbourne, older than Hobart and prettier than Perth, and it has by nature and by acquisition most of the things that visitors remark as typically Australian. Sydney is indeed the most proudly Australian of all cities, and the frankest admirer of Australian ideas. Sydney is alive, impatient to be even bigger and to short-cut ways to be smarter. It is a shop window city. It has more new houses and television sets with fewer new sewerage mains. It has more illustrated advertising painted on higher walls, more moving neon signs, the oldest rows of narrow terrace houses curving into twisting hills in the most picturesque slums. And in such modern palaces of amusement as the musical bar lounges, Sydney carries the contemporary style of the country to its highest intensity.

The Australian ugliness is bigger and better here, but in substance Sydney is only a sharper example of the general Australian townscape. There is beauty to be discovered here, in two categories, natural and artistic, but the trouble is that it must be discovered. The fine things, from the glimpses of magnificent landscape to the rare good buildings, old and new, are all but suffocated by the ugliness. The ugliness also falls into two categories: accepted and unintentional. Australia's accepted, recognised ugliness is no more than the normal blight which afflicts growing communities, especially rich, young, industrialised, growing communities.

Part of it is the blight of age: the old buildings, the slum houses, the leaning fences, hoardings, structures of all kinds that were not very good in
the first place and have long since outlived their prime, but are left behind
to decay as development moves away to new fields. Another part is the
blight of expediency: trees uprooted to save diverting a few yards of drain,
the ill-considered and uncoordinated assortment of posts, hydrants, bins,
transformers, benches, guards, traffic signs, tram standards, a hundred
other necessary public appliances, and neons, placards, stickers, posters,
slogans – all bundled together like an incompetently rolled swag with
loops and tangles of overhead wires. This kind of mess, as made by any
progressive community, sometimes is done unconsciously, without
thought or care. But often it is done consciously, with a little regret, but
with resignation to what seem to be the inescapable facts of industrial life.
The mess is accepted without pleasure or complacency, yet without sufficient distaste to kindle a reaction. It is unfortunate, but it is not tragic.

Unintentional ugliness, on the other hand, has an element of tragedy,
because it comes from better visual intentions. It is the ugliness that
starts in a spark of revolt against the depressing litter of the artificial
environment and ends in an over-dressed, over-coloured, overbearing
display of features.

The Australian ugliness has distinctive qualities, but in substance it
is the same as the thing that has been called: 'the mess that is man-made
America'. These are the words of the London magazine *Architectural
Review* when it devoted an issue in December 1950 to a devastatingly
illustrated attack on American urban and suburban culture. If a means
of arresting this visual blight could not be found soon, the *Review* said,
'the U.S.A. might conceivably go down in history as one of the great
might-have-beens of all time'. And meanwhile the *Review* discovered
that something just as bad was happening at home in England: a world
of universal low-density mess was creeping over the once-lovely English
landscape. *Outrage*, written by Ian Nairn, in June 1955 issued 'a proph-
ecy of doom' – the doom of an England reduced to a universal mean and
middle state, with none of the real advantages of town or country and
the disadvantages of both. Nairn pictured:

> ... an even spread of fake rusticity, wire fences, traffic roundabouts,
> gratuitous notice-boards, car parks, and Things in Fields. It is a
> morbid condition which spreads both ways from suburbia, out into

the country and back into the devitalised hearts of towns, so that the most sublime backgrounds ... are now to be seen only over a foreground of casual and unconsidered equipment, litter, and lettered admonitions.

The mess of the nineteenth and twentieth centuries is no respecter of a country's age, but then in countries older than Australia other centuries still contribute something to the scene. Nowhere yet is it as extensive as in Australia.

Like Sydney, all Australian towns and villages look their best in the longest view – from high in the sky – when the details of the mess are lost and the spaciousness and extent of the private domestic life can be appreciated best. The love of home can be seen in the great speckled carpets spread wide round every commercial centre. The carpet is coloured, somewhat patchily, a dusty olive in Perth, Adelaide and Melbourne: the mixture of terra cotta roofs and greenery in the gardens, and silvery-grey in the north and inland where most of the roofs are corrugated iron or fibrous-cement. By night the carpets are black velvet sprinkled wider with brilliant jewel lights than any other cities in the world with comparable numbers of people.

From the distance there is continuity, unity and the promise of comfort in the mushroom roofs and the bright background of tended green. But as the plane circles lower near the airport it is apparent that the green of the average suburb is a horizontal veneer no higher than the reach of a diligent gardener's snippers: lawn, compact shrubs, annuals, nothing high enough to threaten with shade the pink terrazzo of the sun porch. And as the plane drops closer and lower still one can glimpse occasionally under the eaves of the mushroom roofs and see the battle of the colours and the decorative iron skirmishes. Still the sandblasted koala bears and the yacht-race scenes on the entrance hall windows are not visible. They are not seen until one has landed and is driving through the suburban streets, by which time it is difficult to avoid noticing also the featured columns supporting the corners of the entrance porches and the plasticised silky-oak featured front doors inside the feature porches, and the black plastic silhouette cockatoos featured on the feature doors.

Featurism has low surface tension. It has the quality of penetrating ever further into the artificial make up. Ten years ago all park benches were dark green (sympathetic) or white (challenging). Then they too began to be featured in contemporary colours: a featured red bench, a blue bench. A little later the separate planks or battens of each bench were featured: red, blue, green, yellow alternating. This technique began about 1950 (as far as one is prepared to track it down) in the sudden light-hearted suggestion of a councillor in Prahran, Victoria, who convinced his fellow councillors that this would restore some much-needed gaiety to the drab green foliage of the parks and playgrounds. Within a few months almost every other council in the suburbs of Melbourne had followed Prahran's lead, and later the multi-coloured paint spread throughout the country. It happened at about the same time that garden pergolas, which had been traditionally monochromatic, began to change to many colours, each beam of the pergola featured in a different hot pastel hue. Later the most popular treatment for pergolas, trellises, fences, beer-garden screens and other similar garden adornments was to make them in a squared grid and to feature the inside edges of each square in a different primary.

Colour, this most strikingly single element in the modern Australian scene, is a comparatively new feature. It is a product of the last half of the 1950s decade, the do-it-yourself era, chemical advances, and the keen competition of the largely British-owned paint companies. Heavy advertising has encouraged the idea of happy family painting bees using lots of different pigments on walls and ceilings, and to pick out features. Ordinary colour-cards grew from six to sixty hues in this period. Multi-colouring brightens the creative task of redecorating for the amateur, and ensures the opening of a profitable number of partly required tins of paint. Again, pigment is relished by the pressing and printing machines which produce many modern surfacing materials. But, irrespective of practical and economic influences, strident colour is a direct popular cultural expression of easy living. It is a reflection of the money in the modern pocket, just as equally intense, but heavier, richer colours in wallpaper and gilded plaster reflected the last boom of the 1880 decade. Between the booms pigment was mainly something to hide dirt marks. A drab series of duochrome fashions reflected the comparatively flat progression of the country through the first half of this century. About 1900 the two acceptable colours were brown and cheese. After the First World War they were sometimes green and grey. Cream and green predominated on all paint colour-cards from the

Depression to the war, although the theme was sometimes varied late in this period by the more daring cream and cherry or cream and sky blue in kitchens and entrance porches. Even the rakish jazz-moderne of the pre-war milk bar and picture palace was never a painted style. It indulged in colour only in the neon tubes.

The cream Australia policy lasted for some twenty years, trailing off slowly after the Second World War. For the whole of that time cream was used habitually where other nations would have used white. Most kitchen equipment was not procurable in white enamel. As late as 1955 English manufacturers of stoves and other household appliances and sanitary-ware made special cream models for export to Australia. But by this time cream was losing ground to white or light grey as the neutral base colour, and green was being replaced gradually by a rainbow. Suddenly colour was triumphantly elevated as a feature in its own right alongside vertical boarding and split stone veneer. Now standard household equipment came white, but some manufacturers began making coloured refrigerators and washing machines. Then, as the once-black cars in the streets outside adopted two-tone and three-tone styling, household equipment dropped its reticence. Many manufacturers offered two-tone equipment and others provided interchangeable feature panels on the front of appliances where one's favourite fashion shade could be enshrined, easily to be changed tomorrow when it begins to pall.

Meanwhile, in the commercial streets, where Featurism thrives in the knowledge of its economic justification, the diversion of attention from wholes to parts grew steadily more agitated. Lettering and illustrations, crying for attention to the wares of each little shop, grew from fairly discreet sign writing to huge placards and cut-outs. Hardly a section of external wall in the shopping streets was left without commercial announcements as Australians grew after the middle of the twentieth century into the most vigorous and undisciplined advertisers in the world.

Australians now were more prepared even than Americans to allow anyone with something to sell to take control of the appearance of their country. Nothing like the Fifth Avenue Association, or the Hawaiian Ladies' Organisation, or the American government's control of advertisements on its freeways, could happen in Australia. The typical Australian small, prosperous town is all but smothered with advertising and in extreme examples of holiday towns like Surfers Paradise,

Queensland, or Belgrave, Victoria, the buildings disappear beneath the combined burden of a thousand ornamental alphabets, coloured drawings and cut-outs added to their own architectural features. And meanwhile again the industrial areas keep developing their own separate Featurist style: the featured administration block thrust forward towards the street in front of the plain businesslike works, the featured painting of snow-gums on the feature wall in the featured lobby of the featured administration wing.

And look more closely. Follow the successful Featurist with his neatly creased jacket-sleeves and his four-button cuffs when he leaves the office in his two-tone Holden (light pink with plum feature panel) and goes home to have tea in the feature room: the room he calls the sun-room: the one that he used to call the back parlour, the one the American now calls the family-room.

The room's main feature is not really the feature wall in the yellow vertical v-jointed *Pinus Insignis* boards, nor the featured fireplace faced with autumnal stone veneer, nor the vinyl-tiled floor in marbled grey with feature tiles of red and yellow let in at random, nor the lettuce-green Dunlopillo convertible day-bed set before the Queensland Maple television receiver, nor any of the housewifely features hung on the walls; nor the floor-stand ashtray in chromium and antique ivory, nor even the glass aquarium on the wrought-iron stand under the window. The real feature of the room is the tea-table, groaning with all kinds of good foods set in a plastic dream. The table top features hard laminated plastic in a pattern of pinks resembling the Aurora Australis. The table-mats are a lacework of soft plastic, the red roses in the central bowl are a softer plastic, the pepper and salt shakers are the hardest of all. And, soft or hard, all this plastic is featured in the most vivid primary pillar-box red, butter yellow, sky blue, pea green, innocent of any idea of secondary or tertiary tints, and all strikingly prominent against the pale, hot pastel tints of the flat plastic paint on the walls; all vibrating like a chromatrope beneath the economical brilliance of the fluorescent tubes on the ceiling. The main feature of the feature window is immediately apparent: the venetian blinds featured in a pastel tint. But look again and discover that this is more than one tint; every slat of the blinds is a different pastel hue. And if you look more closely still you may discover, if this is a very up-to-date house, that every aluminium blade of a blind carries a printed pattern, perhaps of tiny animals done in Aboriginal style. Everywhere, the closer you look the more features you see, as in the old novelty picture of a man holding a portrait of himself holding a portrait of himself holding a portrait of himself, until the artist's and the viewer's eyesight fail.

The descent from the sky to a close view of modern Australia is a visual descent from serenity and strength to the violence of artistic conflict in a rich, competitive democracy. Featurism is not of course confined to Australia; it exists to some degree in every free and vital modern society, but in no other country is it more apparent, all pervasive and devastating in its effect. Peasant villages are not Featuristic, nor is Stuyvesant Town nor Stalinallee nor Regent's Park Terrace. A degree of freedom and unruliness is the first essential for its flowering.

If the devastation seems worst in Sydney, this is only because nature provided so much more to start with and the loss is so much more apparent.

THE LUCKY COUNTRY

Donald Horne

1964

Australia is a lucky country run mainly by second-rate people who share its luck. It lives on other people's ideas, and, although its ordinary people are adaptable, most of its leaders (in all fields) so lack curiosity about the events that surround them that they are often taken by surprise. But, being laconic, they can take surprise in their stride. The very scepticism of Australians and their delight in improvisation have meant that so far Australia has scraped through. A nation more concerned with styles of life than with achievement has managed to achieve what may be the most evenly prosperous society in the world. It has done this in a social climate largely inimical to originality and ambition (except in sport) and in which there is less and less acclamation of hard work. According to the rules Australia has not deserved its good fortune. It will be interesting to find out if the rules are wrong.

Everywhere one goes in Australia among sensitive, intelligent people of the middle generation – once the conversation reaches a certain depth – one meets a sense of desperation: What is going to happen next? In the younger generation it reaches a sense of outrage that public images of life should remain so freakishly irrelevant. Those who love their country, or (in the more restrained Australian idiom) are worried about the life their children will lead, or are simply wondering what is going to happen next ... none of these can imagine the future. It is usually seen as a political problem: in the form of Menzies and Calwell the images of obsolescence stand there, improbable but apparently immovable;

succession is seen simply as replacement by the same kind of thing. Among those who are frightened by this perpetual state of Stand Easy – and it is an emotion breaking through political party loyalties – there is a feeling of distrust for their own nation; a fear that responsible, clever people will just not be found; that there will be no breakthrough of new men; things will just go on; no one will do the job. This sense of hopelessness may prove to be an accurate forecast. The conventionalism of Australian elites may prove so strong that it breaks men who have new views of the possible; the desire to preserve certain beliefs and ways of going on may conquer all attempts to react to new demands or define reality anew. There are plenty of good people around but the conventions of the institutions by which power is reached stifle them or repel them. The nation that saw itself in terms of unique hope for a better way of life is becoming reactionary – or its masters are – addicted to the old, conformist.

All the same something is going to happen. The demands of the age will destroy the present conventions – sometime. As Bagehot said of a sudden change in generations, things are not going to stay as they are; the results may be good or evil, success or ruin. It is time in Australia not for consideration of minor change, but for broad, general views of change. These must be based on some sense of reality, but not merely on the practicalism of what is possible for the moment. Very little is possible for the moment. But the time might come when broad views of change that now seem impractical will seem sensible and to the point. A reformer must forget the present occupants of power; they are unteachable. In the irrelevance of the present, he has to look to the future, perhaps produce ideas that may prompt action at some later time. In this situation, to be impractical may be the only way of being practical.

One can hope that events will liberate what is good and progressive in Australians, not perpetuate what is bad; that the relaxation and ease of life and the prosperity will grow; that the ideal of fraternalism will gradually extend to include the Asian races (as it appears to be doing among the young) so that ultimately – but perhaps not for some years – Australia's population problem will be solved in what may be the only way it can finally be solved – by large-scale Asian migration. Then, assuming huge advances in science that will make development possible where it now is not, Australia might really claim the name of continent, a continent for which a second time, but more successfully than in the USA, a new nation will be created with values that have some relation to ordinary human aspiration.

For the present one sees only the impossible. But here again are Australian qualities that can be liberated. The change in generations may meet some of the demands of technology and already there have been the beginnings of a breakthrough for the intellect and, more successfully, the arts. The talent in empiricism might add a new and practical dimension to economic planning, and save it from the doctrinaire. The laconicism and courage of Australians are waiting to be drawn on to face the world outside Australia: this reserve of Australian stoicism has not been summoned for many years but it still seems a feature of the existential young as it was of their fathers and grandfathers. The good qualities of Australians should be described and admired and brought into play. Their non-doctrinaire tolerance, their sense of pleasure, their sense of fair play, their interest in material things, their sense of family, their identity with nature and their sense of reserve, their adaptability when a way is shown, their fraternalism, their scepticism, their talent for improvisation, their courage and stoicism. These are great qualities that could constitute the beginnings of a great nation. This nation should be compelled to display its talents in a sense of reality. Many problems threaten the future of Australia. But we might have good luck. It's worth giving it a go.

AFTER THE DREAMING

W.E.H. Stanner

1968

I n 1932 I went to a remote place in the Northern Territory to study some little-known tribes. It was a broken-down settlement which might well have been the Illawarra or the Hawkesbury of a hundred years or so before. There was an exiguous scatter of farmers, cattlemen and miners with leaseholds over lands still lived on by the remnants of the local tribes, which nevertheless still felt that they had an ancient and unbroken title to the lands.

On the outskirts of the settlement there were a few groups of 'myalls' (bush natives) who were as wild as hawks, timid and daring by turns, with scarcely a word of English, and in two minds what to do: drawn towards the settlement because the break in the tribal structure had reached them too, but unreconciled to the prospect of a sedentary life. Some of them were being tempted in, others pushed away, as the need, fear or expediency of the Europeans dictated in almost Phillipian stops and starts. There was bad blood, frequent fighting, and much talk of sorcery and poison, between the bush and the sedentary groups, and no love between any of them and the Europeans, so that cautious friendship alternated with covert or open hostility. In the space of a couple of years two Europeans in the vicinity were speared to death, and several Aborigines were killed or wounded by others of their own kind.

I have some letters and reports which I wrote at the time. They help to bridge the gap a little, but not wholly. The letters are filled with sympathy for the plight of the natives, with respect for their quality of mind and social personality, and with real affection for several who had become personal friends. But they show very much the same attitudes towards the bushmen I had met, many of whom also had befriended me. It is clear that I gave a lot of weight in the scales of judgement to the hardship, loneliness and privation of their lives, and to their unyielding struggle to keep going. The reports are rather different. Somehow, in them, I seem to have managed to draw a screen over at least the worst things of that frontier. There is no obvious sign of trying to put a good face on things; no indication of saving the eyes or ears of those to whom I was reporting; no palpable effort to write, as it were, for history; but on the other hand a very interesting absence of declamation. The tone of my comments is rather reminiscent of the flat, emotionless remark that Spencer and Gillen had made thirty years earlier when they said that '... taking all things into account, the black fellow has not perhaps any particular reason to be grateful to the white man'. Apparently what lay before my eyes seemed to me a natural and inevitable part of the Australian scene, one that could possibly be palliated, but not ever changed in any fundamental way.

Aboriginal affairs had begun to cause a certain public concern in the middle of the 1920s, because of a series of clashes and atrocities. There had been several inquiries from which authority did not emerge at all well. Our international reputation, which had never been very good, went farther downhill. Humanitarians, mainly in the cities, pressed the authorities hard, and their tracts and pamphlets today make interesting reading: all they ask for are palliatives, better protection, better health measures, better conditions of employment. Few people could think beyond 'protection' and 'segregation'.

Judged by the way in which today's demonstrations go, ours were mild and decorous affairs – beardless too, that is, middle-aged and elderly; youth then could not be dragged to the barricades. They were vigorous for their time but governments scarcely responded; indeed, in the Northern Territory, as late as 1933, after there had been several murders, including that of a policeman, there was immediate talk – official talk – of sending a punitive party to Arnhem Land to 'teach the Aborigines a lesson'. Public indignation prevented that from happening because now almost everyone sensed that the era of an eye for an eye had come to an end. Some sort of new spirit was in the making, but it did not discern at all well where to go. A really clear breakthrough did not come until 1934 when A.P. Elkin and others spoke in downright words of the need for a change from the negative policy of protection and segregation – which, anyway, was obviously failing – to a positive policy.

It seems clear to me now that the change of attitude and policy towards the Aborigines which we trace back to the 1930s was confined very largely to a rather small group of people who had special associations with their care, administration or study. Outside that group the changes made very little impact for a long time and, within the group, it was a case of the faithful preaching to the converted about a 'revolution' which in fact had arrived only for them. The situation has altered very considerably in the last five or six years – witness, for example, the referendum of 1967 – but has a long way to go before we are justified in using words which, like 'revolution', suggest a total change of heart and mind.

Turning this thought over in my mind the other day I asked myself whether it could be tested for truth-value even if only in part. If, for example, the two 'turning points' were not as I suggested distinct and separate, but were connected in some vital way; that is to say, if more than a very few people had been aware of a struggle waged and won in the Aboriginal field, surely (or so I argued) there should have been a marked response from the 'New Australia' that was coming into being after the late 1930s; surely the serious literature from that time on should show some evidence of a consciousness that here was another old, cluttered field to renovate by the new progressive thought.

A partial survey of books written since 1930 is enough to let me make the point that inattention on such a scale cannot possibly be explained by absent-mindedness. It is a structural matter, a view from a window which has been carefully placed to exclude a whole quadrant of the landscape. What may well have begun as a simple forgetting of other possible views turned into habit and over time into something like a cult of forgetfulness practised on a national scale. We have been able for so long to disremember the Aborigines that we are now hard put to keep them in mind even when we most want to do so. It might help to break the cult of disremembering if someone made a searching study of the moral, intellectual and social transitions noticeable in Aboriginal affairs from the 1930s to the 1960s. It seems to me to beg to be written.

One consequence of having given the Aborigines no place in our past except that of a 'melancholy footnote' is both comical and serious. Comical, because one of the larger facts of the day is the Aboriginal emergence into contemporary affairs but about all we can say, on the received version of our history, is the rising twin of that immortal observation, 'from this time on the native question sank into unimportance'. Serious, because the surfacing of problems which are in places six or seven generations deep confront us with problems of decision, but we are badly under-equipped to judge whether policies towards the problems are slogans, panaceas or sovereign remedies, or none of them.

✳

One of the remarkable things about the Aborigines is the mildness which they showed once the main clash was over and their lot was cast. The Aborigines were originally a high-spirited and in their own way a militant people. They were not, however, an organised martial people, and that was why we broke them up so easily. The genius of their society lay in other directions and it was this otherness, fundamentally, that led to their undoing. They had had no need for the larger social and political organisations, the executive leadership, and the skill or wherewithal for operations of scale that channel militancy into martial capacity to serve a flag and a cause. When the time of need came they were at a loss.

We have conclusive evidence from the beginning that they did not – and do not – lack courage, intelligence, endurance or indeed any of the cardinal soldierly virtues. I am not speaking of the military skills, but it is worth saying in passing that as far as minor tactics are concerned there was remarkably little that they had to learn. In other days I was an eye-witness of many fights in which more than a hundred men came to an appointed field. I went away, as I am sure anyone else would, in no doubt whatever about either their personal valour or their battle-spirit. There would be a warming-up period given over to threat-signals and other ritualised gestures of hostility but once the true fighting started it might go on fiercely for hours. The very last thing a man would do would be to leave the battle-line except for honourable cause, such as to get more spears, and then as like as not he would meet his wife rushing up with them. Man for man, under equal and familiar conditions, they were a people who would withstand any comparison.

One of our most difficult problems is to overcome our folklore about them. It tends to run to extremes: canard on one side and sentimentality on the other. There is no point in making them appear better or worse than they were or are. Depreciating them is a way of justifying having injured them in the past and an excuse for short-changing them in the present and future. Sentimentalising them is to go too far in the other direction. We can neither undo the past nor compensate for it. The most we can do is to give the living their due.

What we think of as mildness or passivity is neither of those things. What we are looking at is one of the most familiar syndromes in the world. It is a product mainly of four things – homelessness, powerlessness, poverty and confusion – all self-acknowledged and accumulated over several generations. I will deal briefly with each.

No English words are good enough to give a sense of the links between an Aboriginal group and its homeland. Our word 'home', warm and suggestive though it be, does not match the Aboriginal word that may mean 'camp', 'hearth', 'country', 'everlasting home', 'totem place', 'life source', 'spirit centre' and much else all in one. Our word 'land' is too spare and meagre. We can now scarcely use it except with economic overtones unless we happen to be poets. The Aboriginal would speak of 'earth' and use the word in a richly symbolic way to mean his 'shoulder' or his 'side'. I have seen an Aboriginal embrace the earth he walked on. To put our words 'home' and 'land' together into 'homeland' is a little better but not much. A different tradition leaves us tongueless and earless towards this other world of meaning and significance. When we took what we call 'land' we took what to them meant hearth, home, the source and focus of life, and everlastingness of spirit. At the same time it left each local band bereft of an essential constant that made their plan and code of living intelligible. Particular pieces of territory, each a homeland, formed part of a set of constants without which no affiliation of any person to any other person, no link in the whole network of relationships, no part of the complex structure of social groups any longer had all its coordinates. What I describe as 'homelessness', then, means that the Aborigines faced a kind of vertigo in living. They had no stable base of life; every personal affiliation was lamed; every group structure was put out of kilter; no social network had a point of fixture left. There was no more terrible part of our nineteenth-century story than the herding together of broken tribes, under authority, and yoked by new regulations, into settlements and institutions as substitute homes. The word 'vertigo' is of course metaphor, but I do not think it misleading.

The second part of the syndrome is powerlessness. This condition is anything from three or four to seven or eight generations deep, depending where one goes. The Aborigines did not lack men and women of force and of outstanding, even of commanding, character and personality. I am not thinking of mercurial upstarts like Bennelong but of innumerable others who, having no office or title or rank, nevertheless had sway over large regions and numbers – men such as the great warriors Yagan and Midgegooroo of Western Australia, or Durmugam of the Northern Territory. Some were military leaders, some leaders by their religious wisdom and authority in sacred matters. That there will be others like them I am entirely confident. We do not know exactly what happened to such men in most of the older-settled parts of Australia. Yagan of course was shot and Midgegooroo was executed. Few Australians realise the number of men who were probably potential leaders but who, being seen as trouble-makers, were quietly whisked away to places where they had no influence. This was done until quite recent times. Many of us have talked to men and women whose tribal life broke up in the late nineteenth and even during the present century. From what they said there came a time for all of them when they saw there was nothing else to do but to accept whatever life we offered on our terms. Under those terms it was exceptionally difficult for them to keep or find leaders. It meant unifying heterogeneous and accidental collections of people, who usually felt no reciprocal obligations to each other, for ends few can have seen clearly and by means no one really commanded. To thrust himself forward as a leader is a hard thing for any Aboriginal to do. The idea of a man of authority with right and title to command them over a wide range of many things is foreign to their idea of social life. In this respect their tradition left them very exposed to leaderlessness. I will risk being aphoristic and say that whereas they may tolerate a leader they hate a boss.

Homelessness, powerlessness: there is a third and fatal element. In a hundred local patterns they drifted into a vicious circle of poverty, dependence and acceptance of paternalism. Every act of paternalism deepened the poverty into pauperism and the dependence into inertia. The situation was self-perpetuating and self-reinforcing.

Not many people realise that those whom we least respected – the fringe-dwellers – were precisely those who deserved respect most because they were trying to break out of the circle by refusing to go into institutions. In the conditions of the nineteenth century and the first half of this century any Aboriginal who could go much farther had to belong to the Nobel Prize class of human spirits. Astonishingly enough, there were some who did.

I began by speaking of conflict so I will use that theme to try to bring out the fourth element – the Aboriginal inability to grasp the European plan of life.

I spoke of them as originally a high-spirited and militant people. Their lives together certainly had a full share of conflict, of violent affrays between individuals, and of collective blood-letting. But in some ways they were more skilful than we are in limiting the free play of men's combative propensity.

If we judge by their settled customs, they admitted to themselves that people simply *are* aggressive and that it was no bad solution to allow what could not be avoided, and to ritualise – and thus be able to control, approve and enjoy – as much as possible of what has to be allowed. It is hard to fault their psychology. The subject is a fascinating one but unhappily the research we have done upon it in Australia has neither been plentiful nor distinguished. I cannot, therefore, take it very far, and I can mention a few points only.

The impression I received in watching their large-scale fights was that an invisible flag of prudence waved over the battlefield. There was a tacit agreement to call a truce or an end when a few men on each side had been grievously wounded or at the worst killed. Each life in a small group was a great treasure.

That is not to say there were never occasions on which whole groups were put to the spear, or that there was no lasting bad blood between groups at enmity. It was often so, especially when, by migration or some other cause, neighbour tribes spoke unrelated tongues, or had very distinct customs. But the conquest of land was a great rarity: I do not know personally of a single case. And the war of extermination, with one group bent remorselessly on the complete destruction of the other, as far as I have discovered, was so rare as to be all but unknown. In this sense there were few or no 'total' enemies. It was much more commonly the case that groups which fell out contained a proportion of people who were closely tied by kinship, marriage, friendship, trade, or some other precious bond.

It has seemed to me for some years that two aspects of the Aboriginal struggle have been undervalued. One is their continued will to survive, the other their continued effort to come to terms with us. I will illustrate both by the last two men I met who knew that they must give up the bush life and come more than halfway to strike a bargain with us. One of them, whose tribe had scattered to a dozen places, was an elderly widower whom I saw destroying something in a fire. I asked him what he was doing and he told me he was 'killing his dreaming'. I had never seen nor heard of anything like it before. There is nothing within our ken that remotely resembles it. He was destroying the symbol that linked him with his country, with the source of his own life, and with all the continuities of his people. It was a kind of personal suicide, an act of severance, before he came in to find a new life and a new identity amongst us. The other man was in much the same situation. His people too had wandered away and he was left in solitude except for his wives and children. He told me that he wondered for a long time what it would be best to do. He was a supremely competent hunter and he could have stayed in the wilderness for the rest of his days. But he knew he was getting on in years and in the end he too came in to strike a bargain. What decided him, or so he said, was that he had heard about something called 'a school' and that it was good for children, so he took them in to let them find a new life and a new identity. Neither man was a good model for Henry Kendall's sentimental poem *The Last of His Tribe*. The poet knew and evidently liked the Aborigines but he created a dubious stereotype. Compare the image of his man and those of my two men. Compare also another man I knew who at one time seemed likely to be the last of *his* tribe. I talked to him often about their impending extinction. He had no tears, reproaches or dramatics; instead, he would often laugh in a sardonic way. One day he poked me in the ribs and said: 'When all the blackfellows are dead all the whitefellows will get lost in the bush, and there'll be no one to find them and bring them home.' And he went off laughing. I wish I had the time to enlarge on Aboriginal humour, which comes in part from a wonderful gift, one they did not get from us, of taking us gravely but not seriously. Long may they do so. But I must not pass over the main point of my story about the two seekers after a new life and a new identity.

Over the last thirty years we have been trying to attract them into some sort of union with us. We call it 'assimilation' and think of 'integration' as an intermediate stage or perhaps as a less complete union. But it is easy for us to overlook that a long humiliation can dull the vision, narrow the spirit, and contract the heart towards new things. Some of the Aborigines do not understand our offer; some think it is not genuine; some, that its terms are not very attractive; some prefer to cling to their old identity until they are more sure what identity they would have within our new proposals for them. There are deeper difficulties still. We are asking them to become a new people but this means in human terms that we are asking them to un-be what they now are. But many of them are now seeking to rediscover who and what their people were before the long humiliation. It is a search for identity, a way of restoring self-esteem, of finding a new direction for the will to survive, and of making a better bargain of life on a more responsive market at a more understanding time.

There are many, perhaps too many, theories about *our* troubles with the Aborigines. We can spare a moment to consider *their* theory about *their* troubles with *us*.

RACISTS

Humphrey McQueen

1970

Racism is the most important single component of Australian nationalism. Yet it is in their discussion of racism that the radical historians have failed most seriously because they attempt to minimise its significance even when, like Robin Gollan, they are painfully aware how widespread is its influence. The most Gollan could bring himself to admit in his study of *Radical and Working Class Politics* is that racism 'was perhaps an inevitable aspect of Australian nationalism developing under the conditions we have described'. His use of 'perhaps' and 'inevitable' indicates that he considered it foreign to the solid core of radical nationalism.

Russel Ward is far more brazen in his attempts to relegate racism to the realm of marginal importance. The burden of Ward's defence is that since the typically Australian characteristics were formed before the gold rushes, racism (which he claims came after 1859) is not 'necessarily a part of the Australian ethos'. To which one is forced to add – neither were there many coloureds before 1850 and when they did appear in anything approaching regularity they evoked a racist response from the colonial radicals. What is doubly tragic about Ward's position is that he is genuinely concerned to combat the racism he sees in contemporary Australia; yet he cannot bring himself to accept that it is the linchpin of his precious nationalism.

The racism inherent in Australia's economic and geographic position as the advance guard of European conquest will be explored elsewhere in this work. Three elements discerned are: the destruction of the Aborigines; the dominance of the Pacific; the fear of an Asiatic invasion. This section will deal with only one side of this last factor. It will be concerned with the fear of an unarmed conquest of Australia by cheap Asian labourers who would destroy the labourers' prosperity and prospects. The connection between racism and radicalism was thereby established.

The most usual explanation for racism is precisely this fear of economic competition and the importance of this fear cannot be denied. Without it, racial intolerance could never have become as deeply embedded as it has. But once started it did not stop at purely economic objections. It will be useful if its development is traced from its 'economic base', through its social reinforcements to its articulated acceptance by the workers and the middle classes.

Economic origins of racism

Although by the 1840s British policy was to reserve 'The continent of New Holland as a place where the English race shall be spread from sea to sea unmixed with any lower caste', this had not always been the case. Mattra's 1783 plan for a British settlement in Australia approvingly quoted Joseph Banks' opinion that 'we may draw any number of useful inhabitants from China'. This was modified in Governor Phillip's instructions to the extent that he was permitted to import 200 island women as wives for the convicts. Some reason – racial and/or moral – decided him against it. However, two Maoris were kidnapped in 1793 in the vain hope that they could assist the floundering flax industry at Sydney.

In his *Letter from Sydney*, published in 1829, Edward Gibbon Wakefield struck at the heart of the question by relating coolie immigration to the chronic labour shortage in the colony. It must be remembered that it was this very shortage which produced the high wages, independence and prospects of all-round advancement for the colonists, whether convict or free. This led in turn to their opposition to all schemes of assisted migration, especially transportation, the struggle for the cessation of which was carried over into the fight against indentured Hindus, coolies and Kanakas in the 1840s.

The first Asian labourers appear to have arrived in the late 1830s and worked in the pastoral industry as shepherds; one estimate put the total at over a thousand. While this was of benefit to the squatters, even they had doubts on account of 'paganism' and 'colour'. The depression in the 1840s sharpened working-class opposition to a further move by the pastoralists to indenture still more workers from India. Their petition, sent to the Colonial Office in 1843, was completely in accord with the views of that department's 'Over-Secretary', Sir James Stephen, who had already advised his superiors that they could earn posterity's 'censure if we should colonise Australia from India'. Stephen was looking 'forward for five or six generations' when a white Australia would be of inestimable benefit to Britain and Christianity.

If the decision to keep Australia white found little opposition in England it equally found no want of support in Australia. A motion of the Melbourne Town Council in 1842 declared its opposition to the importation of 'cannibals and coolies'. The tone of this resolution is interesting in the light of Russel Ward's claim that racism was largely a post–gold rush phenomenon.

The adventurer Ben Boyd is a strong contender for the honour of being the first person to use coloured labourers to break a strike in Australia when he prepared to embark with a crew of New Hebridian islanders instead of his regular sailors. Henry Parkes was not far behind. He brought out twenty-five to thirty Eurasian printers to work for four years at £4 a week. His aim was not cheap labour but regular workers. The paper on which they were employed, notwithstanding, attacked Chinese immigration late in December 1850 as 'an act of treason to society'. This too was a pre–gold rush manifestation of something more sinister than a simple desire for high wages.

Nonetheless the gold rushes produced a qualitative change in the nature of this racism: what had been a negative contempt turned to a positive hatred. Disappointed miners blamed not their luck but 'the incursions of a swarm of Mongolian locusts who have forced us to fly with our wives and families from all other diggings in the country until we are obliged to turn at bay upon this our last resting-place – our only hope of establishing a homestead – and drive the moon-faced barbarians away' (*The Miner and General Advertiser*, Lambing Flat, 3 December 1861). Anti-Chinese riots occurred on many goldfields, some of the more serious ones being at Hanging Rock (1852), Bendigo (1854), Buckland River (1857) and Lambing Flat (1861). Juries acquitted European rioters on the grounds that since all Europeans looked alike to the Chinese, individual offenders could not be identified. Eventually Chinese immigration restriction acts were passed in Victoria in 1855 and in New South Wales in 1861, by which time the Californian legislature had passed similar measures to exclude Australians as undesirables.

Even when the Chinese were defended it was in terms which made them objectionable to the labouring classes, with more than one writer praising their 'docility, industry and sobriety'. This industrial docility made them excellent strike-breakers, for which purpose they were used at Clunes in 1873 and in Queensland in 1875. About seventy Chinese were employed as strike-breakers in the Riverina in 1891, prompting 'Banjo' Paterson to the lines:

> *I asked a cove for shearin' once along the Marthaguy:*
> *'We shear non-union here,' says he. 'I call it scab,' says I,*
> *I looked along the shearing-board afore I turned to go –*
> *There was eight or ten dashed Chinamen a-shearin' in a row.*

The Maritime dispute of 1878 is important in this regard not so much because of the large numbers involved, but because of the nature of the response to the shipping company's attempt to have 'aliens of inferior mental and physical capacity or endurance ... supersede ... the indominitable valor of British seamen'. Not only was the opposition to the Chinese expressed in these overtly racist terms, but the strikers also obtained the support of almost every section of the Australian population. Class divisions, such as they were, overlapped and at a protest meeting, 'The Mayor of Sydney was elected chairman, and was surrounded on the stage by many of the best known public men and leading citizens.' At the same time the Queensland government notified the shipping company that if it did not comply with the terms of the 1877 anti-Chinese legislation its mail contract, worth £7000 per annum, would be cancelled.

The Melbourne *Argus* (9 December 1878) reported that:

> a very large anti-Chinese meeting in Hyde Park got out of control, and about 2000 larrikins, bent on mischief marched to lower George Street, the area of principal Chinese residences. They swept up the street with the old Lambing Flat cry "Roll up, no Chinese", and endeavoured to set fire to the Chinese workshops. Before they

were dispersed by the police, several people, both Australians and Asians, were seriously injured.

A few days later, an editorial in the *Illustrated Sydney News* (21 December 1878) went a long way to explaining the intensity of the rioters' hostility:

> It may be a foolish prejudice that neither reason nor religious principle can justify, but we cannot get over our repugnance to the race, whose tawny, parchment coloured skins, black hair, lank and coarse, no beards, oblique eyes and high cheek bones distinguish them so widely from ourselves, and place them so far beneath our recognized standards of manliness and beauty.

Economic fears and pure racism were by now inextricable, with each feeding the flames of the other's fire. So naturally did they go together that at the Fourth Inter-colonial Trades Union Congress in Adelaide in 1886 it was unanimously agreed that coolie immigration should be totally abolished 'because – first, the competition of Asiatic against European labour is entirely unfair; second, it is well known that the presence of Chinese in large numbers in any community has had a very bad moral tendency'.

Social reinforcement

It is possible that economic competition of itself could have generated the cultural racism noted above, such is man's capacity to embroider necessity with myth. But this was not necessary. There was plenty of non-economic evidence that could be used to substantiate the moral degeneracy of the Chinese. Once the Chinese were perceived as an economic threat, the belief in Anglo-Saxon superiority quickly turned Chinese customs into conclusive proof of Oriental infamy. It will now be necessary to examine some of the customs and practices which were thus distorted.

Primary amongst the non-economic factors was Chinese sexual activity. There was but a handful of Chinese women on the diggings, a circumstance which made prostitution and buggery as inescapable as they had been for the white convicts and pastoral workers. However, most of the prostitutes were European and this was interpreted as proof that Chinese men lusted after white women. In 1883, in the pastoral camps of the Riverina, there were 800 Chinese males but only two Chinese females. The balance was hardly restored by the thirty-six European women who were married to Chinese, though it was somewhat redressed by the activities of thirty-seven prostitutes.

The 'right to marry' was never far from the minds of Australia's legislators when they proposed restrictive measures. Henry Parkes raised it in 1888 and the first Labor prime minister, J.C. Watson, could not have been clearer when he told the House of Representatives in 1901 that 'The question is whether we would desire that our sisters or our brothers should be married into any of these races to which we object.' A subsequent interchange between two opposing non-Labor members showed that all three parties were united on this issue. When Mr Lonsdale, a Free Trader, stated, 'We don't want them to marry our white women,' Alfred Deakin, Protectionist, immediately agreed: 'No, we want them to go back to China and marry there.' Indeed inter-marriage was subversive of the racial purity which the White Australia Policy was designed to maintain.

Those who think that 'White Australia' was purely economic could ponder this extract from the Wagga *Hummer* of April 1892 in which a William Lane stressed that while he should not do a black man harm he would rather see his daughter

> dead in her coffin than kissing one of them on the mouth or nursing a little coffee-coloured brat that she was mother to. If this is a wicked thing to say, then I am one of the wicked ones, and don't want to be good either; and I'd pray daily to be kept wicked if I thought there was any chance of my ever getting to think that the colour didn't matter.

In July the same year the Melbourne Trades Hall Council heard a submission from a group of women who were establishing a White Woman's Co-Operative Laundry and were desirous of Union support against Chinese competition. According to a report in *Commonweal* (23 July 1892),

> One woman, Mrs Krossley related how her daughter, fourteen years of age, had answered an advertisement for a nursegirl, the occupants

of the house in Fitzroy to which she applied being Chinese. Now, surely the police can take cognisance of this statement and prevent the defilement of the young girls of our community by the almond-eyed procurer or his leprous associates.

Opium-smoking was another obvious proof of degeneracy. Cases of smallpox and leprosy were discovered amongst new arrivals around 1880; equally alarming was the deportation of Chinese criminals to Australia from 1866 to 1876. Even when the Chinese tried to oblige the Europeans, they often provided evidence of barbarism. In 1883, crates of bones for burial in China were sent from Albury via Sydney where they arrived in a 'stinking' condition. To avoid repeating this offence, the Chinese scraped and washed the next shipment. Unfortunately they did this in the Bungambrawatha Creek which supplied fresh water to a section of Albury.

Trollope's view of the Chinese in Australia as 'thoroughly vicious and inhuman' had a basis in reality. Australians did not invent it, and it was not invented for them. They saw examples of it with their own eyes and, as in all cases of prejudice, they transformed the activities of some into the attributes of all.

While there is ample evidence that the Chinese were extremely law-abiding this did not endear them to Australians as docility was interpreted as something sinister and threatening. Or as the *Bulletin* put it in 1886: 'When he is simply vicious the vice is destructive; when criminal, a menace to the State; when industrious, he threatens revolution to the social structure.' No matter what he did, the Chinese in Australia was bound to give offence simply because he was Chinese.

The Kanakas on Queensland's sugar plantations were far from law-abiding. This was doubtless the result of being totally alienated from their surroundings. In 1891, for example, they represented 1.72 per cent of the population but 5.52 per cent of the gaol population and between 1895 and 1905 they accounted for 45 per cent of the state's executions.

It would be wrong to think of racism in Australia as a response to a small minority of the population. Although the Chinese as a percentage of the total population of Australia remained small there were times and places when they were in the majority. This was the case of some of the southern New South Wales goldfields in the 1860s and at the Palmer River diggings near Cooktown where, in 1877, the Chinese outnumbered the Europeans by 17,000 to 14,000. In Narrandera in the 1880s every second man in town was Chinese. But most important of all was the fact that in the mid-1850s one adult male in five in Victoria was Chinese. These large concentrations served to keep alive the belief that those already here were but an 'advance guard of the great army of coloured men who when they go back to their country as the advance guard of the Israelites did of old, will tell their compatriots of the splendid opportunities which await them in the promised land'.

By the last quarter of the nineteenth century, racism influenced all manner of otherwise unconnected policies. Henry George's Single Tax proposal was opposed as the most 'deadly blow aimed at labour' because its implementation would abolish the 'poll-tax on Chinese', and thus destroy 'the security of labour against Mongolian Immigration'. More directly economic perhaps was the 1896 Victorian Factories and Shops Act in which a factory was defined as any place where four or more persons or one or more Chinese was employed. One of the consequences of this Act was the formation of a Chinese Workers' Union which immediately demanded higher wages. Although they were assisted by the Furniture Trades Union they were refused affiliation with the Melbourne Trades Hall Council.

Responses

If it is true that propaganda alone cannot create racism, it is equally true that propaganda is needed to inflame and direct it. The tribunes of racism in Australia have largely come from the leaders of the Labor Party. Instead of combating racism as a tool of oppression, Labor leaders have almost invariably articulated and reinforced it. Indeed, they must bear responsibility for purveying the filthiest lies and inflaming fears. During the 1901 House of Representatives debate on White Australia, one Labor member claimed that those Asians 'who do raise themselves to the level of the whites get as cunning as foxes, and, notwithstanding our laws and our detective skill, they beat us at every turn'. The Australian Labor Party compares with the Labour Party on the Rand which was the first party in the Union of South Africa to make segregation a plank in its political platform.

Many early Labor leaders such as George Black and William Lane were outspoken racists. Black was a member of the Anti-Chinese Immigration

League in 1883–84 and later a journalist on the *Bulletin*, which eventually took as its motto 'Australia for the White Man'.

Lane was a fanatical racist. It has been suggested that his motive for leaving Australia to found a settlement in Paraguay was his fear of the Asian hordes. Although *A Workingman's Paradise* is his better-known novel, Lane also wrote *White or Yellow? A story of the Race War of A.D. 1908* which was serialised in the *Boomerang* from February to May 1888. The action takes place in Queensland, when wealthy Chinese, supported by some Europeans, have established a dictatorship which is challenged by a 'revolutionary race war' for Australian democracy. Lane's distaste for capitalism was strengthened by his belief that it was the capitalists who encouraged Asian immigration. The tone of Lane's *Boomerang* is well expressed in Henry Lawson's poem 'The Cambaroora Star', which was written to commemorate the *Boomerang*'s closure. The 'Charlie' referred to is of course Lane himself:

> *There was strife about the Chinamen, who came in days of old*
> *Like a swarm of thieves and loafers when the diggers found the gold –*
> *Like the sneaking fortune-hunters who are always found behind,*
> *And who only shepherd diggers till they track them to the 'find'.*
> *Charlie wrote a stinging leader, calling on his digger mates,*
> *And he said: 'We think that Chinkies are as bad as syndicates.*
> *What's the good of holding meetings where you only talk and swear?*
> *Get a move upon the Chinkies when you've got an hour to spare.'*
> *It was nine o'clock next morning when the Chows began to swarm,*
> *But they weren't so long in going, for the diggers' blood was warm.*
> *Then the diggers held a meeting, and they shouted: 'Hip hoorar.'*
> *Give three ringing cheers, my hearties, for the Cambaroora Star.*

The importance of the struggle to end Kanaka labour for the emerging Labor Party in Queensland cannot be overestimated. When Labor won the seat of Bundaberg at a by-election in 1892 on a policy of White Australia, the *Worker* greeted the victory with the headline 'Bundaberg Goes White'. Labor's opposition to Kanaka labour prevented it opposing capital punishment in the first decade of this century, because so many of the executed were islanders. In 1901 the *Worker* commented on one such hanging thus: 'The Queensland Cabinet helped ruin the sugar industry by hanging a Kanaka on Monday and the *Courier* did not protest. If the government go on hanging Kanakas like this, there is a grave danger of Queensland becoming a white man's land.' Or as the minister for home affairs put it in 1918: 'The policy of the country is that the Chinese population shall gradually become extinct.'

Geographic proximity to Asia seems irrelevant to the intensity of feeling. Though Tasmanian Labor was backward in many respects it yielded to none in the fervour of its hatred of the Oriental. The Tasmanian Labor paper, the *Clipper*, habitually wrote of the Chinese in the most offensive terms and suggested, for example, that the abominable Hobart drainage was due to the fact that a 'dirty Chinaman' might have seven votes for the City Council while a white artisan remained disenfranchised. In Zeehan and Queenstown the newly formed Workers Political League scored their earliest successes with boycotts of Chinese laundrymen.

What Lane was fond of calling 'the piebald issue' dominated the thinking of the Labor Party to such an extent that when the objectives of the federal Labor Party were adopted in 1905:

> the cultivation of an Australian sentiment based on the maintenance of racial purity and the development in Australia of an enlightened and self-reliant community

took precedence over:

> the securing of the full results of their industry to all producers by the collective ownership of monopolies and the extension of the industrial and economic functions of the state and the Municipality.

In other words, the Labor Party was racist before it was socialist.

'White Australia' served as a rallying-point which helped unify the first federal Labor Caucus, split as it was on the question of Free Trade and Protection. Free Traders like Hughes completely agreed with Protectionists like the Reverend James Roland from Victoria when he called on Labor members to keep before them 'The noble ideal of a White Australia – a snow-white Australia, if you will. Let us be pure and spotless' and let there be no attempt to 'blend a superior with an inferior race'. This from a Presbyterian clergyman whom the *Age* constantly denounced as unpatriotic and pro-Boer!

Hughes employed his considerable power of invective in a constant advocacy of 'White Australia' which he saw as a major virtue in Federation. Speaking to the *Bulletin* early in 1901 on the Labor Party's proposed attitudes in the new parliament, Hughes made it plain that 'Our chief plank is, of course a White Australia. There's no compromise about that! The industrious coloured brother has to go – and remain away!' But it was no longer the Chinese who were the primary cause of concern. Their place had been taken by the Japanese, who 'by most accounts is able to successfully compete with the white workers in all the skilled trades, whilst at the same time working longer hours for much less wages'. The rise of Japan as a military and industrial power was to have the most serious consequences for Hughes, the Labor Party and Australia, when Hughes split the Labor Party over Conscription in 1916.

Anti-conscriptions in *Labor Call* (26 October 1916) said they

> vote NO because [they believed] in keeping Australia a white man's country. YES would commit Australia to sending 16,500 men away monthly for an indefinite time. Soon all except those utterly incapable of service would be gone, and this country would have to resort to importing labour.

The *Worker* told its readers that 'If we vote to send the white workers out of the country, we vote to bring the coloured workers in.' Frank Anstey felt that the referendum should have been called the 'Coloured Labour Referendum'. Maximum effort was milked from the arrival, a week before the 1916 referendum, of a boatload of Maltese, who, although they 'were not coloured people, but still they helped to prove the point'. During the subsequent election campaign in 1917 the *Worker* once more raised the spectre that a vote for Hughes would 'bring to ruin your White Australia policy'.

Racism was by no means confined to the labouring classes or to the Labor Party. Alfred Deakin, influenced by Professor Pearson, was no less fanatical than Hughes. Some employers feared the competition of Asian business rivals just as much as their employees feared Asian labourers.

It is *Australia Felix* that reveals the degree to which racism became an unquestioned part of the outlook of Australians. Its author, Henry Handel Richardson, never betrays the least qualm at portraying the Chinese as lacking any redeeming feature. She recaptures all the complaints made against them during the gold rushes, the period in which her novel is set:

they use 'extravagant quantities of water'; they 'are not such fools as to try to cheat the government of its righteous dues; none but had his license safely folded in his nosecloth, and thrust inside the bosom of his blouse'; they provide Melbourne's worst 'dens of infamy': and so it goes on until the actual appearance of Ah Sing the vegetable man:

'You no want cabbage to-day? Me got velly good cabbages,' he said persuasively, and lowered his pole.

'No, thank you, John, not to-day. Me wait for white man.'

'Me bling pleasant for lilly missee,' said the Chow; and un-knotting a dirty nosecloth, he drew from it an ancient lump of candied ginger. 'Lilly missee eatee him … Oh yum, yum! Velly Good. My word!' But Chinamen to Trotty were fearsome bodies … corresponded to the swart-faced, white-eyed chimneysweeps of the English nursery.

What is significant about this portrayal is that its author left Australia in 1887 when she was seventeen and returned but briefly in 1912 to gather material. Most likely her childhood experiences were similar to Trotty's. But whatever the source of her image of the Chinese she certainly, in Professor Crawford's phrase, presented her 'Australian material with unerring authenticity'. A fact that has been testified to by the general acceptance that *Australia Felix* has found in this country. Few Australians have been offended by her implicit account of their racist attitudes. Indeed, so widely accepted were these attitudes that it is highly likely that they were not even considered racist. They were just naturally Australian.

AUSTRALIA AS A SUBURB

Hugh Stretton

1970

How much of the Australian way of life is worth having? Most Australians choose to live in suburbs, in reach of city centres and also of beaches or countryside. Many writers condemn this choice, and with especial anger or gloom they condemn the suburbs. Planners' debates often concentrate their disagreements on the same issues: the question of urban density, and the quality of suburban life.

Especially for Australians, residential density presents a true dilemma. It seems to have contradictory effects on life at home and life away from it. If we had to consider only our journeys from home and the quality of the destinations they lead to, then we could easily agree to live as closely as possible together. We could then walk more journeys, make more of the rest by better public transport, and save our cars for the social, impulsive and off-track outings to which they give such marvellous freedom. Cities could save land and money by building shorter lengths of everything. Shorter rails, roads, parking lots, pipes, wires and service distances could all save public and private resources for better uses. Most transport and utility industries are basically dull, for their workers and customers alike. Yet they use what seems an absurd proportion of Australian productivity, a higher proportion than in almost any other country in the world. It would be wonderful to shift some of it back to freer, more interesting uses. Besides money, it would be good to save time. Some of the compulsory travelling and delivering and bury-your-own-garbage time could be distributed to each man's choice of work or play, real privacy or real company; and the shorter routes should bring more varieties of work and play and company within everybody's reach.

The money economies claimed for this scheme are probably illusory, but believers in high density think the expense would be worth it: home life itself would be improved by crowding it. Some say that living close encourages community with neighbours. Others claim that it improves privacy – the city apartment can have a solid door, no fences to peep over, and utterly anonymous neighbours. Its tenants don't have to do much maintenance, and they can share public parks and gardens very sociably. Some Scandinavians crowd into skyscrapers with forest and mountain landscapes all around them. The crowded quarters of other cities are further from the countryside, but often rich in life and urbanity. The culture of assembly and conspiracy, of theatre and gallery and café, of great newspapers and little magazines, of chance encounters and intellectual colonies, is rarely strong in a commuters' city. Once there, such a culture does attract commuters, as well as tourists and various roving international communities. But it needs a residential base. You rarely find it in quarters which empty at night. The great cities are the ones the people live in.

It does often happen that the rich and the writers live there because they want to, and the poor only because they have to. The rich, the volunteers for crowded life, include those who located the jobs which crowd the rest. But the rich themselves usually have plenty of relief from the crowding: a large share of the city's open spaces, a scatter of yachts or country houses, a seasonal round of holiday retreats; country boarding schools or large town parks or private terrace gardens for their children. Rich or not, the writers and painters have often been footloose, disappearing to farms or Mediterranean islands for their most creative work. Or nowadays, to suburbs.

There is a contrasting parody of the chief alternative to crowding, in the urban intellectual's stereotype of suburban non-life.

Suburban vegetation is well damned in song and story. Barry Humphries' Moonee Ponds; Graham McInnes' East Malvern; with only a little misunderstanding by the reader, Patrick White's Sarsaparilla. Less compassionate critics depict dreary dormitories where life shrivels, festers, taps its foot in family prisons. All relations oppress; any love is greedy to own or devour the loved one; conversations if any are boring; neighbours pry. Mum does the dishes, Dad potters and mows, the kids pick their acne between homework and the telly. For relief (they talk a lot about 'relief' and 'satisfaction') Dad has the RSL booze and poker-machines, Mum has the *Women's Weekly*, the young who used to cycle to tennis and become engaged now make use of used birds on the back seats of their used Cortinas.

What these clichés about suburbs call for is really a rejoinder about life. Plenty of dreary lives are indeed lived in suburbs. But most of them might well be worse in other surroundings: duller in country towns, more desperate in high-rise apartments. Intelligent critics don't blame the suburbs for the empty aspirations: the aspirations are what corrupt the suburbs. The car is washed on Sunday mornings because its owner has been brought up to think of nothing better to do, not because suburbs prohibit better thought.

As a matter of fact high-fenced, overgrown quarter-acre gardens can be as free, private and self-expressive as any other private property. With or without the fences you can find in some of them the most creative arts, non-conformist squalor, fertile bohemia, funny eccentricity, busy businesses – and, sometimes, beauty. Most accusations of 'mindless conformity' pick on raw new income-segregated suburbs. Sometimes the accusations are just. More often I suspect they're ritual – conformist imitation is itself a strongish feature of suburban intellectuals' familiar manifestos about suburban life. They often cloud the meaning of 'conformism', which isn't a sin until it includes some element of reluctant or stupid imitation. There have been few serious attempts to sort out the suburban similarities. How many signify independent free choices, how many are coerced, how many are imitative and why is that necessarily wrong, or unfree? The accusers themselves are quite inconsistent in thinking it's the monotony that matters. They don't complain of good monotonies – health, Georgian houses, Paris boulevards, monotonously high incomes or abilities. The similarity of tastes and choices is all right if they are good tastes and choices. Even if not, the similarity is often and above all a sign of *freedom*: more and more people are at last getting what all of them have always, freely, independently, identically wanted. Before we all got the same houses, the contrasts of mansion and slum did not signify individual differences of desire, nor a tenth of the free choices we have now.

Why *do* so many Australians choose to live in a way so unfashionable with intellectual urbanists – twelve or twenty to the acre, halfway between real bush and real city?

It's no problem why they prefer the suburbs to the bush. The cities offer most of the jobs, and most services – not only the deep drainage and garbage removal which are easier to get in many country towns than in most outer suburbs, but also specialised services of every trade and professional kind; the greatest variety of public and private entertainments and social opportunities; the greatest variety of girls to marry, and goods in the shops. A recent survey for the New South Wales Department of Decentralisation and Industrial Development suggests that what people in country towns now miss most of all is higher education that their children can get without leaving home.

But why do so many live sparsely in suburbia instead of densely in real city?

Some don't have much choice. There are only small and diminishing quantities of *cheap* dense accommodation, mostly with bad reputations and worse schools. Law and building economics combine to prevent such slums from expanding either sideways or upwards. Most cheap new housing, public and private, goes to the cheap outer-suburban land where another mixture of law and economics dictates five-roomed houses on fifty-foot frontages. Many new industrial employments go there too. Within reach of them, most of the annual increase of working-class families have to accept the outer-suburban houses because there is no large quantity of anything else they can afford.

But of the majority who *can* still choose freely, why do most still choose the suburbs?

A cottage on its own land is at present the cheapest way to build ten or twenty squares of accommodation. The space around it (though too often badly designed) can be the best and cheapest source of light, air, and insulation against sight and sound. The bungalow's insides can be got into the closest relation with the widest variety of private outdoor spaces. It can be close to its own and visitors' vehicles, for easy or private delivery and loading. Its suburban street carries vehicles, walkers, services and plenty of parking – however unsafe and unattractive its traffic, it economises land and pavement very efficiently.

The 'dilemma of diversity' appears between residential units. Maximum diversity between them may mean maximum monotony within each. With good design, that allegedly monotonous and repetitive suburban quarter-acre can include an infinite variety of indoor and outdoor spaces, further increased if some of the partitions are flexible. Large or small, private or open, sunny or cool, paved or overgrown, efficient or romantic, the rooms in the house and the quarters of its garden can offer real variety of colour, use and mood. Suburb-haters, thinking of people *without* personal resources in *ill*-designed houses and gardens, too often undervalue the free and satisfying self-expression, the mixtures of community and privacy, fond familiarity and quick change and escape, which this minuscule subdivision and diversification of the quarter-acre's spaces can offer to the lives it houses. Compared with it, the private realm of the city apartment is internally monotonous, and its owner more restricted in what he can make of it. He loses a whole field for self-expression, and many chances to adapt his environment to idiosyncratic needs. He has only one escape. That one may be into the crowded city's full and valuable diversity, but he can't go there undressed. The escape is to nowhere quiet or private, to nothing he can kick, dig up, re-plan, encourage to grow, or hang a wet shirt on. In many cities the landless city apartment is where the rich get most neuroses and the poor get most delinquents.

Above all the house-in-garden is the most freely and cheaply flexible of all housing forms. Tents are its only competitors. It can be altered and extended in more ways and directions, with less hindrance from laws or neighbours, to meet more changes of need, than any denser housing can be. Each owner has considerable freedom to choose his own degree of privacy, publicity or neighbourliness. This freedom to alter his house without changing his address is an underrated one. Plenty of people like gardens, and the time they spend at gardening. And many more things than gardening go on behind those fences – there's no need to catalogue the hobbies and small trades and storages, all the arts and crafts and mercifully private disasters that clutter people's backyards. Children's uses of them are probably the most valuable of all – and not only to the children. Home allows the widest variety of outdoor activities and constructions, especially the complicated, continuing, accumulating ones. The players can build their own scenery and sets, and keep them intact for serials. Collectors can house their zoos. Parents, children, visitors, and the relations between them, all share in the benefits. In some urban circumstances (or social classes) children can't 'go out' without due notice, a change of clothes and a minder. But private suburban gardens let them go in and out of doors as they please. Minders can mostly mind their own business, much of which (like writing some of this chapter) is consistent with keeping an intermittent eye or ear on children moving freely about the resources of their own and neighbouring children's houses and gardens.

Where on the other hand children can 'go out' freely, but only to the streets because their mates don't have private gardens either, all parties may lose a good deal. Whether this matters depends on many things. Two extremes of family relation are nowadays under attack. Some parents become their children's slaves, enter incessantly into their games, curry favour (or 'mateship') with them, chauffeur them about. (One ten-year-old is alleged to have said, 'I'm wholesome-choked.') At the other extreme, working or slum-cramped parents have to abandon their children to the streets of the built-up cities to be socialised entirely by their peers – to the horrors of *Lord of the Flies* re-set in Harlem.

Over-dispersed suburbia may help the first extreme, urban density the second. Australia's 60' x 150' suburbia – sparser than much English suburbia, closer than much American – does at least permit three societies to coexist. Child, family and adult life can use overlapping territories without too often getting in each other's hair. There can be subtle gains in the generations' consciousness of each other. They are not imprisoned together inside a city apartment, forced into too much direct, irksome and conflicting relations until one of the other 'goes out' to rejoin its own generation, out of sight or understanding by the other. The house-and-garden gains can include more independence and escape for both, but also more uninterfering observations and understandings by each of the other's world, and frequent but brief invitations into it. Not many activities – least of all children's – can do without ten-minute breaks every hour, and busy streets are not always the best places for such excursions. There are also ranges of perfectly tolerable behaviour (child and adult) which however can't be tolerated either indoors or on public land: building, carpentering, metalworking, digging, hosing, basking, horsing about. There are innumerable games and skills – amusing, educational, utilitarian – which adults and children can't teach each other either indoors or on public land. Altogether the suburbs allow people, if they want and know how to, to enjoy the unoppressive community of generations which many of the English rich shed when they consigned their children to servants and boarding schools a century ago, and some of the city poor lost when they lost their children to the streets about the same time.

Some tough planners object to all this soft stuff. After all, they say, children and adults are the same people. If cities are planned chiefly for the adults, the children will all grow up and get their turn.

But childhood and child-rearing together occupy as much as half of a majority of lives. If you undervalue that half because of its lower economic productivity, you have a funny notion of productivity. It's a matter of opinion how far childhood is 'preparatory', adult life the real thing. I think each year of both has the same value and deserves the same attention, whatever 'mature opinion' says – like most city planning and government, mature opinion tends to come from well-off adult males. It is of course absurd to think that parents have no other roles. But intelligent 'mother-and-child-centred' planning aims to emancipate parents and children from *needless* dependence, and to make it easier for mothers to continue as adults.

One unspoken valuation is concealed in almost all arguments in favour of dense city life. It is that human relations between adult strangers are generally more stimulating and valuable than are relations within families, or within stable neighbourly communities, or between people where they work. Certainly the great value of cities lies in the variety of company they offer; but it is worth looking twice at the common assumption that all intimate, durable relations are 'dull' or 'stifling' while all casual relations are 'exciting'. The 'strange encounter' cult has been rightly ridiculed in its sexual manifestations, only to reappear in more general form in the writings of those who use cities basically as rich consumers' playgrounds. The eternal hope that new faces will bring new revelations does sometimes deserve to be understood as a Casanova complex: a chronic incapacity to give or get much from whatever relationships the sufferer has already. In fact, happy or helpful or creative human relations are not confined to any type. Good and bad relations appear within the closest families, and equally in the busiest open markets. Everyone has an individual pattern of need and response, in relations of both kinds. It is not hard for good cities – especially urban-suburban cities – to offer their members wide and compatible opportunities for relationships of every kind. But any planning theory is silly if it systematically overvalues the strange encounters and undervalues the family and neighbourly and working relationships. The oddest idea of all is the illusion that the strange encounters are always more 'creative'. Life as a long cocktail party is usually for consumers, not creators. Most of the creators I know – poets, organisers, discoverers and other originals – draw inspiration from the depth of a few relationships, not from an incessant pursuit of first nights. They also use a lot of free solitude. If Australian cities developed more of Melbourne's rather private, ruminant character, that might not necessarily be bad, depending on the quality of love and thought that flourished behind the high fences; even if the quality of life there were poor, it wouldn't necessarily be improved by pouring the people out to mix in public places. People need city centres, crowded with opportunities for fun and profit; but as long as they are there within forty minutes' travel, people will be freer and happier in proportion as they also have a generous tract of privacy at home, and steady friends at work.

Some of the effects of suburban life are hard to disentangle from the effects of geographical immobility. A majority of Australians still live in their native cities, in reach of life-long friends and relations. Does it make any difference that many of them still visit their parents where their parents brought them up? What does it do for the parents' felicity, to garden on under the walnut tree their babies slept under, their boys climbed, they all harvested? Mobiles – the four out of five Americans who have left their native states, and often several other states since – have just as high proportions of conformists, and higher proportions of worse afflictions. But the Australians' comparative immobility doesn't seem to impair production. Australians are average mobile from job to job and class to class, and above average productive; but a good deal of both are possible without uprooting because there are only six capitals, historically independent, monopolising most employments, each quite well diversified and self-sufficient. There must be few cities as small as Hobart whose young can nevertheless choose between as wide a range of trades and professions, learn them at day-school while living at home, and practise them right there for the rest of their lives – with grandmother baby-sitting, if not moving in. Certainly the skills may sometimes be second-rate and the familiarities oppressive; but the gains, harder to measure, are less often noticed. Immobility is not a simple cause or consequence of suburban life. The effects of the two are interwoven. However hard to measure, they are obviously important in the structure and spirit of Australian society.

Whether or not you like these effects, others do. From whatever mixture of habit and thoughtful choice, young married Australians are as keen as their elders were on getting their share of private suburban land, wherever they have the choice. They spend more than ever on it. It used to cost a sixth or less of the price of a house – perhaps six months of the buyer's income. In the big cities it is now a third or more of the price of a house – up to two years of the buyer's income – and wherever they can find the land and borrow the money, majorities still think it worthwhile.

MANZONE COUNTRY

Anne Summers

1975

T he first and most influential post-Federation commentator on Australian life was W.K. Hancock whose book
Australia was published in 1930. Hancock's analysis of
Australian history pursued three main themes: the tam-
ing of the land, the emergence of sectional strife and the development
of a nationalism which was democratic and egalitarian.

Most of the standard commentaries on Australian culture have
taken up and reiterated the 'lucky country' theme, portraying a nation
endowed with endless possibilities for national aggrandisement and the
acquisition of personal fortune, a land free from bitter sectarian and
racial conflict, a homogeneous paradise where sun-loving Australians,
beguiled by their belief that they are 'Godzone' continually congratulate
themselves on their good fortune at having been born in, or migrated to,
this best of possible worlds. This vision of Australia has been arrived at
by tabulating the vast physical expanses, the revealed mineral wealth
and the absence of bloody wars or revolutions, and correlating these
with a selective panoramic version of our history: the first country to
receive the secret ballot, the eight-hour day and conciliation and arbitration. The resulting vision dovetailed nicely with the themes elaborated
by colonial literature and gradually a consensus was arrived at. Even
where this did not match the actual experiences of those who read about
it, challenging the happy hegemony meant calling into question not
merely the integrity of the dream-spinners but also of the generations
for whom the vision was some kind of existential prop. The experiences

of the first AIF as well as the industrial struggles of the early labour unions were both integrated into the egalitarian myth and eventually became seen as its basis. Therefore to challenge it involved at least questioning if not actually denying the seminal experiences of a substantial proportion of the male population of Australia.

It is notable that women have rarely participated in this kind of writing; they have written histories and historical biographies but no Australian woman this century has dared to participate in the intellectual exercise of trying to formulate theories about Australian life. A likely reason for this is that the dominant themes which, as we have seen, have been reproduced over three generations with little modifications, are so patently at odds with the life experiences of almost all Australian women.

There is a general assumption that, before the recent upsurge of interest in women's issues, there had been 'nothing written about women in Australia' and yet in 1973 when I compiled a general bibliography on this subject I had no difficulty in amassing a collection, still very incomplete and dealing only with printed works from 1900 onwards, of 523 items. Much material *is* there and the women whose lives it deals with have had existences as various and as difficult to categorise as men's. But to be able to utilise it, to thread it into coherent and illuminating patterns, will require challenging the assumptions and frameworks so far employed by the definers of this level of our culture.

It will mean completely scrapping Hancock's thesis on rural, non-ideological and nationalistic themes and the assumptions of fraternal egalitarianism which they shored up, and developing a concern with family life and social and sexual mores. Already the egalitarian view of our past has received a heavy challenge from the work of people like Humphrey McQueen, and historians of the destruction of Aboriginal society such as C.D. Rowley, Peter Biskup and Lorna Lippmann. But opening up the subject area with respect to Aborigines has not necessarily included a simultaneous recognition that a society dominated by narrowly circumscribed views on individual and group achievements has had other victims as well. It is no longer enough to note the absence of Aborigines or women or any other cultural minority (such as homosexuals) from our official history. We have also to ask what functions their exclusion served, both economically and ideologically, for the dominant hegemony, and whether or not these functions persist.

THE REAL MATILDA

Miriam Dixson

1976

With one of the world's strongest trade union movements, Australia is among the most advanced industrial democracies in the world, while the patriarchal system at the core of that tradition is the most enlightened we have. Yet the overall standing of women in Australia comes close to the *lowest* among Western industrial democracies, having a faintly non-Western flavour (maybe because of the role of the Irish). Australian woman's sense of personhood is among the thinnest, the least robust, within this range. Our short history has bequeathed us a marginally more impoverished stock of 'models' for female identity-formation than has the history of analogous countries.

From the preverbal stages of childhood, the 'once-upon-a-time' months and years, Australian girls begin to acquire a kind of gut knowledge that they are 'outsiders'. It comes across in the looks, the gestures and family customs that constitute the child's first introduction to the values that matter in the big world beyond. So we grow up knowing from way back that to be a woman – an Australian woman, though we imagine that's the only way there is to be a woman – is to be tip-toe, dull, dolly-bird, blank-faced, 'don't crowd me love, I've got my mates'. As in all communities dominated by what Fromm designates as 'patricentric-acquisitive' values, an Australian woman soon develops an awareness that her country values most highly, and rewards accordingly, those qualities which it decrees she must not have if she is to be a 'real' woman: that is, achievement-drive, initiative, autonomy, true dignity, confidence and courage. These she must not display if she is to be a woman sexually relevant in terms of the values congenial to that small but powerful group, 'the pace-setting and boundary creating men'.

In Australia, the pace-setting and boundary creating men tend to be WASPs, that is, white Anglo-Saxon, often Protestant and to all intents heterosexual. They've had a fair, though now waning, success in imposing their cramped style of masculinity on other males. 'Modern society,' Henrik Ibsen once remarked, 'is not a human society; it is only a society of males', and that is of course true in Australian society.

Russel Ward, for example, writing about the 1840s, lists what he believes are aspects of a uniquely Australian outlook. They deserve close attention: their implications are misogynist to the core. In these lines Ward offers

> ... the basic elements of that outlook which later came to be thought of as 'typically Australian': a comradely independence based on group solidarity and relative economic plenty, a rough and ready capacity for 'stringy-bark and green-hide' improvisation, a light-hearted intolerance of respectable or conventional manners, a reckless improvidence, and a conviction that the working bushman was the 'true Australian' whose privilege it was to despise 'new chums' and city folk. We have seen that this ethos sprang mainly from convict, working-class, Irish and native-born Australian sources ...

If we assume for the moment that this is a rough sketch of one major configuration of values in our national identity, we can see that it centres around a special *style* of masculinity. It is a style that reeks of womanlessness: 'group solidarity' should read 'male group solidarity'; 'working bush*man*' is accurate, but the final lines need adjusting: '... this ethos sprang mainly from *male* convict, working-class, Irish and native-born Australian sources ...' And the true Australian had a further 'privilege' omitted by Ward: the 'privilege' of despising not only '"new chums" and city folk' but also human beings who were female. Australian patriarchal society thus threw up a peculiarly limited style of masculinity which owes a lot to that strand of national identity sketched by Ward.

Yesterday's ghosts live on now and help to explain what Ronald Conway describes as 'latent homosexuality on an astounding scale'. Australian women who are close friends with men from other cultures often say Australian men withhold shared humanity from them to a much greater extent, and I suspect this might finally have to be explained in Conway's terms.

If sexuality reflects not only the general but also the specific features of a particular patriarchal society, it is not surprising Australians are increasingly articulating the view that, within the Western democratic context, there is something marginally more impoverished about Australian sociosexual patterns. In 1966 a young and well-travelled journalist, Craig McGregor wrote:

> many Australians ... regard women merely as sexual providers, things to sleep with but not to talk to, and the extraordinary prevalence of phrases such as 'they're all the same in the dark' and 'makes no difference with a bag over her head' illustrates an attitude to women which is narrow, cynical and immature.

The immaturity is ugly and astonishing, and is probably well illustrated by McGregor's remark that 'one of the commonest words used by Australian men to describe sexual intercourse is "a naughty"'.

This immaturity reflects attitudes stemming from an early stage of the individual's development, where sex is often seen as 'naughty' and 'dirty'. But it also stems from an early stage of Australian history, and is in keeping with Hartz's 'fragment' theory. Lacking the tug-of-war from deeply opposing social forces that coaxed and pushed England forward as the nineteenth century unfolded, Australia, a 'fragment' of England ('the whole'), remained in many of its folkways 'frozen' in the archaic postures characterising its formative experiences. And so in describing sexual intercourse as a 'naughty', Australian men are manifesting a retarded quality that is both personally backward and socially or historically backward, expressing attitudes stemming from as far back, perhaps, as the mid-nineteenth century. Thus McGregor explains that many men

> think of women who have consented to sleep with them as 'common' or 'dirt' because, though they desire sex, they regard it guiltily as immoral and rather dirty. It is a fantastic situation, in which a

society accepts a *stern neo-Victorian morality* as correct, transgresses it at every opportunity and then feels guilty about it afterwards. [My emphasis]

Frederick C. Folkard said that 'woman, in a way, has always been a bit of an embarrassment to the Australian. He does not quite know what to do with her. He accepts love casually, is regarded as an inept wooer and shies away from passionate protestations.' In 1967, English authoress Elspeth Huxley attacked the relegation of women 'almost to the status of chattels' in a weirdly segregated 'booze society'. Discussing 'The Girls of Australia', a journalist in *Playboy* wrote during 1969:

> One of the dominant themes in Australian social history has been a strong, intrasexual loyalty among men, an inheritance from the cell-block isolation of the penal days and the outback isolation of the pastoral era, which has led more than one sociologist to suggest it drowns male sex lives in a sublimatory sea of heavy drinking, aggressive masculinity and loyalty not to mistresses but to mates ... Australian girls are treated by their own men with a casualness that borders on sheer neglect.

As recently as November 1974 Al Grassby, special consultant to the federal government on community relations, felt we were still 'tagged [as] a man's country', while another writer saw our recent flowering of 'new nationalism' as marked by some 'utterly Ocker' qualities. The Ocker's way of being a male is so lacking in sensitivity, compassion, gentleness, inwardness and insight, as to render him not just an impoverished, but almost a caricatured, human being.

And increasingly, Australian women begin to spell out their awareness of mainline Australian male definitions of them. Here is *Pol*, making the point (while over-estimating 'the foreigner'):

> The nice thing about the foreigner is that he actually likes women. He doesn't think there's something very weakening about them and that it's much more masculine to be with the boys around the bar. The foreigner also stays and talks to you, gets you drinks and lights your cigarettes at parties too, which is a nice change if you've been used to being marooned with the girls. While the Australian

builds his empire of Fosters and lays siege to it with the boys until it's time to drag you off home to bed.

Jenny Ham, thirty-four, former fashion model, public relations company owner and one-time Melbourne City Council candidate, said this:

For [Australian men] point one in importance is going to the football; point two, putting money on the races; point three, drinking with the boys; point four, conglomerating at a party and talking business or telling risqué jokes while women talk babies.

Rather than feature as a priority at the bottom of this list, Miss Ham prefers the company of European or English men.

One of Australia's leading historians, Manning Clark, points to a significantly underplayed aspect of one of the current larrikin-heroes, Barry ('Bazza') McKenzie: '[He has] ... not the slightest bit of interest in romantic love. His only interest is in how to get it in.' True sexual potency implies a capacity for a fairly sustained and full-hearted human relationship. Our Bazza-heroes, 'stuck fast at a pubescent level of sexual response', interested only in 'getting it in', 'virtual masturbators', must be sadly lacking in such a capacity.

The critic Phillip Adams finds Bazza's creator, Barry Humphries, 'extraordinarily interesting', a 'soulmate' to Patrick White with whom he 'dominates Australia culturally'. There is, to me at least, one similarity of 'soul' which, if these men *are* in any sense culturally dominant, adds up to a devastating comment on the feeling for women in our culture: the similarity of the sense of awkwardness or fear about the flesh of woman one gains from reading them, much as one does from Lawson, Penton, Xavier Herbert, Vance Palmer or Joseph Furphy.

Jeanne MacKenzie, writing in *Australian Paradox*, proposes that one 'rarely' finds 'any expression of rich human emotion, of young love, or any profound relationship between two people of the opposite sex. There are few Australian love poems ... "nearly all Australian fiction reveals some aspect of sexual loneliness"'. In 1973 Max Harris could still endorse a similar view. He wrote:

Geoffrey Dutton has examined the almost complete absence of amatory themes in Australian writing. As far as Australian writers are concerned, right up to modern times, male-female relationships have no potential literary substance. There are no Australian love-poems. There are few detailed studies of women in the Australian novel.

If many Australian writers of high standing deal at best awkwardly with the body, sexuality and women, and often demonstrate aversion and hostility, what does this imply about their sense of woman's humanity? And thus of our own?

Despite their fairly small incomes, women are vital to Australia's economy. In any 'modern economy,' Galbraith remarks, 'the servant role of woman is critical for the expansion of consumption ...' and he concludes that women's 'conversion into a crypto-servant class was an economic accomplishment of the first importance'. This is as true of democratic Australia as it is of any other 'modern economy'. But is it not morally *uglier* because we are so democratic a democracy? Women save private and state employers millions of dollars by virtue of the fact that they produce (give birth to) the producer, then make it possible for him to turn up at work every Monday, clean, clothed and more or less emotionally functioning. This is not paid for, because it is not 'counted'. It is 'woman's work', so it is not 'real' work. But, on an increasing scale, women now also participate directly in the *paid* workforce, though for the most part in its lowest-status and lowest-paid rungs.

In so democratic a democracy as ours, where unions have played such a big part in moulding national values, the historian must find both challenging and paradoxical some aspects of the way women are treated in the workforce and unions. It was not until 10 December 1974 that the Australian government – a Labor Party government – ratified the 1951 Equal Remuneration Convention of the International Labour Organization. As late as 1969, it could be said that women here experienced discrimination in employment, education and training on a scale which 'would receive widespread publicity and outraged condemnation if it were directed in the same overt fashion at colour or religion'.

Women are thus being slowly brought to ask whether there is some curious anthropological male-bonding quality 'imprinted' into trade unionism through the circumstances of its origins in the nineteenth century.

We are internationally proud of our commitment to egalitarianism and justice, which includes justice in the workforce. We have a right to be proud. But in a democracy where trade unions have lodged high in the priority of national values so firm a devotion to wage and work justice, the situation of that large and growing part of the workforce who are female moves beyond mere anomaly to a mockery of those very values. And so, as a committed member of the Labor Party, as an historian of the labour movement as well as of the role of women, I had to ask myself the question: was women's situation in the workforce a mockery of some of our finest values *in spite of* the trade unions or *because* of them? It was not a happy question to find myself asking.

Australian society's unusually low valuation of women, accepted by women themselves, is reflected in the noisy silence, the blank facelessness, of women in most of our decision-making structures. Women have been eligible to vote and stand for federal parliament since 1902, while all states except South Australia conferred the right to stand between 1915 and 1926 (South Australia did so in 1959): but women have made extraordinary little use of this right. In 1972, Don Aitkin, professor of politics at Macquarie University, wrote, in an article headed 'MP – for Male Pigs?':

> In the Australian House of Representatives there is no woman member, and there have been only three since Federation (two of them were wives of former members). Lumping all the Australian Parliaments together there were, in 1960, only 12 women out of 701 members, and there have been less than 40 since Federation. How many women have been Ministers of the Crown? Three.

And does it *really* benefit Australian men that Australian women are amongst the least confident and autonomous in the Western world? Even if our men were to think only in terms of international male rivalry, must it not be keeping them back to receive no astringent perspectives on themselves from women, whose mental universe is 'marginal' to men's and so holds formidable critical potential. In self-interest, should Australian men not think about John Stuart Mill's question: 'Is it imagined that all this does not pervert the whole manner of the man, both as an individual and as a social being?' Australian male friends of mine bewail the dullness of their male compatriots (a sure sign in itself that things are changing), while foreign male friends have done this for years. My Australian men friends say how hard it is to talk about 'inward' matters with their fellows (men students report far less difficulty, by the way).

But inability to contact inwardness and feelings saps us *intellectually*, as is pretty well known. A major cause of this is that Australian males tend to be reinforced in their flatness by Australian women. A man looks into the eyes of a woman. If she were a robust and autonomous being, she would tend to look back with the measured and steady gaze of an independent existent, whose universe was in some ways fruitfully different (even if in other ways complementary). But what the Australian woman actually does, for the most part, is compliantly reflect back at the man his too-often taupe-coloured and boxed-in mental universe, leaving him lonely and as colourless as before. No wonder they don't have much to say to each other.

THE SPECTRE OF TRUGANINI

Bernard Smith

1980

I t seems to me that a spectre has haunted Australian culture, the spectre of Truganini. When she died in 1876 the last of the original Tasmanian Aborigines died. It was the end of a war, the only war that, unaided, Australians have ever won. But it was a complete victory. None of the original Tasmanians survived. Clive Turnbull, the historian of that war, has left us with a vivid description of Truganini's last days:

> King Billy was gone, but Truganini, the 'Beauty of Bruni' lived on, the last of the Bruni Island Tribe, last of all the Tasmanians in Van Diemen's Land. Her uncle had been shot by a soldier, her sister stolen by sealers, her mother stabbed. Her man had his hands cut off in life (and left to drown) and her last compatriot had his hands cut off in death. One by one they had all gone, some shot, some brained with musket-butts, others rotted with drink and disease ... They had been raped, emasculated, flogged, roasted and starved. They had been badgered from place to place, taken from their country to an unfamiliar island and brought back to die in the pestiferous ruins of a gaol. The colonists' lusts had been succeeded by their hatred, and their hatred by their contempt ... Truganini, the old woman, had seen it all, her own story the very story of her race ... Her last years were comfortable, it seems, but there was a shadow over them – her fear of the body-snatchers and mutilation after death ... 'Don't let them cut me up,' she begged the doctor as she lay dying. 'Bury me behind the mountains.'

Since 1788 Aborigines had been treated in their own country as if they were sub-humans. But I do not propose to dwell upon atrocities. Truganini's story must stand, in these talks, for all those that will never be written, but live on in the folk memories of the descendants of the victims. By contrast, white Australians have tried to forget. Indeed at times it would seem as if all the culture of old Europe were being brought to bear upon our writers and artists in order to blot from their memories the crimes perpetrated upon Australia's first inhabitants. In recent years however both sides, black and white alike, have become aware increasingly of the continuing colonial crime, the locked cupboard of our history. It is this new awareness of what actually occurred that, it seems to me, constitutes a central problem for the integrity and authenticity of Australian culture today.

How shall we redeem it from the guilty awareness that these acts of genocide and attempted genocide were being enacted most vigorously at that very time when our own white Australian culture was being conceived and born, and that its very growth presupposed the termination of a black culture which for the rest of the world, apart from ourselves, has come to be regarded as more interesting, coherent, and identifiable as a unique human achievement than our own European-derived culture?

My own approach to this problem, as you may have noticed, assumes a close connection between culture, place and morality. A culture, I would argue, in order to develop and survive must put down firm ethical roots in the place from which it grows. It may become a universal system of moral values, such as Christianity, capitalism or communism, but its vitality and capacity for survival will depend largely upon the quality of the moral values it brings to the solution of human problems during its emergence at a particular place and particular time. A culture cannot live upon other people's universals. It requires moral values born of its own historical experience, values which are continuously tested against the successive challenges of its history. But that is only part of the story, for all cultures are challenged by the ethical values of external cultures, values which may be largely foreign to their own experience but ones which have also been evolved in the continuous struggle to be, and to remain, human.

And what of ourselves? Apart from the Aboriginal component of Australian society, which developed its own ethical systems from an intimate association with the environment during a period of thirty or more thousand years, we are a dependent culture ethically. We brought our moral values, such as they were, from Europe with us, in, so to speak, our travelling trunks; but when tested at the frontiers of Australian experience, in our farms and mines for example, they have become more often than not seriously affected. Australian morality is a history of damaged goods, as that fine historian, the late Margaret Kiddle, was perhaps the first to demonstrate in her history of Western Victoria, entitled *Men of Yesterday*.

Indeed we have succeeded in creating only one system which was relevant, in some small way, to our own environmental and historical experience. This is the doctrine of mateship fashioned from the experience of rural workers in the Australian bush, formulated in the works of such writers as Lawson and Furphy, and disseminated by the *Bulletin* throughout the country during the last two decades of the nineteenth century. The doctrine was adopted by C.E.W. Bean to give a unity to his account of the first AIF, and its history has been written by Russel Ward in his *Australian Legend*. Mateship was an ethics of situation, distilled from a century of coping and surviving in the bush. 'The greatest good was to stand by one's mate ... the greatest evil to desert him.'

The mateship ethic has been rightly criticised for its limitations. It was racist. You couldn't have a Chinaman for a mate; it was intolerant of independent behaviour and women played little part in it. Mateship ethic has long ceased to be – if it ever was – fashionable among Australia's urban *élites*, whether social or intellectual. Yet the mateship ethic, despite its limitations, does reveal a survival capacity wherever Australians experience hard living conditions and collective action becomes the only form of rational action available: in the unions, in the armed forces in war-time. Some aspects of the ethic have been taken over by contemporary communities experimenting with alternative lifestyles, and in a debased, commercialised form, it animates the ideology of the Australian Ocker.

Despite the amused scepticism which the mateship ethic arouses among many today, it is to be noted that it was in the years when that ethic flourished that Australia became known internationally as a leading nation in social and political reform, in fields such as manhood suffrage, the secret ballot, votes for women, the abolition of plural voting, graduated income and land taxes, age pensions and an indexed basic wage. In such matters Australia played, in the years before the First World War, a role of world significance, gained a reputation for being not only an advanced democratic society, but a humane and compassionate one.

The greatest weakness of the mateship ethic however was that it did not include the Australian Aborigine. For white Australians the Aborigine was not a human being; he was an embarrassing joke. When Mary Gilmore was twenty-two and Lawson nineteen she suggested to him that he might go outback and study and write about the Aborigine, but he replied saying that he 'wanted to stay in the city ... to mix with people ... educate his mind by contact with other minds'. Writing about the Aborigine, he told Mary, would only be laughed at or ridiculed, and he wasn't 'going to be laughed at or ridiculed by any one'. For Joseph Furphy the Aborigines were a doomed people, doomed because they were incapable of innovation, caught in their own unchangeable rituals and myths.

Furphy's rejection of a future for the Aborigine reveals the influence upon his thinking of an ethic stronger than mateship, the ethic of social Darwinism which became powerful in Australia around 1870, and dominated cultural attitudes until the 1920s. I see it essentially as an ethic of conquest, providing the basic moral justifications for dispossession – those best able to exploit and land, or anything else for that matter, have the best right to it. Such views have been under strong attack in recent times, notably from the Conservative movement, but they remain highly influential. Social Darwinism erected an almost impenetrable barrier between the deep spirituality of Aboriginal culture and the materialism of our new, white Australian culture. Although it is possible to trace throughout our early history a thin line of concern for the plight of Aboriginal society, it is not until the 1920s and 1930s that our own culture was able to produce a few pioneering writers with a sufficient technical command of language, and compassionate imaginations powerful enough to built the first bridges across the morality gap that had been established between black and white in this country. Before these bridges were established the new Australian culture was not in a position to speak on behalf of the human condition in this part of the world, but only about the private hopes and fears of the victorious white component of our society. That perhaps is why in our arts and letters we have tended to cultivate the lyric, and the satire, the comic and the pastoral (often with bushranging banditti to enliven the action) but to avoid tragedy. The tragic muse was an old Aboriginal woman, surviving precariously as a fringe-dweller in some unknown country town.

✳

Australian culture is suffering from a guilt problem. Since the beginnings of white settlement Aborigines have been steadily dispossessed of their lands upon which their well-being, self-respect and survival have depended. It is a story of homicide, rape, the forcible abduction of children from their parents; and it is remembered in the folklore of the survivors.

But for most white Australians it is a nightmare to be thrust out of mind. Yet like the traumatic experiences of childhood, so with the childhood of a nation. As Freud has put it: 'It is universally admitted that in the origin of the traditions and folklore of a people, care must be taken to eliminate from the memory such a motive as would be painful to the national feeling.' I want to consider in this lecture some of the ways in which the crimes committed against Aboriginal society have been suppressed and removed from our nation's memory.

One way was to pretend that the murder of Aborigines was not murder at all but more like clearing land or killing animals for sport. As one commentator put it in 1847: 'Regret concerning the disappearance (of the Aborigine) is hardly more reasonable than it would be to complain of drainage of marshes or the disappearance of wild animals.' Such attitudes are not confined to colonial times. In his recent autobiography, Charles Perkins records how 'White station owners would go on regular hunts for Aborigines. "Instead of having a kangaroo hunt today, we'll have an Aboriginal hunt." They would go out and shoot men, women and children. My mother saw this happen as a girl.'

It is fallacious to argue that such examples of advanced moral degeneracy were inherited from Europe when white people first settled here. On the contrary, it might well be argued that the eighteenth century in its social philosophy and jurisprudence developed a higher respect for human rights and human dignity than has occurred either before or since. The American Declaration of Independence, the French Declaration of the Rights of Man, did much to codify that respect. Captain Cook sailed into the Pacific with similar ideas as those expressed in those Declarations firmly in mind. You may recall that the Royal Society and the British government sent him in 1768 to observe the transit of Venus, at Tahiti, and discover new lands in the South.

The President of the Royal Society, James Douglas, fourteenth Earl of Morton, after whom Moreton Bay in Queensland is named, gave Cook detailed advice as to how he should treat with peoples encountered on the voyage. Let me quote:

> shedding the blood of those people is a crime of the highest nature. They are human creatures ... They are the natural, and in the strictest sense of the word, the legal possessors of the several Regions they inhabit. No European Nation has a right to occupy any part of their country, or settle among them without their voluntary consent. Conquest over such people can give no just title: because they can never be Aggressors.

Cook's official instructions from the Admiralty also stressed this need for prior consent. He might take possession of 'convenient situations in the country' only with the 'consent of the natives'. But Cook did not follow those instructions. On 22 August 1770, on Possession Island he took possession of the whole of the East Coast of Australia in the name of George III without having gained the consent of any Aborigines anywhere along that coast. At Botany Bay he had been met with spears; at Endeavour River they almost burnt his encampment down. Cook acted according to an older naval tradition, of the adventurer who goes beyond his instructions hoping for justification later. He was quite frank about it. To a young French admirer some years later he wrote: 'a man would not accomplish much in discovery who only stuck to orders'. So far as I know his act of possession was never explicitly condoned during his lifetime; though of course he was never taken to task for it.

My point is this. It was not at the centre, not in London, but in Australia, that the principles of universal justice championed by the philosophers and lawyers of the Enlightenment began their long process of degeneration. If it was upon the frontier that our mateship ethic evolved it was also upon the frontier that the Enlightenment ethic began to crumble. Frontiers are not places, except in Antarctica, where men meet nature but where they confront other cultures, and systems of law conflict. Malinowski has called such frontiers a 'third cultural reality'; and they produce in Professor Stanner's words 'a queer set of shapes'. Les Murray has described them as a 'gulf of style'.

There isn't much degeneration in Cook really; just the signs that he is prepared to take the law into his own hands when he guesses he can get away with it. In Australia at least he had taken no lives; had no reason to project his guilt upon his victims; indeed he held a high opinion of Aboriginal society.

In a much-quoted statement, he wrote:

> They may appear to some to be the most wretched people upon Earth, but in reality they are far happier than we Europeans, being wholly unacquainted not only with the superfluous but the necessary Conveniences so much sought after in Europe, they are happy in not knowing the use of them. They live in a Tranquillity that is not disturbed by the Inequality of Condition. The Earth and sea of their own accord furnishes them with all things necessary for life, they Covet not Magnificent houses ... they live in a warm and fine Climate and enjoy a very wholesome Air, so that they have little need of Clothing, and this they seem to be fully sensible of ...

Nowadays when historians quote this passage they usually qualify its significance by saying that on this occasion Cook was not himself the cool dispassionate observer, but had fallen victim to the myth of the noble savage. It does not occur to them that Cook may have been simply reflecting upon a condition of happiness which he had personally observed. Cook's view has in large measure been vindicated by Geoffrey Blainey's account of Aboriginal Australia contained in his book *The Triumph of the Nomad*. Indeed Cook's comment could serve as a suitable epigraph to Blainey's book. Support for Cook's view also comes from a surprising quarter. To read the autobiographies of living Aborigines such as Jack Davis, Jimmie Barker and Dick Roughsey is to be impressed by the great happiness which they obviously enjoyed as children growing up in the bush in their own communities, a happiness they have treasured throughout life. Had Cook found it necessary to take lives in Australia, however, he might have found more to criticise in Aboriginal society. It usually works that way.

At any rate confronted by the realities of the colonial frontier, the murder, rape, abduction and servitude for victuals and clothing amounting to slavery, colonists turned away from the principles of universal justice enunciated by their European fathers and grandfathers, to take refuge in primitive tribal myths that lay at the heart of their own culture, in order to justify themselves. Did not the Bible inform us that the Aborigines were the descendants of Ham? And were not the sons of Ham cursed for all eternity to be his elder brothers' servants, simply because Ham had got a fit of the giggles when he saw his old father Noah lying half-naked on the ground stiff with the grog? Tough punishment indeed you might say for laughing at Dad's genitals; but there is more to the myth of Ham than that. In its original form it is rather different from the edited Biblical version. It is Ham's young son, Canaan, who castrates his grandfather during his drunkenness; and this is the excuse which the Israelites invented for themselves to justify the conquest of Canaan, their prom- ised land, and the enlistment of Canaanites as slaves. So that the myth of Ham is from the beginning a dispossession myth, and came to serve the same purpose for the pastoralists of Australia as it served the sons of Abraham almost 4000 years before.

The Ham myth was bad enough, but it did at least admit that Aborigines were human. Things however got worse. Charles Darwin's theory of natural selection reduced the status of the Aborigine from that of a perpetual servant to that of an entrapped animal about to die. It is important to be clear about this. Darwin's theory was a *major* sci- entific achievement and remains so. But it is a biological theory, selection occurs by means of biological inheritance. It offers no expla- nation, except by analogy, for social change. But in the hands of the popularisers of the theory of natural selection such as Herbert Spencer, social analogies were seized upon. A man with a gun was fitter to sur- vive than a man with a spear; the murderer was fitter than his victims.

Darwin himself cannot be exonerated entirely from the charge of vulgarising his own theory, by using biological analogies to explain social change. As a young man he had arrived in Hobart in 1835 aboard *HMS Beagle* shortly after the few surviving Tasmanian Aborigines had been moved to Flinders Island. The rapid decline in the Aboriginal population was seen by him not as the product of a white settler policy but as a biological process. 'The varieties of Man,' he wrote at the time, 'seem to act on each other in the same way as different species of ani- mals – the stronger always extirpating the weaker.' And much later he wrote in his *Descent of Man*, 'how can we feel sure that an old dog with an excellent memory and some power of imagination as shown by his dreams, never reflects on his past pleasures and pains in the chase?' This he concludes would be 'a form of self-consciousness'. 'On the other hand,' he continues, 'how little can the hard-worked wife of a degraded Australian savage, who uses very few abstract words, and cannot count above four, exert her self-consciousness, or reflect on the nature of her own existence.' The conclusion is inescapable: Truganini possessed less intelligence than Darwin's dog.

Reflections of this kind by the man who has rightly been called the Newton of biology, plus the work of popularisers like Spencer, helped to justify the atrocities of the Australian colonial frontier. In a similar fashion the vulgarisation of Marxian theory has been used to justify the extirpation of kings, capitalists and peasants. In both cases moral issues are reduced to natural processes. Herbert Spencer's social Darwinism sought to explain Aboriginal society as a natural process rather than as a social formation. The Aboriginal culture came to be conflated with the Australian bush itself. It is well known that white settlers tended to perceive the bush as mournful and melancholic. Historians have, I believe, misunderstood this phenomenon, treating it as a kind of nostalgia for England when it was more the product of fear and guilt. When Marcus Clarke writes that 'the Australian forests are funereal, secret, stern. They seem to stifle, in their black gorges, a story of sullen despair' we might ask ourselves whether it is the black gorges or guilty colonial hearts that sought to stifle the story of despair, projecting their fear and guilt upon nature itself.

By still deeper processes of repression and projection it became possible to write the history of the pastoral occupation of Australia, despite the fearful atrocities of the 1830s and 1840s, as if it were an Arcadian idyll, with squatters singing the 23rd Psalm as they led their flocks into green pastures, like Abraham into the promised land.

The ironic logic of history is at times incredible. It was none other than James Collier, for many years Herbert Spencer's own literary assistant, who wrote, after his migration to Australia, the first history of the pastoral expansion. Called the *Pastoral Age in Australasia* it appeared in 1911. John Macarthur was the hero. 'He shines through that murky dawn,' Collier wrote, 'like a hero of Corneille.' It is not difficult to guess who the murky dawn was. Collier's book is a highly competent history, an impassioned hymn of praise to the pastoral enterprise, and he does not flinch from recounting some of the atrocities of the frontier. But this champion of social Darwinism reduced the great moral tragedy to a natural process. I quote:

> There can be no question of right and wrong in such a case. The only right is that of superiority of race, and the greater inherent capacity on the part of the whites; the only wrong on the part of the blacks is their all-round inferiority and their inability to till the ground or even make use of its natural pastures. All other wrongs were incidental and … trivial. This was the capital offence, and it was irredeemable.

Such was the theoretical position. But if the Aborigine was to be put thoroughly out of mind it was desirable that he be removed as a visible element from the landscape.

In policies, adopted by all the new Australian colonial governments established after 1850, Aborigines were driven from their traditional lands, their tribal structures destroyed and their families herded into missions and government reserves, where even children required a permit in order to visit their parents, and the superintendents, as often as not, roamed about with stockwhips. Professor Rowley has compared these institutions to Solzhenitsyn's well-known image of the Soviet prison camps as the Gulag Archipelago; spread throughout the country but virtually invisible to all but their inmates. Les Murray in his poem *Beside the Highway* has, in a gentler fashion, captured the despairing inertia of these reservations:

> Beside the Settlement, Mad Jess sits down,
> In the withered grass and contemplates her shoes
> The Settlement eats corned beef and boiled potatoes
> Drinks tea, chews bread and treacle,
> Stares at walls.
> Another day half done.

The reservations helped to throw a white blanket of forgetfulness across the central tragedy of Australian settlement. Generations of Australians grew up in cities that had never seen an Aborigine let alone spoken to one. In the 1880s such people began to create a new Australian culture.

With the Aborigines banished to hidden reserves and the old melancholy of the bush absent, Australian nature could at last be approached in a radiantly happy mood. Sunny Australia, the Lucky Country, was at last our own. Hugh McCrae wrote:

> *I blow my pipes, the glad birds sing.*
> *The fat young nymphs about me spring ...*
> *I am the lord,*
> *I am the lord.*
> *I am the lord of everything!*

The Heidelberg painters and their successors were now able to consolidate the pastoralist dream of a sun-kissed Arcadia. Some hoped that Australia might become the centre of a new white civilisation, 'the Delos of a coming sun-God's race', freed from the injustices of old Europe. Others reacting against the crude materialism of white Australian society discovered for themselves the imposing edifice of European arts and letters. Between 1880 and 1914 the foundations of a new white Australian culture were laid down; and its achievements are considerable but, seen from the perspectives which we have been exploring, it was a closed house into which the first inhabitants of this country were not invited to enter.

Those who looked to Europe were led by Norman Lindsay who developed, after reading Nietzsche, a great hatred of all so-called primitive cultures. The influence of Nietzsche in Australia is crucial for an understanding of the mechanisms of forgetfulness. Nietzsche was deeply influenced by Darwin and Herbert Spencer, but he developed his own eccentric brand of evolutionary theory. Human evolution in his view was a matter of mind, not of a process of biological selection. It was advanced by the creative geniuses of society, the artistic supermen. So the followers of Nietzsche tend to establish pantheons and canons of genius: Shakespeare, Michelangelo, Rubens, Pope, Dickens and so forth, as standards. Such men they praise, and write poems to. They, and they alone, are their true mates.

Lindsay's vitalism and the influence of Nietzsche continued in the work of a talented galaxy of poets, Brennan, Slessor, Baylebridge, Hope, McAuley and their numerous academic disciples. The main achievement in this body of poetry, which is considerable, lies in the lyric and in satire. Tragedy, or a sense of moral commitment to anything other than the traditional forms of poetry and the more traditional forms of the Christian religion, is rare if not non-existent. Patrician and personal in temper it has no place for working-class, folk or popular culture which it either patronises or ignores and, as Judith Wright has pointed out, the tradition has been pursued as if the Aborigine had never existed. Slessor even managed to write one long poem about Captain Cook without mentioning the Australian Aborigine. Cook's intention in discovering Australia was apparently, if we are to take Slessor seriously, to make it possible for white men to write poems here. The Hawaiians, who killed his hero, are described as 'puzzled animals', 'cruel birds', and they possess 'goatish flanks'.

And as with our poetry so with much of our history. Professor Stanner has noted that in the writing of Australian history 'a cult of forgetfulness' has been practised 'on a national scale' so far as Aboriginal society is concerned. Since then this neglect has been defended by one historian, Professor Frank Crowley, who maintains that 'the Aborigines just were not important in the early history of white settlement'.

But their degree of importance surely depends on the kind of questions one asks. If one, for example, is mainly interested in the growth of the rural and manufacturing industries and the establishment of European-type institutions, the Aborigines might well be treated as the 'fringe-dwellers' of our history or ignored altogether. But history of this kind can easily become history written for Caesar, victory history: nectar drunk from the skulls of the slain. No doubt much of this kind of history will be written as we ride in triumph towards our great white jamboree of 1988. If so, this will be a pity, for 1988 might well be a time of atonement.

THE END OF CERTAINTY

Paul Kelly

1992

The story of the 1980s is the attempt to remake the Australian political tradition. This decade saw the collapse of the ideas which Australia had embraced nearly a century before and which had shaped the condition of its people. The 1980s was a time of both exhilaration and pessimism, but the central message shining through its convulsions was the obsolescence of the old order and the promotion of new political ideas as the basis for a new Australia.

The generation after Federation in 1901 turned an emerging national consensus into new laws and institutions. This was the Australian Settlement. Its principal architect was Alfred Deakin who became recognised as Australia's greatest prime minister. The feature of the Australian Settlement is that it was bipartisan and was accepted, sooner or later, by Liberal, Conservative and Labor politicians. Its universality provided the bonds for eight decades of national unity and progress despite its defects.

At its inception Australia had no Bill of Rights or Declaration of Independence as a focus of national identity. The nation was founded not in war, revolution or national assertion, but by practical men striving for income, justice, employment, and security. The Australian Settlement was their creation. It is an achievement second only to the creation of Australian democracy, and its operation within that democracy has offered for most of this century the best definition of nationhood. But this Australia is in transition – in the 1980s, the Settlement ideas underwent a process of creative destruction from which there is no return.

The ideas which constitute the Australian Settlement, though devoid of formal definition, may be summarised under five headings – White Australia, Industry Protection, Wage Arbitration, State Paternalism and Imperial Benevolence.

Australia was founded on: faith in government authority; belief in egalitarianism; a method of judicial determination in centralised wage fixation; protection of its industry and its jobs; dependence upon a great power (first Britain, then America) for its security and its finance; and, above all, hostility to its geographical location, exhibited in fear of external domination and internal contamination from the peoples of the Asia-Pacific. Its bedrock ideology was protection; its solution, a Fortress Australia, guaranteed as part of an impregnable Empire spanning the globe. This framework – introspective, defensive, dependent – is undergoing an irresistible demolition.

The foundation idea of the Australian Settlement was White Australia. It was the unique basis for the nation and the indispensable condition for all other policies. It was established in the first substantive law passed by the federal parliament – the mark of national individuality in an Empire of coloured races. White Australia was not just a policy, it was a creed which became the essence of Australian nationalism and, more importantly, the basis of national unity. It was endorsed by Labor and Conservatives, employers and unions, workers and housewives.

The first prime minister, Edmund Barton, predicted the demise of Western colonialism and the rise of new states in Africa and Asia. But Barton drew a false conclusion: he saw White Australia as a bulwark against this future age, not as its inevitable victim.

But the greatest exposition of the policy came from Deakin:

> The unity of Australia is nothing if that does not imply a united race. A united race means not only that its members can intermix, intermarry and associate ... but implies one inspired by the same ideas ... of a people possessing the same general cast of character, tone of thought, the same constitutional training and traditions ... Unity of race is an absolute to the unity of Australia. It is more actually in the last resort, than any other unity. After all, when the period of confused local politics and temporary political divisions was swept aside it was this real unity which made the Commonwealth possible.

Deakin's words betrayed, however, the insecurity lurking behind the assertion of White Australia. He said that Japanese should be excluded 'because of their high abilities' and that they 'would be our most formidable competitors'. With reference to Japan, Deakin said, 'It is not the bad qualities but the good qualities of these alien races that makes them dangerous to us.' This was the premonition of a challenge which would face Australia throughout the century. It surged with Japan's 1905 defeat of Imperial Russia, reached its zenith in the Second World War, and was reinvented in its contemporary form when Japan became an economic colossus.

White Australia, as Deakin also implied, transcended negativism and served as a dynamic basis for national action. It was notable for the eloquence of its defenders – Henry Lawson, the poet who created the mythology of the Australian identity; the liberal intellectual Frederic Eggleston; the socialist writer Vance Palmer; and Australia's longest serving prime minister, R.G. Menzies. White Australia was the first and greatest ingredient in Australian nationalism; it was the chief motive driving Australian imperialism. It was the first principle in the first platform devised by the Australian Labor Party caucus in 1901. Its last great racist champion was ALP leader Arthur Calwell, who, as architect of the post-war immigration programme, embodied in these contradictory impulses – immigration and racism – its final gasp.

White Australia fell victim to decolonisation, the demise of Empire and the transformation of Australian national interests. At its 1965 National Conference, the ALP abandoned its commitment to White Australia. In March 1966 the policy was abolished by the Holt coalition government. But its interment was accompanied by funeral obsequies which revealed that the principle of a homogeneous Australia remained alive. The nation had merely decided that racially based discrimination was officially unacceptable. There was no alternative vision to replace White Australia nor any intention to permit significant non-white immigration.

In 1973 the Whitlam government abolished the final vestiges of official racial discrimination. In the late 1970s the Fraser government supported a major influx of refugees from Vietnam. This was the trigger which prompted an alternative national credo from Malcolm Fraser in the early 1980s – multiculturalism – which became the official definition of national direction. But for most people multiculturalism could never serve as an adequate or a sufficient re-definition of national identity.

It was the legacy of the post-war immigration programme and the transformation of the Asia-Pacific from a region of military threat to one of economic progress which forced Australia to substitute multiculturalism and regional integration for the original idea of White Australia. Australia's future living standards are tied, in part, to the success of Australia's integration into the Asia-Pacific. It is the rise of a massive and prosperous middle class in the Asia-Pacific which will trade, travel and live in Australia that is the ultimate guarantor of a new identity. This involves changed immigration patterns and settlement policies, joint Australian–Asian ventures, a major tourist influx, greater foreign investment from Asia, educational exchanges, and the mutual search for new products and markets.

In short, it means a greater Asian presence in Australia and a greater Australian presence in Asia. It means, above all, more people-to-people intimacy and dialogue. In the 1980s Bob Hawke's declared objective was to 'enmesh' Australia in the Asia-Pacific, his term for the widest possible contact and intimacy. This transition in national identity has been uneven and stormy but the change is inevitable. The ultimate issue is the reconciliation between the growing Asianisation of Australia and maintenance of the dominant Anglo-Saxon Judaic-Christian value system.

The second pillar of the Australian Settlement was Protection. Its appeal transcended that of an economic policy. Protection was both a creed and a dogma. It was a philosophy that would make Australia powerful, secure its prosperity and assuage its insecurity. For its disciples, Protection was a policy for both war and peace. Protection and White Australia became fused into a self-reinforcing bond. Protection was the core of Australia's consciousness.

The first issue resolved within the new Federation was the contest between Protectionists and Free-Traders, symbolised in the struggle between Alfred Deakin and George Reid, the respective leaders of these groups. The victory for Protection was swift and decisive; Deakin was lionised and Reid was humiliated. The first moderate tariff was established in 1902, a more stringent tariff adopted in 1908 in the third parliament, both delivered by Protectionist governments with support from a divided Labor Party.

Deakin was a Victorian and Reid was from New South Wales. These two colonies in the second half of the nineteenth century had chosen opposing solutions to the employment demands from the post-1850 trebling of Australia's population. Victoria had chosen Protection while New South Wales opted for Free Trade. But the Victorian model prevailed in the new Commonwealth.

As early as 1875, Reid had attacked Protection using arguments which his intellectual inheritors would still be promulgating more than a hundred years later. Reid said the core of Protection lay in its neglect of principle, its resort to expediency and its refusal to address whether solutions were right or wrong.

The Deakin–Reid battle was the first wet–dry contest in Australian national politics. It was a struggle not just over trade policy, but over competing visions of the new Commonwealth and whether its development would rest upon the principle of government intervention or that of individual enterprise. Deakin's victory was comprehensive and Reid slouched off as High Commissioner to London – a trail-blazer for the vanquished. It would be another eighty years before Reid's position would be vindicated.

The victory of Protection was sealed in three ways. First, Deakin's Liberals had been able to secure a coalition of support to put the Federation on the Protectionist path. Second, the Labor Party, initially divided and uncommitted on the issue, finally settled for Protection. Third, when the non-Labor forces merged in 1909 – the Deakin Protectionists and Reid's Free Traders – the newly created Liberal Party was pledged to Protection. Labor and non-Labor was Protectionist; the circle was all but closed.

The final step occurred in the early 1920s which saw the emergence of the Country Party. The non-Labor Nationalists under W.M. Hughes established the Tariff Board and then legislated for the highest and most comprehensive tariff schedules. This reflected the expansion of Australia's industrial base during the First World War. But the decisive event of this period was the subjugation of the Country Party to Protection. It proclaimed a rebellion but settled for compensation. After threatening to attack the Protection edifice as a burden to primary producers, the Country Party was bought off.

During the 1920s the Country Party, under its first great leader, Earle Page, joined the Protection compact. The cost was a system of statutory marketing, growers' boards, public subsidies, price fixing and industry levies. The 'man on the land' who had promised to subvert tariff-raising and wage-fixing, was harnessed to the chariot wheels of

Protection. Now a national stance of 'Protection All Round' was underwritten by the three major parties.

From its inception Protection was seen as the basis for nation building. Deakin declared: 'No nation ever claimed national greatness which relied upon primary industry alone.' Protection was a policy which industries sought in their self-interest. It entrenched sectional interests and sectional politics and was justified by national leaders as a policy to build industrial strength.

The flaws in the Protection edifice were known from the start and received periodic fanfare. In 1929 the Brigden Committee, reporting on the tariff, made an appeal for moderate protection but warned that 'the tariff has probably reached the economic limits and an increase ... might threaten the standard of living'. It said that the burden of the tariff fell upon Australia's lifeblood – wool, wheat and mineral exports. In fact, the average tariff level almost doubled in the decade to 1920 and doubled again by 1932 to become one of the world's highest.

The impact of Protection was known but unheeded – one industry's Protection became another industry's cost through higher prices, thus forcing the second industry to demand, in turn, greater Protection as compensation. Two works published in 1930 exposed the practice underpinning Protection: Edward Shann's *Economic History of Australia* and W.K. Hancock's *Australia*. But ideas could not penetrate the political edifice of self-interest and perceived national interest. Indeed, during the post–Second World War era, Protection experienced a resurgence under the leadership of a political giant, John 'Black Jack' McEwen, the toughest figure in post-war politics.

McEwen lived by the personal philosophy that 'a man who can't inspire fear in his opponents isn't worthy of the fight'. His vision was succinctly expressed: 'I have always wanted to make Australia a powerful industrialised country as well as a major agricultural and mining country. This meant that I was bound to favour broadly protectionist policies.' McEwen championed this vision throughout his twenty-nine years as Country Party deputy and leader – including twenty-two years as the minister responsible for secondary industry. He is the only post-war politician whose name was given to an economic philosophy – McEwenism. By 1970 Australia, apart from New Zealand, had the highest manufacturing tariffs within the industrialised world.

When McEwen retired in 1971, his apparently immovable Protectionist structure was under threat from an apparently irresistible anti-Protectionist tide, furious at the longevity of its denial. It was during the 1970s and 1980s that the structure fell to successive assaults. The final timetable for Protection's virtual dismantling was announced by the Hawke government in March 1991. It offers a wonderful symmetry: that Australia will enter its second century as a nation in 2001 liberated from the Protectionist shackles which stifled its first century.

Trade Protection did not exist alone because its triumph involved the capture of the entire economy. The power of Protectionism derived from its alliance with Arbitration, the third institution of the Settlement. This alliance, in fact, was called New Protection: its meaning was precise – the legal obligation upon employers who benefited from protection to redistribute their profits to their employees in wages and working conditions provided upon a 'fair and reasonable' basis. New Protection left a legacy as powerful as any political idea in Australia. It was the device which tied both capital and labour to the post-Federation consensus. The Commonwealth Arbitration Court, later the Conciliation and Arbitration Commission, then the Industrial Relations Commission, became the forum for its entrenchment.

The depression of 1890s had been the dominant economic influence on the Australian Settlement. Its legacies were Protection and Arbitration and above all their fusion in the principle of New Protection. Arbitration was an Australian institution based upon the most distinctive of Australian ideas, the 'fair go' principle. It was Australian in its effect to restore order after the class conflict of the 1890s which neither unions nor employers wanted to repeat, in its egalitarian ethos, and in its solutions through bureaucratic legalisms.

The father of the Arbitration Bill was the South Australian liberal, Charles Kingston, but it was introduced by Deakin in a tour de force of lyricism:

This bill marks, in my opinion, the beginning of a new phase of civilisation. It begins the establishment of the People's Peace ... which will comprehend necessarily as great a transformation in the features of industrial society as the creation of the King's Peace brought about in civil society ... imperfect as our legal system may be, it is a distinct gain to transfer to the realm of reason and argument those industrial convulsions which have hitherto involved, not only loss of life, liberty, comfort and opportunities for well-being.

The Bill provided for conciliation between unions and employers and, if necessary, compulsory arbitration in the form of an award made by a new court which would determine the 'right' in industrial disputes. It was passed, finally, in 1904 after a series of political crises and re-drafting, becoming the major achievement of the second parliament.

The philosophy of the Arbitration Act was that industrial relations required an umpire and could not be left to employers and employees. The aim was to remove the need for industrial action by paying workers a fair wage and guaranteeing equity across industries. The Australian system was unique because 'it provided regulation not only of the process for settling disputes but also direct regulation of the outcome ... based on specific views about wage equity'. This led to a system of national wage regulation and institutionalised comparative wage justice, an idea which defied the contrasting economic performance of different industries in varying regions. The Act enshrined trade union power and encouraged the growth of unions on a craft rather than an industry basis.

Arbitration was part of Labor's first federal platform in 1901. But the Labor Party, the beneficiary of its creation, did not establish the Arbitration system. It was an initiative of the Deakinite Liberals and it was secured, finally, by an alliance of Free Traders and Protectionists. It was supported by the Labor Party and the trade unions and resisted by the employers.

The influential president of the Commonwealth Arbitration Court from 1907 to 1921 was Henry Bournes Higgins, a middle-class radical and social reformer, appointed to this life's work by Deakin. Higgins, as an outsider but a friend of the Labor Party, became attorney-general in the first federal ALP government in 1904. For his biographer 'it was as though the working class was being officially received into the corridors of power with Higgins as its guide.' Higgins was a rich lawyer and a man of fierce independence.

In his first case as president, Higgins put his stamp upon the Arbitration Court – the *Harvester* judgement of 1907 which enshrined New Protection. Excise duties were to be waived for manufacturers if the Court certified that they were paying 'fair and reasonable' wages. The parliament had left the Court to interpret this definition and Higgins chose Sunshine Harvester as the test case. He could not think of 'any other standard appropriate than the normal needs of the average employee.' He calculated them on the Melbourne household budget for about five people to which he made extra allowance for 'light, clothes, boots, furniture, utensils, rates, life insurance, savings, accident or benefit societies, loss of employment, union pay, books and newspapers, tram and train fares, sewing machine, mangle, school requisites, amusements and holidays, intoxicating liquors, tobacco, sickness and death, religion or charity.'

The result was a wage of forty-two shillings a week, a calculation influenced by Pope Leo XIII's *Rerum Novarum* encyclical, fairly primitive maths, and the worker's right to plan for a family of five. This established a wage fixation system based on human need, not on profits or productivity. It entrenched the idea that wages should be set by judicial decree. It enshrined the idea of a minimum wage which was sacrosanct and introduced the notion of family welfare into wage setting. It established the notion of cost-of-living as a basis for wage movements and underpinned the regulated wage structure. It was the rock upon which Higgins built his Court. This basic wage evolved as a wage for the unskilled with margins paid above it. Having taken his stand, Higgins was ruthless in its prosecution. This was revealed in the case involving BHP in 1909.

Higgins told BHP that if it could not pay the minimum rate then it would be preferable to shut down the mine: 'If it is a calamity that this historic mine should close down, it would be a still greater calamity that men should be underfed or degraded.' Unemployment, by implication, was preferable to cheap labour.

Arbitration's dedication to wage justice and equity was an institutional bulwark against the growth of class warfare which a market system would have imposed, given the huge fluctuations in Australian's national income from commodity price movements. Yet the rejection of wage flexibility was also an institutional flaw for a nation whose export revenue depended upon fluctuating commodity prices. Higgins' interest was class power, not market forces. He said that Arbitration was needed to impose justice; to check the 'despotic power' and bourgeois spirit of employers.

Higgins encouraged workers to trust Arbitration and strengthen their unions to utilise its advantages. The employers, after their initial resistance to the Court, were incorporated, finally, within the system. Arbitration grew in a turbulent but relentless manner as a joint federal–state structure of courts with union and employer organisations. The failure of the effort to abandon federal Arbitration by the coalition government of S.M. Bruce in 1929 which saw his government defeated and the loss of his own seat, only reinforced the political weight of the system.

Arbitration was the greatest institutional monument to Australian egalitarianism and its quest for social order. It was an heroic endeavour founded in optimism that man could defy the anarchy of the market-place and impose a system of just prices to secure his material dignity. Its longevity is a tribute to its ability to incorporate its opponents. But in the 1980s the conflict between the international economic pressures on Australia and centralised wage-fixation became irresistible. Higgins' effort to insulate wages from the international market finally began to collapse.

The Liberal–National coalition reversed a lifetime of virtual acqui-escence in Arbitration when, in the 1980s, it declared its intention to dismantle the system. In the early 1990s the Labor Party and the trade union movement announced their own intention to move towards an enterprise bargaining system – evidence that the primacy of the central court and its system was crumbling.

The fourth element of the Australian Settlement was State Paternalism – individual happiness through government intervention. It originates not with Federation but from the white man's arrival in 1788 to establish a prison. Belief in state power was rooted in a society shaped by former convicts, military officers and a 'colonial secretary' mentality. From the start the state was involved in every form of commercial activity. The entrepreneur was divorced from the mechanism of the market. The individual looked first to the state as his protector, only secondly to himself.

This statement was reinforced by the growth of nineteenth-century democracy. Australia's political consciousness was developed after the Industrial Revolution and the French Revolution. It fell into that period when the entire direction of politics was to demand political rights and secure economic benefits from the state. In Australia this process, cul-minating in the triumph of the Labor Party, was facilitated by the absence of countervailing forces in the form of a property-owning aris-tocratic or entrenched ruling class.

The triumph of democracy in Australia was as comprehensive as anywhere in the world. But its nature involved a greater fusion between the interests of the individual and the state than in most other nations. During the 1890s and early 1900s Australia became a pioneer in progressive social laws which meant, in effect, the advancement of state power.

Deakin's liberalism was creative and dynamic. It was dedicated not just to the 'destruction of class privileges' but to the erection of laws and institutions to advance the individual through state power. Deakin declared:

> State socialism I fear only because of the weakness of the old social idea in us ... run by selfishness nothing could exceed the corruption likely to be bred under a system of State Socialism but safeguarding this I have no desire other than to extend the sphere of State interference and control.

The Labor Party supported Deakinite liberalism until it was strong enough to seize power from Deakin. Labor built upon the Deakin inheritance. It harnessed class power to the instrument of the state. Deakin sympathised with Labor but he could never join Labor. Deakin's liberalism was an appeal to the common interest but Labor campaigned on a class interest; a new appeal for a new century. Labor marched into the seats of the Deakinite liberals and stole the working-class votes on which they had relied. Deakin saw the inevitable and opined that 'the rise of the Labor Party is more cosmic than the crusades'.

The Australian Settlement had been achieved on the basis of Deakin's parliamentary alliance with the Labor Party; in effect, a Liberal–Labor alliance which is the key to the Settlement's longevity. It meant that faith in government power was shared by non-Labor and Labor as the century unfolded.

In 1930 when W.K. Hancock sought to capture Australia's political tradition he wrote:

> Australian democracy has come to look upon the State as a vast public utility whose duty it is to provide the greatest happiness for the greatest number ... to the Australian, the State means collective power at the service of individualistic 'rights'. Therefore he sees no opposition between his individualism and his reliance upon Government.

The most penetrating account of state socialism came from Frederic Eggleston who held several Victorian state ministries on the non-Labor side in the 1920s. Eggleston noted that Victoria's public services 'in proportion to the size and the economic standing of the community, constitute possibly the largest and most comprehensive use of state power outside Russia'. After a detailed review of banking, railways, roads, water supply, electricity, agriculture, forests, transport, ports and other services, Eggleston concluded, indeed he claimed to have proved, that state intervention was failing.

Eggleston was a disillusioned interventionist convinced after his ministerial experience that the Victorian model required a retreat of state power, a diagnosis that was never implemented. His central argument, documented in detail, was that state socialism in practice undermined individual initiative and responsibility.

It was this same belief, in fact, which drove the 1980s campaign to secure smaller, less interventionist government and a more competitive Australia. It was driven by the need to foster a more dynamic individual citizenry. Its symptoms were a public sector surplus, an attack on government regulations, privatisation of public enterprise, needs-based welfare, deregulation of the labour market, and micro-economic reform to achieve better results in the economic lifelines that had been dominated by the state – energy, communications and transport.

For example, in its 1988–89 report, the Industries Assistance Commission (IAC) estimated that an extra $12 billion annually would flow to GDP from more efficient transport, aviation, communications and energy services. The key to this lay in a reduction in government intervention. In its 1989–90 report the IAC complained that governments had distorted markets for much of Australia's history and insisted that 'greater exposure to competition – both at home and abroad – is the surest means of securing higher productivity'.

The final pillar of the Australian Settlement was Imperial Benevolence – the belief that Australian prosperity and security was underwritten by the Empire. In 1901 the six states united in a Commonwealth under the British crown. It was a union achieved by practical politicians who saw no conflict between being both British and Australian. They sought to make Australia strong by refurbishing the bond with Britain. A strong Empire meant a strong Australia; nationalism and Empire loyalism were bedfellows. The Royal Navy was the guarantor of White Australia.

British finance and trade preference underwrote Australian growth. Federation created a nation but it could never create a sense of national identity or purpose.

Australia was a constitutional entity with a spiritual void at its core. It longed for a test of national character. That came at Gallipoli which, in turn, became a legend that was asked to do too much – to sustain a national identity. The Australian psychology was trapped between the aspiration to independence and the comfortable dependence upon Britain. It is extraordinary that it took Australia until the 1972 election of the Whitlam government to begin to bury its inferiority complex. This glimpse of genuine national confidence was fractured but the sentiment returned with firmer foundations in 1990. It was exhibited in the serious and growing movement to celebrate the centenary of the Commonwealth in 2001 by the declaration of a republic. In 1992 Paul Keating became the first prime minister to campaign for a shift in Australia's identity from a constitutional monarchy to a republic.

Two trends coalesced during the 1980s – the internationalisation of the world economy in which success became the survival of the fittest; and the gradual but inexorable weakening of Australia's 'imperial' links with its two patrons, Britain and America. The message was manifest – Australia must stand on its own ability. Australians, in fact, had waited longer than most nations to address the true definition of nationhood – the acceptance of responsibility for their own fate.

The upshot is that the 1980s was Australia's decade of creative destruction. It witnessed business shake-out, financial excess, economic restructuring, individual greed, the making and breaking of fortunes and, for many, a struggle to maintain financial and family security. Despite the hopes it engendered, the decade closed in pessimism. But the significance of the 1980s transcends this pessimism; the decade saw the collapse of the Australian Settlement, the old protected Fortress Australia. In the 1960s it was shaken; in the 1970s the edifice was falling; in the 1980s the builders were on site fighting about the framework for the new Australia.

The 1990s will answer the fundamental question raised by the 1980s – whether this decade laid the foundations for a new settlement or was merely a misguided aberration. It will resolve the battle between the reformers and the traditionalists; between those looking towards a new order and those merely tinkering with the old. It will determine whether

Australia has the courage and insight to remake its political tradition or whether it buckles before the challenge and succumbs to an economic and social mediocrity.

FROM THREE CHEERS TO
THE BLACK ARMBAND

Geoffrey Blainey

1993

What has been good and what has been bad in the history of Australia? I selected this topic because it raises several difficult and dovetailed issues. Moreover, these issues are central in Australian politics and indeed in the nation's own sense of itself and where it is going.

Everyone will draw up a different balance sheet. It will depend partly on the historian's own experience and assumptions and bias. The exact balance sheet depends partly on the year when they happen to draw up the credits and debits, for some years are more buoyant than others. In this short time I will not attempt to draw up a full balance sheet but concentrate on several vital facets of European and also Aboriginal history.

To some extent my generation was reared on the 'three cheers' view of history. This patriotic view of our past had a long run. It saw Australian history as largely a success. While the convict era was a source of shame or unease, nearly everything that came after was believed to be pretty good. Now the very opposite is widely preached, especially in the social sciences.

If you first went to school in the 1930s you learned little Australian history but you accepted that the pioneers were at least as worthy as their inheritors. This was the view handed down to the young through school lessons or papers or radio. A nation fighting for its life usually sees that life, present and past, as very much worth defending by persuasion as well as arms. The left wing and the right wing were alike in their congratulations, though they rarely congratulated the same events.

There is a rival view, which I call the 'black armband' view of history. In recent years it has assailed the generally optimistic view of Australian history. The black armbands were quietly worn in official circles in 1988, the bicentennial year. Until late in that year Mr Hawke rarely gave a speech that awarded much praise to Australia's history.

Even notable Labor leaders from the past – Fisher, Hughes, Scullin, Curtin and Chifley – if listening in their graves in 1988, would have heard virtually no mention of their names and their contributions to the nation they faithfully served. Indeed the Hawke government excised the earlier official slogan, 'The Australian achievement', replacing it with 'Living together' – a slogan that belongs less to national affairs than to personal affairs. The multicultural folk busily preached their message that until they arrived much of Australian history was a disgrace. The past treatment of Aborigines, of Chinese, of Kanakas, of non-British migrants, of women, the very old, the very young and the poor was singled out, sometimes legitimately, sometimes not. These condemnations of Australia's past treatment of various categories of people were so sweeping that at times close to 80 per cent of the population was in the 'hit list' – a suspiciously high percentage, you must admit, when this really was one of the world's most vigorous democracies.

My friend and undergraduate teacher Manning Clark, who was almost the official historian in 1988, had done much to spread the gloomy view and also the compassionate view with his powerful prose and his Old Testament phrases. For Manning Clark, Australia was the land where the money-changers had recaptured the temple – a biblical takeover in reverse. Clark spoke of 'the sickness of society at large', and the perpetual rule of the tough and the ruthless. Australia, he wrote, is a nation which throughout its history had equated 'material achievement with public virtue'. These are powerful views, and some evidence can be found to back them, but I do not think, with all respect, that the evidence is strong enough.

Even Australia's material achievements of the past are under the hammer; and some recent books by historians see mainly injustice in the present, and poverty and inequality in the past. Why a million people a year were clamouring to enter such an unattractive society, and why so many people had been eager to come across the world in the majority of past decades, was a point not quite explained. Now schoolchildren are often the target for these views. In contrast, the general public for the most part remains proud of the nation's history, or what they know of it – their affection stood out in Sydney on Australia Day, 1988.

To some extent the black armband view of history might well represent the swing of the pendulum from a position that had been too favourable, too self-congratulatory, to an opposite extreme that is even more unreal and decidedly jaundiced.

Australia – until, say, the last quarter century – was one of the great success stories in the economic history of the world. In the economic realm Australia was more successful 100 years ago than it is today; but it still must be classed as successful. It is in the top twenty-five, using virtually every definition, and by some economic observers it stands in the top fifteen. Whether such high places will be retained on the world's ladder is difficult to forecast. Australia is likely, on present evidence, to decline further in the next ten years.

We should measure economic success partly by the steepness of the mountain that had to be climbed. This was a tough country to colonise. I'm sure the Aboriginal pioneers found it difficult and in many ways they succeeded. The British also found it difficult. It was far from their homeland. The return voyage was hazardous: the sea route past Cape Horn was the main route from Australia for about ninety years. Australia was probably the finest triumph of long-distance colonisation the world so far had seen.

The newcomers found that the various climates of this continent were strange. The climates remained a riddle. The first settlement at Sydney was made on the basis, understandably, of a blunder about climate. An additional shock was to discover that so much of the continent was arid. This shock was still being felt by explorers in the 1870s. We still do not know what is a normal run of seasons.

Australia is the world's largest museum of soil deficiencies. Farming here, compared to North America, was a lottery because the soil, so deficient in phosphate and other minerals, seemed exhausted after only a few crops. Of course the land had natural advantages – sweeping grasslands in which the natural predators were not prolific and a winter climate that did not require the penning of livestock under a roof.

All in all it was a great achievement to turn Australia into one of the world's great producers of foods and fibres. The natural fibres are costlier and less in favour in this era of synthetic fibres but in the cold winters of the northern hemisphere, how many hundreds of millions of lives were made more liveable or even prolonged by Australian wool? Likewise Australian-grown food is not so urgently needed at present but its era will probably come again. Meanwhile, in a reasonably favourable year of the last decade Australia was probably producing enough food to sustain – on a modest intake of calories – close to 100 million people here and overseas. That is a remarkable achievement in a continent where probably fewer than one million people could feed themselves in Aboriginal times.

The story of mineral production in Australia needs no comment, except to say that it depends more on effort, imagination and efficiency than on luck. If luck really is all-important, why did the Aborigines have so little luck as miners? The phrase 'lucky country' is plainly misleading when applied unthinkingly to any primary industry, let alone to the whole economy.

When you place the obstacles on one side and the economic achievements on the other, you have to give three cheers – or if you are mean, two and a half. It is true, as many critics point out, that the wealth produced has not been evenly spread. At the same time those regimes which, like the Soviet Union, claim to have been successful in spreading wealth have failed dismally to produce enough wealth to spread. For most of the last hundred years it was better to be a poor Australian than a middle-income member of most other nations.

The heyday of Australia's economic success was in the period from the end of the first gold boom to about the eve of the First World War. The late Professor N.G. Butlin of the Australian National University placed Australia's living standards at the top of the world at about the start of this century, and this verdict is proudly passing into Australian folklore. It is difficult to know whether this verdict is valid: international comparisons are so hazardous. I myself would call it a powerfully argued guess. Moreover, his calculations excluded the Aborigines. At the same time, Australians almost certainly stood on one of the top four rungs of the world's ladder of prosperity in most years from 1870 to 1914.

Why has Australia, while still standing high on the world's economic ladder, been forced to step down so many rungs? A significant part of the descent took place in the last decade, and can be explained by poor economic management, more in Canberra but also in the tall glasshouses of Melbourne, Sydney, Adelaide, Perth and Brisbane. But the major descent from the top rungs of the ladder began even earlier. Two reasons for the relative decline between 1914 and 1950 were geographical. In a period when the world moved steadily from firewood and coal towards oil, we lacked our own supply of oil: so an energy-rich country lost its advantage. Moreover, the climate in south-eastern Australia, so important to the rural economy, was relatively dry.

Over a longer period, our economic decline owes much to cultural factors reinforced by political decisions: a reluctance to save money, partly because of the increase in social security; a high preference for leisure; and a work culture which is more laid-back than our powerful and vigorous sports culture. The difference between our Friday and our Saturday values is almost a cultural iron curtain.

Beyond dispute, the colonising of Australia since 1788 has done great damage to the environment, mostly in the areas of urban and agricultural settlement. What we call economic progress took place with such speed and with such scant knowledge of the environment. There was a heavy toll, including the destruction of rare species of plants and animals, the increasing salinity of irrigated lands, the clearing of forests and the deliberate introduction of new animals – rabbit, cat, fox and many others – that displaced or preyed on native species. On the basis of damage for each 100 square kilometres, we cannot feel sure whether greater alteration was made to Australia than to Europe in the last 200 years, though in the last 2000 years Europe has probably been altered the more, simply because of the sheer density of its human settlement.

There are various ways of measuring comparative ecological damage just as there are of defining democracy. Do you apportion the blame for ecological damage partly by counting the damage done in relation to the number of lives lived in the region, or the damage done for each 1000 square kilometres of a nation's territory, or the relative vulnerability of the environment to damage of certain kinds? For example, a small population occupying a large area that is not very vulnerable does not necessarily deserve high marks for inflicting less harm on the species and landscape. No doubt the settled regions of south-eastern Australia are one of the world's areas damaged the most in a short space of time. Admittedly, it was one of the more vulnerable areas, even before the First Fleet arrived. The Aboriginal record of damage was also high, when one considers their simple technology and the fact that so few new species were introduced in addition to human beings and dingoes.

I count democracy as one of the major credits on the national balance sheet. Australia was an early convert. By 1860, the overwhelming majority of Australia's population lived in democratic territory – Western Australia and most of the Aboriginal people were the exception. I guess I'm the originator of the statement, now creeping into wider usage, that Australia is one of the five or six oldest continuous democracies in the world, but I am only too aware that it is one of those statements that passes muster so long as it is not inspected too closely. After all, what is a democracy? What was called a democracy in the time of Disraeli or Bismarck might not be called one today. What proportion of adults must possess the right to vote if their land is to be called a democracy? If 50 per cent is required, then there was no democracy in the history of the world even as late as 1890.

Even when nearly all the adult men had the right to vote in the election of representatives to a lower house – and Australia had reached that stage by the 1860s – their ultimate power, and their legitimate title to the word democracy, was in effect limited by a variety of countervailing powers. The checks and limits included the monarchy and its colonial representative who was the governor. They included the power to conduct foreign policy (a power largely residing in Westminster), the courts, a restrictive upper house and uneven electorates. Even allowing for the variety of such checks which operated in virtually all European or colonial democracies as late as 1890, and even allowing for the different checks operating in the republic of the United States (including the fact of slavery), Australia is by any reasonable definition one of the oldest continuous democracies in the world. The word *continuous* is important because many European democracies were crushed by Hitler.

There is a valid case for arguing that Australia is the oldest continuous democracy in the world, for in 1903 it became the first national parliament to permit women both to vote and to stand for election. I did not hear in the bicentennial year of 1988 our national leaders refer even once to this long and remarkable democratic achievement of the country they were allegedly celebrating.

In Australia democracy is less in favour in intellectual circles today than thirty years ago. The more emphasis that is placed on the rights of minorities, and the need for affirmative action to enhance those rights, the more is the concept of democracy – and the rights of the majority – in danger of being weakened. Likewise, the High Court in recent years might be seen as a quiet challenger to democracy. At times it is beginning to see itself as a third and very powerful house in the federal system of government. The 1988 referendum, fortunately rejected, was a subtle attempt by the federal government to increase those powers.

Australia won democracy with relative ease in a series of bloodless steps. We tend to take it for granted and to think that it is an easy system to operate. It is not, however, so easily operated. In fact it depends partly on a society which emphasises individual responsibility as much as individual rights. We became a rights-mad society in the 1970s and 1980s, forgetting that there will never be enough rights to go around. A firm right granted to one person or group is often a loss of a right to another person or group. The Bill of Rights that nearly passed through the federal parliament in 1986 was a traffic jam of competing rights. It would be unwise, indeed complacent, to see democracy as a permanent victory for Australia.

Many Australians see the treatment of Aborigines, since 1788, as the blot on Australian history. Fifty years ago, fewer than 50,000 Australians probably saw this as the blot. Now maybe several million are convinced that it is the main blot and maybe half of the population, or even more, would see it as highly regrettable. Irrespective of whether deep shame or wide regret is the more appropriate response, this question will be here to vex or torment the nation for a long time to come.

My own view on this question is much influenced by my own particular interpretation of Australian history. My starting point you might disagree with, but I have held it for some twenty years, have often reconsidered it, and will hold on to it until contrary evidence arrives.

The meeting of the incoming British with the Aborigines, at a thousand different parts of Australia spread over more than a century, was possibly a unique confrontation in recorded history. No doubt a version of the episode happened somewhere else, hundreds of years earlier, on a smaller scale. But there is probably no other historical parallel of a confrontation so strange, so puzzling to both sides, and embracing such a huge area of the world's surface. If we accept this fact we begin to understand the magnitude of the problem that appeared in 1788, puzzled Governor Arthur Phillip, a man of goodwill, and is still with us. It will probably remain with us for the foreseeable future, defying the variety of quick-fix formulas that sometimes attract the federal government, tempt the High Court, and tantalise thoughtful Aboriginal leaders.

In 1788, the world was becoming one world. Europe's sailing ships had entered nearly every navigable sea and strait on the globe, and the ships' crews were alert for anything that was tradable, and so they were sure to return to any place of promise. In 1788, the industrial revolution was also beginning. Here landed representatives of the nation which had just developed the steam engine, the most powerful machine the world had known, and also the semi-mechanised cotton mill. On the other hand Australia represented the way of life that almost certainly prevailed over the whole habitable globe some 10,000 years earlier. The Aborigines had no domesticated plants and animals and therefore a very different attitude to the land – this is part of the long painful background to the *Mabo* case. They had no pottery, they had implements of wood and bone and stone but none of metals, they had no paper and no writing, though they were skilled at a variety of other signs. They had no organisation embracing more than say 3000 people, and probably no organisation capable of putting more than 200 people into a battlefield at the one time. They had few, if any, permanent villages, and only a token ability to hoard food. They believed in a living, intervening god – here was a close resemblance – but not the God seen as the correct one. It was a society with many distinctive merits, often overlooked, but it was startlingly different to the one that supplanted it.

In 1788, Aboriginal Australia was a world almost as remote, as different as outer space. We now think of Aboriginal Australia as having a unity, but it had even less unity than Europe possesses today. There were countless economic and social differences, and an amazing variety of languages. Accordingly the idea, widely voiced now, that the incoming British could have – and should have – signed a treaty with *the* Aborigines, and so worked out rights and compensations, rests on a faith in the impossible. Any treaty would have been one-sided, with the Aborigines as losers.

Even if the First Fleet had brought out not the dross but the wisest and most humane women and men in England, and even if the Aborigines whom they met at Sydney Harbour were the wisest of all their people, how conceivably could a treaty have been signed – given the differences in language and understanding? And if a treaty were signed, how far inland and along the coast would it have extended? The north and south sides of Sydney Harbour, then as now, had different languages and tribal arrangements. (I do not use this argument, incidentally, to comment on the question of whether there should or should not be a treaty today.) There was a huge contrast between the two cultures, the incoming and the resident. Every Australian still inherits the difficult consequence of that contrast.

How can we fairly summarise this complex and delicate question: was the treatment of Aborigines an ineradicable stain on Australian history? There are many answers, each of them a part answer.

The Aborigines probably enjoyed a very high standard of living, so long as their population remained low. My belief – I have set it out elsewhere – is that they were a highly successful society in the economic sphere, and that the typical Aborigines in 1788 had a more varied and more secure diet than the typical Europeans. This kind of semi-nomadic society once existed everywhere in the inhabitable world, but in the years of the neolithic revolution it had vanished from every large landmass except Australia. A highly skilled system, it was extravagant – and we are too – in the use of space and land and resources. A huge area was needed to support few people. Such were the land needs that the whole globe in the time of the hunters and gatherers perhaps supported only one per cent of its present population.

Such a form of land use was bound to be overthrown or undermined. The world's history has depended heavily on the eclipse of this old and wasteful economic way of life – wasteful in terms of human potential though not wasteful in terms, modern terms, of the whole range of living things. There is no way it could be preserved. The miracle is that it survived until 1788 and later. It was tragic for the generation that had to lose it. Any idea that the Aboriginal way of life of 1788 could have been retained for centuries more is a daydream. It is strange that the Australian version of land rights almost tries to restore this archaic and untenable way of life.

After the British arrived, the treatment of Aborigines was often lamentable: the frequent contempt for their culture, sometimes the contempt for the colour of their skin, the removal of their freedoms and usually the breaking of their precious link with their tribal homelands. And also the killing of them, in ones and tens and even occasionally in the hundred. In 150 years it may be that as many as 20,000 Aborigines were killed, predominantly by Europeans but sometimes by Aborigines enrolled as troopers.

After many attempts to help Aborigines, it came to be widely believed by about 1850 that nothing effective could be done to preserve or rescue them. So dramatically were their numbers declining that they were expected by learned opinion in Europe and the Americas to die out. Learned opinion was mistaken. Interestingly, this mistaken view was in part self-serving but it was the considered view of science at a time when science was being enthroned as king. Charles Darwin, the greatest biological scientist of his day, believed that the Aborigines were doomed. It is ironical that science, which transformed Australia and made it so productive, was so astray on a matter so vital to the Aborigines.

Oddly, the vilification of Aborigines by Europeans who lived in the nineteenth century is now almost matched by the vilification of those same Europeans at the hands of the present-day moralists, scholars, journalists and film-makers. Again and again we see and hear the mischievous statements that the Aborigines' numbers were drastically reduced by slaughter. In fact, diseases were the great killer by a very large margin.

It is also timely to recall that the loss of life in traditional Aboriginal society – whether through infanticide or through warfare and other kinds of violence – was probably on a large scale. There is a tendency today to treat traditional Aboriginal society as especially peace-loving, a view to which I do not at present subscribe, though the evidence is sparse. The Aborigines were and are human beings with the same capacity as Europeans to live in peace or to make war. At present there is a tendency, maybe a welcome tendency, not to look too closely at traditional Aboriginal society. Certainly it was grossly over-criticised in the past. At the same time, it is unwise and unfair if the temporary drawing of the blinds over that society is accompanied by crude propaganda directed at the equally vulnerable European society which pushed aside the Aborigines.

Even on recent issues the accounts of the treatment of Aborigines have little relation to fact. How often, for example, do we now hear it said that the Aborigines had no vote until 1967? Credit should be given for attempts to redress past wrongs.

It is not easy to draw rules for the handling of such explosive questions. We have to try, however, to be fair to both sides – the early Australians and the Europeans who arrived later. Understanding is needed on all sides, and neither I, nor anybody else, can claim an adequate understanding of such a complicated and unusual question. Nothing does less to promote discussion than the constant use of the word racist. It is often a correct word but it is also becoming the favourite word of the prejudiced, the ignorant and often the intellectually unscrupulous.

Anyone who tries to range over the last 200 years of Australia's history, surveying the successes and failures, and trying to understand the obstacles that stood in the way, cannot easily accept the gloomier summaries of that history. Some episodes in the past were regrettable, there were many flaws and failures, and yet on the whole it stands out as one of the world's success stories. It is ironical that many of the political and intellectual leaders of the last decade, one of the most complacent and disappointing decades in our history, are so eager to denounce earlier generations and discount their hard-won successes.

Many young Australians, irrespective of their background, are quietly proud to be Australian. We deprive them of their inheritance if we claim that they have inherited little to be proud of.

THE FUTURE EATERS

Tim Flannery

1994

Culture means many things to different people, but one of its key elements is the embodiment, in beliefs and customs, of actions that help people survive in their particular environment. This is not to say that all cultures are in tune with their ecology, indeed it could be argued that the great majority of the world's cultures are not. This is because cultures that we can call 'ecologically attuned' are the result of many thousands of years of experiencing and learning about a particular ecosystem.

The problem of cultural maladaptation seems to be particularly acute in Australia. For it has the highest number of new settlers of any of the 'new' lands, and it has an extremely difficult and unusual ecology. Perhaps this accounts for what outsiders perceive as the obsession Australians have with defining themselves. But to Australians, that obsession makes perfect sense. It arises from a frustration born of the long-felt inability to live in harmony with the land. It comes from the dismay one feels when seeing the extraordinary beauty and complexity of unique environments wither – even from an apparently gentle touch by a European hand – and from the floods and bushfires that constantly remind Australians that the land does not hold them comfortably. Finally, and most importantly to many, it arises from the great gulf of culture and understanding that exists between Aborigines and other Australians.

As a result of these feelings, Australians have long struggled with the issue of national identity; yet they have done so without really trying to understand the nuts and bolts workings of their land. It is, I think, now clear that any lasting notion of Australian nationhood must arise from an intimate understanding of Australian ecosystems.

Throughout the 1980s and 90s the struggle of Australians to define their sense of manhood has intensified. Until recently, the image of the suntanned stockman – laconic, self-reliant, but a dependable mate – has been the role model for Australians; their way of defining themselves. But is the stockman a true Australian? Do the ideals he encapsulates help us survive in modern Australia? The same question, I argue, must be asked of our other cultural icons: our flag, oaths, anthems; and policies such as multiculturalism, a haven for large-scale immigration, and the relatively new idea of becoming part of Asia.

The stereotype of the stockman was born on the Australian frontier at a time of rapid expansion into a hostile land. Pioneers had to be tough and self-reliant and had little time for recreation. But most importantly they had to stick together, for hard times could see all perish if the community was not cohesive. Thus, mateship was esteemed above almost any other value.

The great Australian writer Henry Lawson saw mateship as a central tenet of Australian culture and through his writings extolled its importance in Australian life. His sense of its importance arose in part from his own experience of various crises – particularly droughts – while he travelled through the Australian bush in his youth. His works are full of references to the vulnerability of Australia's pioneers to these disasters. His poem 'Bourke' is a classic example:

No sign that green grass ever grew in scrubs that blazed beneath the sun;
The plains were dust in Ninety-two and hard as bricks in Ninety-one.
On glaring iron-roofs of Bourke, the scorching, blinding sandstorm blew,
No hint of beauty lingered there in Ninety-one and Ninety-two.

It is easy for contemporary, urban Australians to forget the importance of the social bonds inherent in the ideal of mateship. After all, most of the time people were busy trying to live their lives away from the scrutiny of their near neighbours and to avoid the petty conflicts that arise as a result of living in such close proximity. But the Australian environment will not permit even urban Australians to escape indefinitely from the difficulties faced by the pioneers. The Sydney bushfires of January 1994 are a good example, but El Niño-Southern Oscillation–spawned flood and fire have, at one time or another, devastated parts of virtually every major Australian city. In such circumstances, mateship suddenly re-emerges *en masse* in the suburban wilderness and people do extraordinary things to help those whose lives have been affected.

I find it both intriguing and heartening that European Australians should seize upon the ideal of mateship so quickly after colonising their new home. That it should persist for so long in an environment as adverse as the sprawling Australian suburbs is little short of a miracle. Such caring is the very sweetest of the uses of adversity. Perhaps there is something quite fundamental about such social obligations that makes them indispensable in the Australian environment. There is no doubt that Aboriginal culture, particularly as it existed in the more hostile environments, had this sense of sharing. Aborigines had, and indeed still have, social obligations which link people over thousands of kilometres. In times of crisis, these social obligations could see people sharing their few resources with visitors from even more severely affected areas. It is perhaps a tribute to the harshness of Australian environments that these two human groups, which are so different in so many other ways, should both develop and maintain such an onerous system of social obligation and sharing.

To return to the stockman, the key thing about him is that he is an image from the frontier. The frontier was created when people introduced cattle to grasslands that had lacked large herbivores since the diprotodons vanished at least 35,000 years ago. The uneaten grass of their rangelands was an enormous resource which could not be fully exploited by humans in the absence of large herbivores. For only herbivores could turn its energy into meat and hides. Following the extinction of the diprotodon, and in New Zealand the moa, the resource lay essentially untapped, or at least vastly underutilised, by humans in Australasia – until the coming of the Europeans. In New Zealand, it was the shepherd with his flocks that turned the grasses into gold. In Australia, the stockman was foremost, although shepherds, particularly in the nineteenth and early twentieth centuries, played a vital role as well.

Contrary to popular opinion, the stockman is not uniquely Australian. Give him a moustache and *mate*, broaden the brim of his hat and you have an Argentinian gaucho. Give him fringed leggings and a six-shooter and you have a North American cowboy. It is no coincidence that stockman, cowboy and gaucho all come from newly settled continents. For just as the Australian grasslands were cleared of their diprotodons by the first invaders, the prairie and the pampas lost their native elephant, horses, camels and sloths when the first Indians arrived 11,000 years ago. Thus, the grasslands of all three continents presented a bounty that had not been reaped for millennia. The stockman/gaucho/cowboy arose to take advantage of a particular, short-lived ecological niche which resulted from this situation.

Today, the first bounty of the open range has long been exhausted, rendering the ecological niche untenable over vast regions. More intensive land uses have now taken over in these areas. In addition, changes in Australian society, such as increasing urbanisation, feminism, multiculturalism and the declining role of agriculture in the Australian economy, are all acting to render the image of the stockman anachronistic. Yet despite this – perhaps as a result of the inherent appeal of his independence and mateship – the image of the stockman still has immense emotional value to many Australians.

If the stockman arose out of a special and short-lived window of economic opportunity and was not entirely a uniquely Australian phenomenon, at least it arose as a response to local conditions. But there are many aspects of Australian culture that developed in the enormously productive, highly seasonal and 'weedy' ecosystems of Europe or east Asia which have, to our detriment, thrived in Australia. Given the differences in environment, it is remarkable how tenacious these European traditions and views have been in the new land.

Science has not been exempt from the Cultural Cringe and this has already cost Australians dearly. I have a number of colleagues who graduated from Australian universities during the late 1940s and early 50s, following war service. It was at this time that the very last of the bridled nailtail wallabies, pig-footed bandicoots, lesser bilbies and many other Australian mammals were becoming extinct. I have asked several of my older colleagues why they did not devote their studies to preserving these unique elements of Australia's natural heritage. The answer given has always been the same. They were, they said, absolutely riveted by the developments occurring in biology overseas. One must not forget that this was the time when Watson and Crick were unravelling the secrets of DNA, when major advances were being made in evolutionary studies and when the names Oxford and Cambridge reigned supreme in academia. Thus, despite repeated warnings that the Australian fauna was in dire trouble, our promising young graduates left the country one by one to pursue the 'big questions' in biology. With them left the last hope of preserving Australia's unique and vanishing fauna.

Today, the Cultural Cringe seems to be most evident in the reticence of Australians to develop a strong, vibrant and unique culture of their own. Instead, the government produces policies such as multiculturalism, or we talk of becoming a part of Asia. Neither of these options will help Australians to live comfortably in their own land. Indeed, pursued to their logical ends, these policies could destroy the slow process of adaptation between humans and their environment which is currently occurring in Australia.

No one seems to have defined what it means for Australia to 'become part of Asia', yet many Australians accept it as an imperative. It is clear that Australia can never be like Asia in an ecological sense. Therefore, our economy and culture must always differ fundamentally from that of the Asian nations. There are certainly excellent arguments for Australia increasing its trade, cultural, scientific and other links with its Asian neighbours. Indeed, provided our overall population does not grow as a result, there is no disadvantage in having a large proportion of the Australian population derived from people of Asian ancestry.

Even if this were achieved, Australia will always be startlingly different. For the El Niño-Southern Oscillation, soils and biology will begin to change people of Asiatic origin into Australians just as surely as it has done with Europeans. It is clearly a great challenge to forge links with Asia. But the greatest challenge will be to fit Australia's uniquely shaped bit of the world economic jigsaw into the puzzle as a whole. In order to do that, we must know the shape. An unthinking push to 'become part of Asia' will not help us with that.

And what of the government policy of multiculturalism? Although widely adopted and believed in by many Australians, the community concept of multiculturalism is fuzzy. Many people confuse it with immigration. But these concepts are in fact quite separate. Australia's population is so diverse today that a cessation of immigration would have no effect on multiculturalism.

In fact, the government policy of multiculturalism simply means that it is a national goal that people with diverse cultural practices should live side by side in Australia without obliterating each other's culture. From a biological perspective there is absolutely no reason why this should not happen, as long as all cultures modify the few of their practices that can adversely impact on the Australian environment. These, in general, relate only to family size, some agricultural practices, the harvesting of wild resources and attitudes towards the bush.

In the face of the challenges outlined above, Australians have begun to search more deeply for symbols of their identity. Increasingly, they are looking towards 'the bush' to provide them. From a biological per- spective this is a good thing, for hopefully it will build strong links based upon understanding between Australians and their environ- ment. Such links are vitally important, for Australians are caretakers of a disproportionately large share of the world's biological riches and Australia is a land that tolerates few mistakes. If Australians do not possess a culture that values these things, they will be lost to the world.

The production and consumption of meat is a notoriously conserva- tive area of human behaviour and provides many major examples of cultural maladaptation. Indeed, so conservative is this area of human behaviour that modern Australians are almost entirely dependent for meat from mammals upon the three species (cattle, sheep and pig) that were initially domesticated in the late stone age of western Asia some 8000–10,000 years ago. I find it remarkable that despite a shift in conti- nents and the space of 200 years, with some minor exceptions, Australians have not added a single new source of meat to their limited diet.

Despite this conservatism, Australian primary producers support, albeit inadvertently, a vast array of edible animals on their grazing properties. A typical grazing property in western New South Wales supports large populations of three or four species of kangaroos, sheep, goats, cattle, feral pits, rabbits, dogs, horses and emus. All of these spe- cies are highly edible, and all are esteemed by one or more cultural groups somewhere in the world. Yet the traditional Australian attitude to them is strange and highly wasteful, for most Australians consider that only sheep and cattle are fit for human consumption. All the rest, which often constitutes a substantial part of the meat produced, is ignored, shot, or poisoned and left to rot where it dies, breeding blow- flies which further reduce the productivity of sheep.

One of the most striking of all European maladaptations concerns our management of fire. As was discussed earlier, the pioneers quickly wrested control of the firebrand from the Aborigines and with it control of productivity in Australian environments. Graziers have long controlled fire. In many areas they burn more frequently than is good for the ecosystem. In these cases hollow logs and other shelter needed by wildlife is destroyed and soil nutrients lost.

In forests and urban areas Europeans initially (and indeed even today) often had no fire policy, resulting in a massive build up of fuel and the ignition of fire storms that scorched, with monotonous regularity, millions of hectares, resulting in massive losses of life and property. Such devastating fires climaxed in south-eastern Australia in the 1920s and 30s, and it was then that a policy of fire exclusion was implemented in many areas, combined with protective patch strip burning. Although initially successful at containing wildfires, the policy resulted in fuel building up to unprecedented levels. Bushfires of extraordinary ferocity followed.

Slowly, Europeans learned that throughout much of Australia, one must fight fire with fire. Prescribed burning was thus used extensively from the 1950s onwards. But even this policy has often been applied lackadaisically, with little thought being given to overall fire management. Indeed, the Sydney bushfires of January 1994 show how fragile the Australian control of fire is; and not surprisingly they have kick-started development of a better fire policy. It is to be hoped that, after 200 years of ignorance, modern European fire management techniques are coming to resemble Aboriginal firestick farming, or even reconstituting the older, less fire-prone Australia of pre-Aboriginal times.

The highly urbanised nature of contemporary Australia is another example of maladaptation. The problem of catering for continued growth in Australian cities seems almost insurmountable. The only solution offered so far is to increase urban density. This, of course, results in a dramatic decline in urban wildlife, and in generations of young Australians growing up in concrete jungles without any opportunity to learn first-hand about or experience their unique wildlife heritage. Without that, there is little hope for the future indeed.

But the cities present even more severe problems in terms of nutrient and energy transfer. At present they act as vast nutrient and energy sinks for the surrounding countryside. The nutrients and minerals are quite literally stripped from the hinterland and are freighted *en masse* to the cities or overseas for export. The nutrients, once accumulated in the urban areas, become an enormous problem in the form of sewage and other pollutants, which cannot be easily dealt with given current funds and technology. A.D. Hope, Australia's Poet Laureate, saw this with remarkable prescience when he wrote 'Australia' in 1955:

> *And her five cities, like five teeming sores*
> *Each drains her: a vast parasite robber state*
> *Where second-hand Europeans pullulate*
> *Timidly on the edge of alien shores.*

The list of examples of cultural maladaptation is almost endless, but Australia's beach-oriented culture (with its coincident appallingly high rate of melanoma), its taxation and banking practices as applied to rural areas (with its potential for financial and ecological ruin) and its economic addiction to home ownership and construction (which adds pressure to continue with population growth) are a few. Doubtless many, many more will become apparent as the process of cultural adaptation continues.

The period from the 1950s through to the end of the 1980s has seen a backwards march from the goal of developing an environmentally attuned Australian culture. My grandfather ate more native animal foods than I do, for he loved his mutton birds more dearly than chicken. My grandmother and her family knew more about native birds than I, for she lived in the countryside and kept an assemblage of cockatoos, magpies and other birds about the house. Most of my predecessors had a better feel for nature as children than my children do, for few grew up in such a densely urbanised and highly regulated environment as my son and daughter.

I find it sad that so much of the energy of the debate about what it means to be Australian is misdirected. Many Australians would consider that the person eating the meat pie is more 'Australian' than the one eating the souvlaki. Yet no one cares to ask whether the meat has come from kangaroo or cattle, or how much soil was lost in the production of the wheat products used to wrap the meat. Likewise, many people worry about whether immigrants come from Asia or Europe, yet never for a moment think of the effect of Australia's total immigration intake on population growth.

It is ignorance of the past that dooms each new wave of immigrants to the 'new' lands to be future eaters. So certain are they of their superiority; so sure of their ability, that they do not think to learn from those who have gone before them, nor do they take the time to read the signs of the land until disaster has overtaken them. We, perhaps, are the first generation of future eaters who have looked over our shoulder at the past, but we have done so quite late in the process of environment destruction. If we can change our ways before we have consumed all of the future that we are capable of, then we will have achieved something very precious.

It is true that the most recent immigrants are slowly being shaped by their new homes, but like Aborigine and Maori before them, the process is costing dearly in terms of biodiversity and sustainability. This, in turn, is severely limiting the future for their children. More than sixty years ago, Sir Keith Hancock wrote in his great work *Australia*:

> When it suits them, men may take control and play fine tricks and hustle Nature. Yet we may believe that Australia, quietly and imperceptibly … is experimenting on the men … She will be satisfied at long last, and when she is satisfied an Australian nation will in truth exist.

If Australasians are happy to progress towards adaptation at the imperceptible pace of change at which evolution proceeds, it will be a long time indeed before an Australian or a New Zealand nation will in truth exist. But humans are different from all other creatures. We can think, understand, and act to make our lives better. Yet despite all of our advantages – our technology and our intellect – we seem to have made as disastrous a series of mistakes as any other species. Even now, we seem to be seeing only the very first glimmer of the change that Sir Keith foretold. For the moment, I hope that Australasians one and all will begin to ask the right questions. For this is the first, necessarily wobbly step on the road to discovering what it means to be custodians of the wonderful and enigmatic 'new' lands.

A SPIRIT OF PLAY

David Malouf

1998

When Europeans first came to this continent they settled in the cooler, more temperate parts of it. This was where they could reproduce to some extent the world they had left, but it was also because they saw themselves as cool-climate people. The wisdom, fifty years ago, was that white men would never live and work in the north.

Well, we seem to have re-invented ourselves in these last years as warm-climate people. Not only do we live quite comfortably in the north, it is where a great many of us prefer to live. If present population trends are anything to go by, a large part of our population in the next century will have moved into the tropics, and Queensland, our fastest growing state, will be our local California.

This is a change of a peculiar kind. A change in the way we define ourselves and our relationship to the world that is also a new way of experiencing our own bodies. And the second change I have in mind is related to this. It is the change in the living habits of Australians that we can observe any night of the week in Lygon Street in Melbourne, in Rundle Street, Adelaide, in various parts of Sydney: people eating out on the pavement under the stars in a style we recognise immediately as loosely Mediterranean, a style that has become almost universal in these last years, but which fits better here than it does in Toronto or Stockholm.

It seems to me to be the discovery of a style at last that also fits the kind of people we have now become, and that fits the climate and the scene. But the attitudes it expresses, also loosely Mediterranean, make the sharpest imaginable contrast with the way we were even two decades ago, the way, in that far-off time, that we saw life and the possibilities of living.

Look at these diners. Look at what they are eating and drinking: at the little dishes of olive oil for dipping their bread, the grilled octopus, the rocket, the tagines and skordalia, the wine. Look at the eye for style – for local style – with which they are dressed and their easy acceptance of the body, their tendency to dress it up, strip it, show it off. Consider what all this suggests of a place where play seems natural, and pleasure a part of what living is for; then consider how far these ordinary Australians have come from that old distrust of the body and its pleasures that might have seemed bred in the bone in the Australians we were even thirty years ago. These people have changed, not just their minds but their psyches, and have discovered along the way a new body. They have slipped so quickly and so easily into this other style of being that they might have been living this way, deep in a tradition of physical ease, a comfortable accommodation between soul and body, for as long as grapes have grown on vines and olives on trees.

But half a lifetime ago, in the 1950s, olive oil was still a medicine and spaghetti came in tins. Eating out for most Australians was steak and chips at a Greek café if you were on the road, or the occasional Chinese meal. We ate at home, and we ate pretty much what our grandparents had eaten, even those of us whose grandparents came from elsewhere: lamb chops, Irish stew, a roast on Sundays. It would have seemed ludicrous to take food seriously – to write about it in the newspaper, for example – or to believe that what we ate might constitute a 'cuisine', something new and original, a product of art as well as necessity, an expression, in the same way that 'Waltzing Matilda' or 'Shearing the Rams' might be, of a national style and of the local spirit at play.

As for those other changes – of attitude, ways of seeing ourselves in relation to one another and to the world – I shall mention only two. Both were once so deeply embedded in all our ways of thinking here they might have seemed essential to what we were. We could scarcely have imagined an Australia without them.

The first was that belied in racial superiority and exclusiveness that went under the name of the White Australia Policy, but was really, until the end of the Second World War, an exclusively British policy. As the *Bulletin* put it with its usual brutal candour: 'Australia for the Australians

– the cheap Chinese, the cheap Nigger, and the cheap European pauper to be absolutely excluded.'

These sentiments, this sort of language, which was common to the *Bulletin* and to later popular papers like *Smith's Weekly* right up to the early 1950s, expressed the policy of *all* political parties, left and right, and seemed not only acceptable, but unremarkable. Both the attitudes and the language were inextricably tied in with our concept of nationhood. Or so it seemed. Yet the White Australia policy, when it disappeared in the 1960s, did so almost without argument. This great tenet of the Australian dream, of a single superior race on the continent, had grown so weak and theoretical by the 1960s that it simply vanished as if it had never been, and, despite recent rumblings, seems to me to show no signs of revival.

So, too, amazingly, did what had been from the beginning the strongest of all divisions among us, the sectarian division between Protestants and Catholics.

When I was growing up in Brisbane, in the late 1930s and early 1940s, Catholic and Protestant Australians lived separate lives. They might have been living in separate countries. The division between them, the separation, the hostility, was part of the very fabric of living; so essential to life here, so old and deeply rooted, as to seem immemorial and impossible to change.

Catholics and Protestants went to separate schools and learned different versions of history. Secondary students even went to different dancing classes, and when they left school they played football with different clubs, joined different lodges (the Order of Ancient Buffaloes or the Oddfellows if they were Protestant, the Hibernians if they were Catholic), and debutantes came out at different balls. People knew by instinct, at first meeting, by all sorts of tell-tale habits of speech and attitude, who belonged to one group and who to another, just as they knew which corner shops or department stores they should patronise. And these divisions functioned institutionally as well as at street level. Catholics worked in some areas of the public service, Protestants in others. In Queensland, the Labor Party was Catholic; Protestants were Liberal. In the two great referenda over conscription, in 1916 and 1917, the country divided not on party but on sectarian lines – Protestants for, Catholics against – although in the end the 'no's' won; and one should add that serving soldiers were as likely to be Catholic as not.

Part of the bitterness behind all this was that Catholics were almost exclusively Irish, so that the division had an ethnic and historical element as well as a religious one. It was a continuation on new ground of the history of Ireland itself, based on ancient resistance to English invasion and tyranny, and on the English side on fear of Irish subversion and a deep-rooted contempt for Irish superstition and disorderliness. All this created its own mythology. The suggestion, for instance, that bushranging in Australia was a new version of Irish rebellion. It is true that most of the best-known bushrangers, real and imaginary, have Irish names, but as so often, what is told and strongly felt is not necessarily what is true to fact. The Kelly gang was Irish, but so were Kennedy, Scanlon and Lonigan, the three troopers they killed at Stringybark Creek. So were the police who hunted them. Then, too, to be Irish here did not always mean that you had Irish forebears.

My father's people were Melkites, Greek Catholics who recognise the authority of the Pope. Since there was no Melkite church in Brisbane when they arrived there in the 1880s (or anywhere else in Australia for that matter), my father and his six brothers and sisters went to the local Catholic church, St Mary's, and were sent to school with the nuns. Despite their name and background, they grew up as Irish as any Donohue or O'Flynn, taking on with the religion all the peculiar forms of Irish Catholicism, its pietism, its prudery, its superstitions and prejudice. To be Catholic in Australia in those days was to be Irish, wherever you came from.

And what exactly was at stake in all this? To a Protestant militant like John Dunmore Land, the continent itself.

For Irish Catholics in Australia, Protestants were not only in the ascendance as they been At Home, but in the majority. For Protestants the fear was that this happy condition might one day be reversed; that they might wake up one morning and find they had been outnumbered and that this great continent had fallen overnight to Rome and to Mariolatry.

That Catholics did become the majority at last in the late 1980s, and nobody noticed, is a mark of how large the change had been. Young people today not only feel none of the old hostility. For the most part they have never even heard of it. And this is not only because of the increasing secularity of our society although that too is part of it. It is because these differences no longer matter. The whole sorry business is worth recalling now for only one reason, and it is this. If Australia is basically, as I believe it is, a tolerant place, that tolerance was hammered out painfully and over nearly 150 years in the long process by which Catholics and Protestants, the Irish and the rest, turned away from 'history' and learned to live with one another in a way that, for all its bitterness of distrust and resentment, was never murderous as it had been elsewhere, even in times of the greatest stress: during the Easter Uprising of 1916, for example, and the Irish Civil War of the early 1920s; or, before that, during the Home Rule controversy of the 1880s, or before that again, in 1868, when a suspected Fenian named O'Farrell tried to assassinate the visiting Alfred, Duke of Edinburgh, at Clontarf.

This rejection of the move from hostility to murder is important. The smell of blood is not easily forgotten. The stain of it is hard to eradicate and the names of the dead are always there to be reiterated and to become the source of a new round of violence.

Something in the tone of Australian society has been unwelcoming of extremes, and if this makes for a certain lack of passion, a lack of the swagger and high rhetoric that begins as theatre and ends as terrorism and war, it has also *saved* us from something. In contrast to some other mixed societies, like Ireland itself, central Europe in the 1930s, and, most recently Lebanon and Bosnia, some final sanction has always operated here against the negation of that deep psychological work that over something like six millennia has made it possible for us to live with strangers and, however different they might be from ourselves, make neighbours of them.

And isn't this, finally, what holds civilised societies together? The capacity to make a distinction between what belongs, in the way of loyalty, to clan or sect or family, and what to the demands of neighbourliness; what belongs to our individual and personal lives and what we owe to *res puplica* or Commonwealth, the life we share with others, even those who may differ from us in the most fundamental way – skin colour and ethnicity, religious and political affiliation, customary habits. It is the capacity to make and honour these distinctions, out of a common concern for the right we have, each one of us, to pursue our own interests, that is essential to the life of cities, and beyond that, to their more precarious extension as states.

On the whole, we have done well in this. Not only in creating a society in which these distinctions *are* recognised and honoured, but in creating a tone that those who come here from places where they are not, quickly learn to value and accept. There is something to be said for mildness. It leaves people the breathing space, and the energy, to get on with more important things. As George Nadel puts it in speaking of the fight for decent working conditions in Australia: 'The fact that it appeared within reach of everyone made democratic experiment safe, and the working classes were satisfied to secure their share by enjoying a greater return for less labour rather than by political radicalism.' That is, there have been no revolutions in Australia, no blood, at least in this instance, has stained the wattle.

The world these days is global. Australians have not escaped the pressures of the complex present; we will not escape the pressures of an even more complex future. In daring to become a diverse and multi-ethnic society, an open experiment, we run more risk perhaps than most places of breaking up, of fragmenting. But we have faced danger before. What saved us on those earlier occasions was neighbourliness, the saving grace of lightness and good humour, the choice of moderation over the temptation to any form of extreme. These characteristics of our society are still visibly alive in the present; in occasions we take for granted, so much so that we fail sometimes to see how rare they are.

Consider the atmosphere in which election days are celebrated here. The spirit of Holiday hovers over our election boxes. As the guardian angel of our democracy, it seems preferable, and might even be more reliable, than the three or four bored paratroopers who descend to protect the ballot-boxes in even the smallest village in a place as politically sophisticated as Italy. Voting for us is a family occasion, a duty fulfilled, as often as not, on the way to the beach, so that children, early, get a sense of it as an obligation but a light one, a duty casually undertaken. And it can seem casual. But the fact that voters so seldom spoil their vote, either deliberately or by accident, in a place where voting is compulsory and voting procedures are often extremely complicated, speaks for an electorate that has taken the trouble to inform itself because it believes these things matter, and of a citizenship lightly but seriously assumed.

I ended my first chapter with the description of an audience, a mixed convict and military one, at a Sydney performance of Shakespeare's *Henry IV Part One*. What I wanted to see in it was a first attempt here at a society in which all sorts of divisions between groups, but also between individuals, might be resolved by the fact that, in becoming an audience, this heterogeneous crowd had also, for the duration of the occasion, become an entity – and perhaps a single occasion, single occasions, is the best we can hope for, and is enough: a recognition that unity is there as a possibility. It does not have to be sustained as long as it is available when we need it to be.

Let me end with another audience, one in which what was promised in that earlier audience seems to me to be marvellously fulfilled, under more complex conditions and on a vastly larger scale.

An audience comes together of its own volition, unlike a rally, for example, where there is always some element of compulsion, if only a moral one of commitment or duty. An audience simply appears, as the 700,000 or so people do who turn out each year for the gay Mardi Gras procession in Sydney. They have no reason for being there other than interest, curiosity, pleasure, and they are an audience, not simply a crowd, an audience that has been created and shaped by the society it is drawn from, and in which the faculty of watching, listening and judging has been sharpened to an extraordinary degree.

What impresses me about this audience is its capacity to read what it is presented with and come up with an appropriate response: to greet extravagant glitter and camp with delight and a degree of humorous mockery; to see that deliberate provocation is best dealt with by a shrug of the shoulders or live-and-let-live indifference, but that a more sober note is being struck when people incapacitated by AIDS are being wheeled past, and that what is called for by the large throng of their nurses and carers is the acknowledgement of service with respectful silence or applause.

No one has trained this audience in its responses: they come naturally out of what has been picked up from the society itself, they reflect its 'tone'. It is, as an audience, as mysterious in the way it appears and reconstitutes itself for each occasion as any other. No one twenty years ago could have predicted its arrival, but there it is.

As for the actors in this street theatre – could anyone have guessed, back then, that it would be just this group that would call a popular audience into being? Another mystery.

What seems extraordinary here, is that what, until recently, had been a marginal group, mostly invisible, has not only made itself visible but has made the claim as well to be central – that is, as central as any other – and has created that audience for all of us. Open, inclusive, the parade is made up of virtually every strand in our society: the various ethnicities, including Asian and Pacific people and Aborigines; members of the armed forces, the police, and of every other profession, including sex-workers. In being multiple itself, such a parade offers the crowd a reflected image of its own multiplicity, and all within a spirit of carnival, a form of play that includes mockery and self-mockery, glamour and the mockery of glamour, social comment, tragedy and a selfless dedication to others, as if all these things were aspects of the same complex phenomenon – as of course they are. It is called life.

Carnival deals with disorder by making a licensed place for it, and with the threat of fragmentation by reconstructing community in a spirit of celebratory lightness. It takes on darkness and disruption by embracing them. Forces that might otherwise emerge as violence, it diverts through tolerance and good humour into revelry and sheer fun.

Such carnival occasions have ancient roots. They go back to the pagan world, and to medieval festivals, days of licence, Fools' Days, when the spirit of mockery was let loose and a place found for disorder within the world of order and rule. For all its contemporary glitz and high jinks, our version of Mardi Gras retains much of its ancient significance. As a popular festival it reinforces community. It recovers for us, within the complexities and the divisiveness of modern living, a sense of wholeness. And there is a connection here between the carnival world it celebrates, its vulgarity, its flaunting of the flesh, and that first convict performance of *Henry IV*.

Falstaff, the randy, disreputable anti-hero of that play, is the great embodiment in our literature of the spirit of carnival, the direct descendant of the Vice that larked about at the centre of the old morality plays, and before that of the Lords of Misrule, who presided over medieval Fools' Days. Falstaff, and the disorder he represents, is what has somehow to be included in the world of Rule. 'Banish plump Jack,' he tells Prince Hal, 'and banish all the world.'

Falstaff, with his shameless insistence on the flesh, his dirty jokes and phallic shenanigans, is a necessary aspect of what it is to be alive. So is the challenge his non-conformism offers to the coldness and impersonality of the law. Finding a place for Falstaff, acting imaginatively in the spirit of lightness he represents, is the way to wholeness; and wholeness, haleness, as the roots of our language tell us, is health.

HOME-GROWN TRADITIONS

Inga Clendinnen

1999

We have some magnificent home-grown traditions. Our way of memorialising our war dead seems to me unique in its sadness and its absolute denial of military vainglory. Anzac Day dramatises not the glamour of military might, the glory of victory or the injustice of defeat, but the irreparable nature of loss. In that First World War, the Great War, about half of all our men between eighteen and forty-five enlisted in the AIF. One in five was killed. Few households escaped. And we learnt an enduring lesson. War is not glorious. War kills. I suspect our tradition is unique in that steady, tender focus on young men dead before their time. It is also worth remembering that during that war Australia twice rejected a referendum to establish conscription for overseas service. The troops at the front voted 'no' too.

Ours is a very secular grieving. Ken Inglis, who has written a fine book on our sacred monuments, records a First World War cartoon. A digger is being asked 'What are you? Church of E, RC, YMCA, what?' Answer: 'AIF, mate.'

Inglis tells us that the favoured local monument in Australia after the war was the obelisk, the simple four-sided shaft which was relatively inexpensive, which mattered to the little communities who had to raise the money, yet had space enough to record the name of every local man who volunteered. Being ready to take the risk was what mattered. What I remember is the second most favoured monument, the marble Anzac, life-size but looking smaller, drooped over his reversed rifle in all those country towns with its small metal plaque, every one of them representing a loved individual. Nothing grandiose. Nothing larger than life. Just the exact and terrible size of death.

I wish we still had the tradition preserved well into my adult life when at the eleventh hour of the eleventh month, at the low wail of a siren, the whole country stilled. I remember the spreading silence as the city hushed, as trams and cars stopped, as people stopped, bowed their heads, remembered. And then, after what seems a long time, the city would start again. We had a fine and truthful tradition there, as we have in our Anzac Day remembering still. The Anzac march goes on, and it's getting bigger, because these home-grown ceremonies of war easily integrate new arrivals. Many of them know better than we do the cost of glorifying war.

From war to heroes. I like our local heroes, those very secular saints. They tend to be tough physically, but tougher morally, men of action (they are usually men) but not of violence, men who deflate aggression by intelligence and wit. Not a ham-fisted, bone-headed John Wayne among them. Humour is a rare characteristic in heroes, who are usually sullen types. I think of Weary Dunlop, a real Australian hero who commanded the respect of everyone, and of a fictional one, and don't pretend you don't like him, Crocodile Dundee. I think of a semi-fictional one like John Clarke – yes, I know he's a New Zealander – as a distinctly Australian hero. He knows how to handle himself, not by violence, but by a disarmingly ironic wit. Popular Australian-heroes-at-war films like *Gallipoli* and *Breaker Morant*, whatever the murky actuality, catch the scepticism in the face of bombast which to my mind is still central to Australian society. We are also chronically sceptical about intellectual abstractions, chronically unresponsive to rhetoric.

Somehow connected to that aversion to pomposity and our obstinately horizontal view of society is our connection to our convict past, to the men and women exiled to a land 'designed to punish', but which, as Robert Hughes puts it, was 'renamed with the sign of freedom'. These men and women left behind the invisible shackles of class, and the iron shackles of servitude were soon enough struck off. Australian unionists fought for the eight-hour day, and they won. By 1907 a legally enforceable basic wage was in effect across the country. By 1909 women had the vote in every state. D.H. Lawrence, visiting Australia more or less by mistake in the early twenties, had been in the country for only a few days when he knew 'the instinct of the place' to be 'absolutely and flatly democratic', and therefore intolerable to a natural aristocrat like himself. The total absence of deference made his English heart blench: 'In Australia,' he observed gloomily, 'authority was at a discount.'

These days I spend half the year in Far North Queensland, and I like it. On the use of a much-challenged word: I like it when someone calls me 'mate'. He's often a workman, he might be softening me up, he might be about to tell me something I'm not going to like, but I like being called 'mate'. I know people say that between men the word can be a prelude to aggression. When it's used to me, an elderly middle-class woman from the south, it is anti-division – anti-class, anti-gender, anti-generational, anti-regional. It says something like 'we're in this mess together – mate'.

It is often enough said that we non-Aboriginal Australians are city-living coast-dwellers who know nothing of the interior. Even a hundred years ago, 70 per cent of us lived in towns, so I suppose most of us don't know much about the bush or the desert. But we think we do. We feel its presence, in part through representations – through literature, through paintings, increasingly through film. We learned something about the courage of the men and women who live inside the great Australian loneliness from our old school readers: remember 'The Drover's Wife'? I had dismissed Henry Lawson as a sentimental old party, and too often a drunken one as well, until I happened upon 'The Bush Undertaker', and discovered in its antique and disreputable central character a very Australian hero, along with a deep comic nihilism which makes Samuel Beckett seem anodyne.

As for the painters – I saw a Russell Drysdale exhibition not long ago, and for the first time really saw what he was up to. Consider perhaps his most famous painting, *The Cricketers*: the mad insouciance of those sticklike figures, the jubilant shadows cast on the parched earth, on the flaking masonry wall, shadows and wall equally impermanent in that indifferent landscape – but the shadows vividly, imperishably human: the obsessed cricketers, in the middle of what should have been nowhere, engrossed in their game and so making 'nowhere' home. For me, Drysdale's outback people, black and white, standing quietly in that implacable landscape, speak of a modest daily heroism, a resolution to endure that which must be endured afresh each day.

My own pleasure in our landscapes has only intensified with travel overseas. I love the fragility of the marks of human habitation on this land – the windmill by the one tree, the collapsing cottage beside the old water tank, the galvanised iron shed vanishing into the flat blue shimmer of a noonday sky. I find those scratches on the face of the land beautiful, because they speak of an obdurate enduring, a parsimony of gesture, an interiority which matches the land itself. Landscapes elsewhere, like the human marks upon them, seem altogether too noisy.

We also know the land because so many of us travel through it. I didn't know that until I began spending time in the North, and saw the stream of pilgrims travelling through to places west and further north, and felt the mood of their travelling. There are a lot of footloose young people, most of them concentrating more on the sexual than the physical landscape – but there are others, too: whole tribes of retirees, people on long service leave, and, noticeably and movingly, recent migrants, who have lost the land of their childhood, and are seeking to steep themselves in the land they have chosen as their own.

These people travel as if travelling had come to obsess them, especially travel into remote regions. They are not celebrating white triumphs over dark places: they flee white structures, except for petrol stations. I think they are paying homage to the continent itself: to its mute and mesmerising beauty. And they come back recognising the land's essential connectedness with its most competent human inhabitants. They clutch their paintings and speak with awe and pride of the continuing presence of the people who accepted this various and difficult country as it is, and simply lived in it.

Another strength: to his point our post-war immigration programme has been a resounding success. This might be due to the dignity with which our migrants suffered the pains of the migrant experience for the first difficult years, in their own communities and behind closed doors, but it also has a great deal to do with the humanity and inventiveness of our primary and secondary schoolteachers and our nurses. They are our front-line assimilators. We underestimate and undervalue both groups. Some of it is also due to luck: the social structure of our suburbs, the rhythms of our economy. But it also owes something to the geniality of the receiving population, a geniality displayed, for example, in the public and inclusive nature of our pursuit of sport and pleasure.

If a great deal of America surfaces at the baseball stadium, a great deal of Australia surfaces at the beach. You remember how it was a decade ago. We would see families – Italian, Greek, Turkish, very occasionally Vietnamese – spilling out of station wagons, unpacking tablecloths and chairs, and setting up elaborate picnics beside the car in the carpark, the little girls in starched dresses, the granny's chair carefully set in a patch of shade.

After a summer or two, they would graduate to a decorous meal among the tea-tree, and the men might swim. Now they are part of the dishevelled mob on the beach, with soccer competing with cricket for the packed sand, the little girls splashing in frilled lycra suits, and the grandmother, in her first bathing costume, frolicking in the shallows with the baby.

As for migrants' gifts to us – they are multiple. Some irascible people might say: 'only cafés and cooking', but anyone who lived in Australia through the 50s knows that cafés and cooking are life-transforming. Their best gift to us is a multiplicity of intimate connections, by marriage, friendship, business, with other people and places in the world, and other ways of living in the world. I remember the joy of teaching at La Trobe University in the 70s and 80s, and the zest in the classrooms as different cultural experiences, expectations and styles collided.

There are also more deliberate gifts distilled from their own earlier histories. I will cite only one example. The Jewish Holocaust Museum in Elsternwick, Victoria, is a voluntary organisation of survivors of the Nazi persecution. These people choose to turn away from their sunny present back into their terrible past on their scheduled days every week, because they believe in the power of history, too, and because, despite their own and their families' experiences at the hands of the Nazis, they continue to believe in the goodwill and the humanity of strangers: that if they can show their fellow citizens honestly and accurately what was done in the course of the Holocaust, they will reject such actions forever.

We all share the democracy of the beach. I know from experience the applied egalitarianism of a rather less public corner of the nation: the Liver Transplant Unit at the Austin Hospital in Melbourne. We know that in some countries there are horrors in the transplant trade. Almost everywhere there is the bitter injustice of wealth overcoming need. In Australia, however rich they are, no one can buy a transplant. No one can jump the queue. Patients are medically assessed, and ranked according to need. And then they wait. They wait for the miracle of altruism which will lead some unknown family, in the midst of affliction, to gift the organs of their dead loved one to strangers.

An encounter with any one of these experiences is to my mind conducive to civic virtue: to developing trust in one's fellows, to strengthening the view that all we need is the light rein of the law, not membership of self-protective vigilante groups, to order relationships between people who might be different from one another, but who are certainly neighbours, and potentially friends, potentially family.

I have mentioned the Aboriginal inhabitants of Australia only obliquely to this point. They do not fit easily into this amiable picture. Nonetheless, they add crucially to it. I'm not talking, or not at this stage, about the art or about the myths, that web of stories which holds this great recalcitrant continent within the net of human intelligence. I point to a simpler thing, which as it happens is very evident around Townsville. Under all the blows that living alongside whites have dealt them – the evictions, the forced resettlements, the separation of families – many Aborigines maintain loyalty to a highly demanding notion of kin obligation. You see it when individuals and groups travel long distances with minimal cash and no security to see a brother or son or cousin in prison, a grandmother or a child in hospital. That knowledge of the importance of active love in times of adversity, the durability of that generous sense of family obligation, is a gallant thing to see.

I think there are unobvious connections between my possibly idealised portrait of the egalitarian white Australian, and what I am coming to see as the systematic injustices still being inflicted on Aboriginal Australians today. Most of us tend to think of 'culture' in terms of decorative items for public display, like special costumes and dances – what I call the Sunday Hat notion of culture. I suspect that the hidden springs behind what is often taken to be white racism is a fixed image of the vanished tribal Aborigine, the nomadic hunter with spear and throwing-stick and body-paint, and therefore the denial of Aboriginality to anyone not fitting that model. This artificially narrow notion of culture combines with a passionate egalitarianism to oppose any extension of benefits to the Aboriginal poor beyond those available to impoverished whites. Simultaneously, perhaps perversely, growing acceptance of multiculturalism also tends to work against Aborigines. We say, 'Let them have their culture: let Aboriginal dance troupes perform, let didgeridoos roar, even give them first place in the procession – they are, after all, our indigenous culture. But do not give them anything more.'

On the island where I live for part of the year, a third of the population voted for One Nation in the last state elections, for a conglomeration of reasons, none of them particularly disreputable. One large one was rage against abstract talk and the condescension of politicians and of southern intellectuals. On the matter of the future employment for their children, a daily terror, they were fed vague, expansive promises – promises insulting in their vagueness. They would ask a straightforward question about native title claims and get a bucketful of moral exhortation or a gush of rhetoric about the wickedness of impeding Australia's march towards prosperity emptied over their heads. Predictably, Pauline Hanson's persistent 'please explain, explain properly, don't fob us off as if we are fools just because we are not professional intellectuals' won wide support.

They were also having hard times, with the rural decline and cuts in government spending. They are not ungenerous, as their response to the victims of natural catastrophes makes clear, yet their response to Aborigines is profoundly ungenerous. Until very recently the label 'Aborigine' was applied at the whim of white administrators, and was used to enforce curtailments of freedom not easily imagined by non-Aborigines. Now, when it might possibly carry some small benefit like support for children trying to stay at secondary school, it rouses a hot jealousy – especially when those benefits are promoted by smooth-talking southerners, especially when, as they believe, Aborigines are no worse off than they are, when 'Aborigines' are not real Aborigines at all. Their egalitarianism, an explicit, cherished and central value, is outraged, and gives energy to their protest.

They are also pragmatic people who mistrust statistics and, indeed, argument. Instead they trust their own experience. They know their daughter can't get a job, they hear about a Vietnamese newcomer who has a job, they conclude that immigrants take Australians' jobs. And even when whites live in close geographical proximity with Aborigines, they remain largely ignorant of the daily realities indicated by those terrifying statistics. Instead they generalise from the moments they do see. A housewife outside Woolworths sees a mob of Aborigines piling into a taxi-bus with their vast shopping as she begins to drag her loaded trolley across the dusty parking lot to her car. She does not consider that the Aborigines live fifteen kilometres out, that their cars are often unreliable, that a group taxi is their cheapest mode of transport. Instead she thinks: 'Aborigines take taxis whenever they want. It's not fair.' And she concludes, on no evidence at all, that 'the government' is paying for it.

To label such people 'racist' is to miss the point. Their egalitarianism and their obstinately independent empiricism are strengths – but strengths easily corrupted to bad conclusions. So what is to be done? They won't be bullied by moralisers. Abuse, exhortation, rhetoric won't work with them. Their powerful sense of justice, were it better informed, might, if they could hear some true stories to expand and to context their own observations, and to understand the 'why' of the present circumstances of Aborigines. They will also have to be persuaded that culture is not a Sunday hat to be displayed on great occasions, but an internalised set of strategies for managing life's difficulties, always in intimate interaction with the changing circumstances of life; that one's culture, like one's present circumstances, is the product of one's history.

OUR RIGHT TO TAKE RESPONSIBILITY

Noel Pearson

2000

I f we are to survive as a people, we have to get passive welfare out of Aboriginal governance in Cape York Peninsula. We have to get rid of the passive welfare mentality that has taken over our people.

The right to self-determination is ultimately the right to take responsibility. Our traditional economy was a real economy and demanded responsibility (you don't work, you starve). The whitefella market economy is real (you don't work, you don't get paid).

After we became citizens with equal rights and equal pay, we lost our place in the real economy. What is the exception among whitefellas – almost complete dependence on cash handouts from the government – is the rule for us. There is no responsibility and reciprocity built into our present artificial economy, which is based on passive welfare (money for nothing).

Passive welfare has undermined Aboriginal law – our traditional values and relationships. When you look at the culture of Aboriginal binge drinking you can see how passive welfare has corrupted Aboriginal values of responsibility and sharing, and changed them into exploitation and manipulation. The obligation to share has become the obligation to buy grog when your cheque arrives, and the obligation of the non-drinkers to surrender their money to the drinkers. Our traditional value of responsibility has become the responsibility of the non-drinkers to feed the drinkers and their children when the money is gone.

Passive welfare and grog and drugs are finally tearing our society apart. We were dispossessed and discriminated against before we were in-cluded in the welfare state, but our law – based on trust, respect and mutual help – was better honoured during those times of hardship and guardianship than it is today. Our struggle for rights is not over and must continue – but we must also struggle to restore our traditional values of responsibility. We have to be as forthright and unequivocal about our responsibilities as we are about our rights – otherwise, our society will fall apart while we are still fighting for our rights. We do not have a right to passive welfare. Indeed, we can no longer accept it. We have a right to a real economy; we have a right to build a real economy.

Aboriginal society in Cape York Peninsula

It is a sad but clear fact that Aboriginal society in Cape York Peninsula today is not a successful society. There are numerous indications that our communities are severely dysfunctional.

These are just some of the signs that our society is not functioning successfully:

- Our people die twenty years earlier, on average, than other Australians;
- Our health is by far the worst of any group in the Australian community;
- Our people suffer from diseases that other Australians simply do not have;
- Our children do not participate in the education system anywhere near as successfully as other Australian children;
- We are over-represented in the juvenile justice system, in the criminal justice system and the gaols;
- There is more violence amongst our people than in other communities in Australia.

We need to face up to this reality. The kind of society we inhabit today and the lifestyles our people lead are ridden with problems. Whilst other communities and groups in Australia, and indeed across the planet, suffer from many of these same problems, the degree to which our Aboriginal society suffers from these problems is extraordinary.

We should not romanticise the way things were in the past. Life was certainly not easy for our people in the years before citizenship. Nevertheless, it is also obvious that in a number of important ways our situation has deteriorated over the past thirty years. Probably the clearest indication of this is the decline in life expectancy. Perversely, this social deterioration occurred despite the vast improvement in the material circumstances of our communities that resulted from the transfer of resources that came in the wake of our citizenship and the recognition of our material poverty by the state since 1970.

There are Third World societies which are materially far worse off, but which appear much more successful than Aboriginal society in Cape York. Those societies are not gripped by such despair and helplessness as our people are. Access to material goods and cash is not itself a guarantee of success. Anastasia Shkilnyk, in *A Poison Stronger than Love*, her account of the Grassy Narrows Indian community of Ontario, describes an indigenous group in Canada, a First World country which, like Australia, can afford welfare provisions for its indigenous peoples. Shkilnyk pointed out that this community's situation was more parlous than more materially deprived societies. She wrote:

> I could never escape the feeling that I had been parachuted into a void – a drab and lifeless place in which the vital spark of life had gone out. It wasn't just the poverty of the place, the isolation, or even the lack of a decent bed that depressed me. I had seen worse material deprivation when I was working in squatter settlements around Santiago, Chile. And I had been in worse physical surroundings while working in war-devastated Ismailia on the project for the reconstruction of the Suez Canal. What struck me about Grassy Narrows was the numbness in the human spirit. There was an indifference, a listlessness, a total passivity that I could neither understand nor seem to do any thing about. I had never seen such hopelessness anywhere in the Third World.

Shkilnyk here describes our future. Whilst no communities in Cape York Peninsula have deteriorated as badly as the Grassy Narrows described by Shkilnyk, Cape York communities are increasingly exhibiting the very symptoms she observed there.

Despite the fact that ours is one of the most dysfunctional societies on the planet, none of the current discourse on the subject gives me any satisfaction that the underlying issues have been grasped, let alone confidence that the right measures are being taken to change this situation.

Facing the social and cultural pathology of grog

We all know that the problem of grog in Cape York Peninsula is of an incredible dimension. Yes, it is true that diet, smoking and stress are other key factors in our atrocious health situation and increasingly early death – but the relationship between grog and all of these other 'lifestyle' problems is obvious. For younger people in the Peninsula, the problem of drugs is as bad as grog. Drug dependency and petrol sniffing amongst the young were unknown in Cape York Peninsula not too long ago. Drugs are now rife and communities are reporting outbreaks of petrol sniffing.

We need to see clearly what is involved in Aboriginal binge drinking. When you look at a drinking circle you see people who are socialising around grog. Social and cultural relationships between the drinkers are expressed, reinforced and reiterated whilst people are engaged in drinking. Everyone involved in the drinking is obliged to contribute resources – money – for the purchase of grog. Everyone is obliged to share the money and the grog.

These social and cultural obligations are invoked at every turn by members of the drinking circle. These invocations are very heavy indeed and they most often draw upon real obligations and relationships under Aboriginal laws and customs. What, when people are not drinking but hunting, is a cultural obligation to share food with countrymen, is turned into a cultural obligation to share grog. In fact your fellow drinkers will challenge your Aboriginal identity in order to establish your obligation to contribute money to buy grog: 'Come on, don't be flash! We not whitefellas! You-me black people!'

When you look at the obligations which are set up around the drinking circle, you see the drinkers under reciprocal obligations to contribute to buying the grog. When I have money, it's my turn to shout. When your money comes, it's your turn to shout. Outside of this drinking circle are the women and the children and the old people and the non-drinkers. The resources of these non-drinkers are used to feed the families – including those who have spent most or all of their money on grog – when they are hungry. But more than that, these non-drinkers are placed under tremendous social and cultural pressure to contribute resources to the drinking circle for buying grog. So the drinking circle becomes a hole into which the family's resources are sucked. Wives and girlfriends, parents and grandparents, are placed under tremendous pressure – social and cultural and ultimately through physical violence – to contribute to this pathological behaviour. Whilst the relationships between drinkers are reciprocal ('We share our grog because you-me brothers – one mob'), the relationship between drinkers and non-drinkers is not reciprocal. The drinkers take, the non-drinkers are forced to give.

Looking back, in the 1970s it was mainly the men who formed these drinking circles. The children, the youth, the women, the old people, stood outside of these circles but were affected by their behaviour and forced to supply resources to the drinkers. Then in the 1980s, you started to see younger women despair and join the drinking circles. And now it is the old people – yes, mainly the women – who are keeping the society fed, and who have an anxiety for the future of these children and their community. Who want to change things.

How is it that our society has been so corrupted?

The manipulation and corruption of Aboriginal values and relationships

Whilst we understand that colonial society has taken a toll on the structures and principles of our society in Cape York Peninsula, there is no discourse among our people about how we can reconcile what remains of our traditional culture with the development of a successful society. When we recognise elements of our traditional social arrangements and values in our current arrangements, we assume that they are right and should be maintained because traditional society was successful. But there are problems with this assumption. By simply assuming that everything that we think of as 'Aboriginal' or 'traditional' is good, we fail to analyse the deformities that these arrangements and values have undergone. Clearly the traditional obligation to share resources has been corrupted.

It was during discussions with Mervyn Gibson from the Hope Vale community that I came to understand the social and cultural manipulation and distortion that is involved in Aboriginal drinking. When you grow up in a family, a community and a society in which the society's values and relationships are daily being exploited by pathological behaviour – to such an extent that this becomes the social norm – you tend not to see that we are being badly manipulated by the drinkers. But you realise that it is manipulation – not culture, not tradition, not identity, but manipulation – when you look at how other obligations and relationships are ignored or abused. What about the obligation towards children? Why are all of the family's resources going to fulfil so-called obligations to cousins and uncles for drinking, when the children have nothing to eat? What about the old people, what about our obligation to look after them? How is it that they end up with the total responsibility to look after all of us?

What about our social and cultural relationships with other people, people outside of the drinking circle? What about their needs? What about our obligations to them? What about these values? If you talk about identity, what kind of Aboriginal are you if you are not caring for your children and your old people? The culture of Aboriginal drinking ignores these questions. Indeed, drinking circles are seen as essential Aboriginal behaviour – by the drinkers themselves, and by those (black and white) who see Aboriginal drinkers as pitiful victims, and thereby perpetuate and sanction the corruption of Aboriginal values and relationships.

It is well known to us that Aboriginal drinking results in the breaking of Aboriginal law. Relationships under Aboriginal law and custom are daily corrupted by drinking. Wrong people socialise together. Inappropriate behaviours ensue. So rather than drinking being a true expression of Aboriginal social and cultural values and relationships, it is a blatant corruption of them.

Those who are caught in the misery of social and cultural
corruption – and those who deliberately perpetuate it

Of course, most Aboriginal people we know in the Peninsula – our cousins, our friends, our uncles, our brothers – who are involved in the pathologies of drinking and gambling are caught in an economic and social system not of their choosing. The suction hole of these drinking and gambling coteries, and all of the social and cultural pressure that they bring to bear on people, are almost impossible to avoid. This is not a matter of blame. People are caught in an economic and social system that precipitated this misery. But it is a matter of responsibility. Our people as individuals must face their responsibility for the state of our society – for respecting and upholding our true values and relationships, our own laws and customs.

Whilst the great majority of our people are unconsciously involved in a system which involves exploitation and manipulation, there are those, black and white, who cynically exploit this pathology. These are the white publicans and canteen owners, the air-charter companies, the taxi companies, the store owners who cash cheques for profit, who sell methylated spirits to known alcoholics. These are the black and white sly-grog sellers who charge $50 for a flagon or $200 for a carton of beer. These are the people who sell drugs to our children, and get them to deal on their behalf.

Often the people who are involved in, say, selling sly grog are themselves not heavy drinkers. Perfectly sober people will exploit this pathology, and sly grog is a highly profitable business. These are the parasites feeding on the misery of our people. And we allow them to. It is a testament to the degree to which our values and our Aboriginal law have been overborne that we tolerate this exploitation in the midst of our own society.

The unravelling of Aboriginal law

The High Court's ruling in the *Mabo* case has now recognised Aboriginal laws and customs as part of the legal system applicable to Aboriginal society and Aboriginal lands. This is a fundamentally important step in the right direction.

Central to the recovery and empowerment of Aboriginal society will be the restoration of Aboriginal values and Aboriginal relationships, which have their roots in our traditional society. Even as our traditional society was ruptured by colonial invasion and our people underwent an ugly colonial history, we survived. At least in a spiritual sense our ancestors prevailed over this colonial bastardry and inhumanity. Our ancestors struggled to keep our society alive against an onslaught which even the colonists believed would end in our extinction as a people.

And the thing that we retained – even if we lost our lands and our economy and our rights, and even if our families were torn apart – was our law: our Aboriginal values and relationships. From the bush to the country towns to the working suburbs, these values and relationships make us a rich people. They have shielded our people against loneliness and provided sustenance during desperately mean times. They still do. But when we look at our society in Cape York and the nature of our problems, it is these very values and relationships that are now unravelling before our eyes. It is passive welfare that has caused this social dissolution. Dependence on passive welfare is our most urgent problem.

The passive welfare paradigm

Passive welfare has several aspects, which together constitute what I will call 'the passive welfare paradigm'.

Firstly, passive welfare is an irrational, 'gammon' economic relationship, where transactions between the provider and the recipient are not based on reciprocity. The principle in this relationship is 'money for nothing' or 'help for nothing'. Essentially it is charity. Unlike commercial transactions, no mechanisms promote rational and constructive behaviour, either on the hand of the recipient or on the hand of the provider, which is usually the government. As Immanuel Kant wrote in *The Conflict of the Faculties* in 1798: 'Welfare, however, has no principle, neither for him who receives it, nor for him who distributes it, one will place it here and another there ...'

Secondly, welfare is a method of governance. Welfare involves a superior power having all of the rights and all of the responsibilities to make decisions and take actions on behalf of relatively powerless people. People on the ground are seen as passive recipients, clients or customers. They are provided 'services', essentially on a plate, by far superior people (white and black) with greater expertise and knowledge. Those with power will jealously and steadfastly work to keep it. Invariably, all initiative and resources are concentrated in the hands of the people who are supposed to save and serve the hapless and the helpless. As a method of governance, welfare is increasingly becoming a means of managing marginalised groups at minimal cost without even maintaining the fiction that a lasting solution to their problems is sought.

Thirdly, welfare is a mentality. It is a mentality that accepts the principles underlying the economic relationship and the method of governance described above. This mentality is internalised and perpetuated by recipients, who see themselves as victimised or incapable and in need of assistance without reciprocation. This mentality says that it is their right to have assistance without reciprocation. But this mentality is also held by people in power (white and black). The bureaucracy views people on the ground as incapable – and therefore, instead of simply providing resources and facilitating decision-making and action at the ground level (especially concerning social programmes), it hoards power.

Following are some of the problems with passive welfare:

- It is a poor substitute for participation in the real economy, psychologically, socially and economically. Welfare is never enough to live properly on. Rather than providing the opportunity for a proper place in the wider economy and society, passive welfare confines the recipient to her or his stagnant environment;
- It pacifies recipients rather than invigorating them into social, political and economic action to secure a better deal for themselves and their children;
- It reproduces these same problems in following generations.

Many of the passive welfare programmes are in fact aimed at overcoming the very problems which passive welfare created in the first place. The problems caused by passive welfare give rise to a whole set of other problems, so more passive welfare is administered to try to alleviate the original problems that it caused. And so on.

The welfare paradigm has been particularly destructive in the governance of Aboriginal society. The passive welfare mentality results in:

- Our people thinking that the solutions to our problems lie outside of ourselves. We think that 'somebody else' will address the problems, be it the government, white people or other Aboriginal people – but not ourselves;
- Our people failing to take responsibility for ourselves as individuals, for our families and for our communities;
- The promotion of a victim mentality amongst our people;
- The expectation that assistance will be provided to people without us doing anything in return;
- The devaluation of resources that are important and which

should be properly valued and used to develop our communities. Passive welfare cheapens money. Welfare money does not have the same value as personally earned money.

These effects of passive welfare are well known.

The nature of passive welfare and its relationship to our social breakdown

The nature of passive welfare (which today is nearly our sole material resource) explains our social crisis. It explains why, even as our material condition improved over recent decades, our social condition deteriorated. Passive welfare has come to be the dominant influence on the relationships, values and attitudes of our society in Cape York Peninsula. This influence soon came to be directly at odds with our traditional relationships, values and attitudes – our Aboriginal law – which our ancestors had hitherto managed to keep alive, and which gave structure and strength to our families and communities in the face of ill treatment by the wider society. Invariably the outcome of the ongoing conflicts between our traditions and the economic base of our society is that our traditions succumb and are eroded daily. Indeed, we are now at a stage where many of the traditions we purport to follow are too often merely self-deceptions (that we care for each other, that we respect our Elders, that we value our culture and traditions) and the 'traditions' which we do follow are in fact distortions conditioned by the pathological social situation which passive welfare has reduced us to: that we sit around in a drinking circle because we are Aboriginal; that you are trying to be a flash whitefella if you are not giving your brother money for grog.

The resources of passive welfare are fundamentally irrational. Whereas the dollar earned through a commercial or labour transaction has a rationale, the dollar given as a matter of course has none. Everyone in a passive welfare economy is susceptible to irrational (mis)appropriation and (mis)expenditure of money, because that is the very nature of the money. Money acquired without principle is expended without principle.

When people have only one means of existence, the nature of that income obviously influences their whole outlook. The irrational basis of our economy has inclined us to wasteful, aimless behaviour. Like other people who can't see any connection between their actions and their circumstances, we waste our money, our time, our lives. We neglect our material possessions, our education, our social and economic development. We do not seize opportunities that arise. There always comes another day and another cheque. No one feels the need to use a sum of money for a meaningful investment, or to use a day to build something that will last.

The worst consequence of this lack of meaning and purpose is that it has compounded the effects of dispossession and trauma by making us susceptible to an epidemic of grog and drug abuse. This epidemic now has its own momentum and in turn makes it inevitable that our scarce resources increasingly finance irrational and destructive behaviour. We must now deal with both passive welfare dependence and substance abuse simultaneously, as these two problems feed off one another and undermine all efforts toward social recovery. The notion underlying most discussion about substance abuse, the theory that substance abuse is only a symptom of underlying social and psychological problems, is wrong: addiction is a condition in its own right, not a symptom.

Passive welfare alone would not have caused our social disaster. But the combination of passive welfare dependence and the grog and drug epidemic will, if not checked, cause the final breakdown of our traditional social relationships and values. Grog and drug abuse coupled with an outlook determined by a passive welfare economy is a fatal combination. The intrinsic force in the grog and drug epidemic is now stronger than the force of our traditional social norms and values. People motivated by their addiction to grog or drugs now regard and treat other people in our society in the same way as they regard the passive welfare money: these people (wives, girlfriends, parents, grandparents, children, relatives) are not valued and respected. They will always be there and the addicted do not have to take any responsibility for them. These people are simply a source of resources (money, shelter, food, comfort and care), and they are treated accordingly.

Those who are concerned about the social problems in Cape York Peninsula need to have a clear understanding of our economic history, because the relationship between economic circumstances and social problems is critical. There has been too much of a separation of the social from the economic when we consider our problems. The fact is, every economic relationship is also necessarily a social relationship, and underlying many of our social problems are these economic relationships and issues. The relationship between government and the community, and between government and the individual, is perpetuated and recreated in all of the internal relationships of our society. The principles upon which money circulates within the community carry with them all of the inherent values of the original passive welfare.

Welfare dependency is the result of colonial history

European colonisation took away the self-sufficiency of Aboriginal society. The land and its resources were appropriated during the colonial period. The means for our people to sustain our traditional society were taken from our ancestors. The Aboriginal economy was fundamentally disrupted by colonisation. In a short time, options for Aboriginal people were reduced to:

- Trying to survive by moving between the traditional economy where possible and working in the white economy (this itinerant existence became increasingly difficult and, in time, impossible);
- Begging for scraps on the fringes of the white economy and being exploited as prostitutes and slaves (and therefore soon dying out);
- Being removed from white society and its slave economy to missions and government settlements;
- Finding a more stable situation in the white economy, usually as exploited labour at the lowest end of the economy (for instance in the cattle industry or as domestic labourers).

The reduction of Aboriginal people to fringe-dwelling beggars whose only economic option was charity from whites was a prescription for genocide. For there was no charity. Aboriginal society survived where it was isolated from the white economy, on settlements where people could endeavour to provide for themselves with the assistance of missionaries and 'protectors' by creating an institutional subsistence economy, or where they could find some more stable place at the lower end of the white economy. This lower end of the white economy amounted to an informal system of slave labour. However, the Aboriginal participation in this economy, though the circumstances were harsh and cruel, was not on the basis of passive welfare or charity.

This situation persisted until the late 1960s. The Aboriginal people of Cape York Peninsula moved between the institutional economy of the settlements and the real economy. Therefore men resident on the missions had to leave the settlements to seek work in the pastoral, agricultural, mining and fishing industries. Up until the 1970s, the Aboriginal people of Cape York Peninsula participated in the real economy at its meanest level.

The welfare take-over since the 1970s

Social welfare as provided by government since the 1970s produced a revolutionary change in the Aboriginal economy of Cape York Peninsula. Aboriginal people withdrew from participation in the real economy. People came back home to work nominally in the institutional economy of the mission – an economy which was becoming more and more dependent on government funding. The impact of the equal wage decision on Aboriginal labour in the cattle industry was decisive. People lost their place in the pastoral industry and were forced into the increasingly welfare-based economy of the settlements.

The assumption of responsibility for Aboriginal affairs by the federal parliament after the 1967 referendum and the recognition of the rights of citizenship of Aboriginal people resulted in an increase in welfare provisioning by the Commonwealth government. The people and communities of Cape York Peninsula are now almost completely dependent on passive welfare. Most income is from government payments to individuals and to Aboriginal organisations. The economy of the communities is artificially sustained by government funds. This funding also creates the few job opportunities that are available in the communities.

Our confrontation with racism through history

I have suggested that the nature of the passive welfare economy is reflected in our social relationships, but our social problems are most often interpreted as the legacy of our colonisation. In discussions of our historical legacy there are three general themes that arise: racism, dispossession and trauma. These are said to explain our position in Australian society and are seen as the origin of the problems this paper is seeking to confront.

Our recent history can be seen as a sequence of phases, characterised by the different roles played by dispossession, trauma and discrimination at different times. Initially, we were for a brief period simply formally dispossessed. Dispossession followed the initial judgement that we were inherently less capable to use this land for the good of ourselves and for humanity.

A phase of traumatic confrontation necessarily followed as that judgement was acted upon, since we were in fact inextricably linked to our land. The destruction of our traditional society through frontier wars, murder, sexual enslavement and abduction was compounded by the spread of diseases against which we had little resistance.

Official discrimination was then the dominant aspect of the third phase of our confrontation with racism, the recent period after the breakdown of traditional society when we became a 'protected' people. The survivors of the traumatic confrontations were suppressed as an underclass, unable to claim their traditional homelands and working for almost nothing. Whilst discrimination had been present from the moment of colonial intrusion, it was during this protection phase that institutionalised discrimination became the dominant aspect of racism. An enormous legal and bureaucratic apparatus was developed in order to manage the remnants of the beaten peoples. This system regulated the smallest movements and events in our lives and we were still being traumatised, but more often through administrative decisions, for example in relation to the removal of children, and less so by violent assaults.

Today, during the current phase of our confrontation with racism, official discrimination has been abolished, though there has been something of a return in recent years, the Commonwealth parliament's amendments to the Native Title Act being the most blatant. Dispossession is still in place. Traumatic decimation of our people and disruption of our culture and families are the dominant factors in our collective psychology, and trauma is daily recreated in our dysfunctional communities. Whether today's unofficial discrimination is just a regrettable residue of past official discrimination or fulfils the same function of holding us down is a matter for dispute. But it is there.

Racism: an impediment but not a disability

In the light of our experience, it is understandable that racism is offered as the main explanation for our present situation. One of the strong but unstated reasons why we justify passive welfare amongst able-bodied Aboriginal people, in spite of the obvious harmful effects on our society, is that we consider racism a disability.

Make no mistake, racism is a terrible burden. It attacks the spirit. It attacks self-esteem and the soul in ways that those who are not subjected to it would have not an inkling of. Racism is a major handicap: it results in Aboriginal people not having access to opportunities, in not recognising opportunities when they arise, and in not being able to seize and hold onto opportunities when they recognise them. Australians concerned about the position of Aboriginal people in this country should not underestimate the decisive role that racism plays in the well-being of Aboriginal individuals and society. Australians need to stop kidding themselves that 'racism isn't all that bad – black people should just get over it and get on with it'. If you are black in this country, you start life with a great and crushing burden. Most non-Aboriginal Australians do not appreciate how crushing this racism has been and continues to be. They do not understand how destructive it is. Only if they could take on the identity of an Aboriginal person for a while would they gain some understanding of the central role racism plays in the oppression of Aboriginal people as individuals and as a community.

In addition to this direct experience of racism, we sense that we are excluded from the domains of real power, political and economic. I understand only too keenly the paralysing effect of this burden. But my argument in this paper is that, though racism looms so large that it is tempting to characterise it as a disability, we should not and must not treat it as such. The minute we treat racism as a disability, we concede its power over our lives and over our future. As bad as racism is, we cannot allow it to reduce us to being treated – and seeing ourselves – as if we are not fully capable people in our own right. Though our people have it harder than others in society because of racism, we must not succumb to the racism that is latent in the welfare paradigm – the idea that though we seem to be fully able-bodied people, we need to be treated by the state as if we are not.

Conclusion

Our parents, grandparents and great-grandparents were severely victimised, abused and discriminated against. They suffered more than we have. Yet they survived, not by seeing themselves as victims or by seeing their salvation in whitefella charity or pity, but by struggling. If we make our recovery as a people dependent on what the *wangaarrngay* should, and one day might, do for us, we are deluding ourselves. Pity, goodwill, charity – these are all poor substitutes for our people taking our fair share and our rightful place in the country.

The thing about passive welfare is that its effect on us is more insidious than any other external threats. The injuries and bruises our people suffer at the hands of Australian society are considerable. The wounds are real and damaging, but we can see that racism and dispossession threaten our survival, and that we must fight. But passive welfare seems to us to be an asset, not a threat. Who doesn't want labour-free income? For this reason, the dangers of passive welfare are difficult for us to see and the condition is harder for us to confront and treat. Our society is weakened and destroyed from within, without us even understanding what is happening to us and why.

Having said this, I am also conscious that many of the ideas set out in this paper have been expressed by many of our people before. The truth is that in our guts we have known that passive welfare was no good. The call for responsibility in this paper is not anything that mothers, grandmothers and old people do not say every day to their children and grandchildren – but they have been, more and more, railing against the wind.

THE NEW LIBERALISM

Judith Brett

2004

T he Australian Legend was a term coined by the radical historian Russel Ward in the 1950s to describe a set of distinctive Australian character traits forged from the nineteenth-century settlers' experience of the land: egalitarianism, practical improvisation, scepticism towards authority, larrikinism, loyalty to mates, generosity. Ward claimed that the Australian tradition was inherently radical and that ordinary Australians were naturally left-wing. The itinerant rural labourers who formed the first Labor parties embodied the virtues of the Australian Legend, as did the Australian diggers of the First World War, and it captured aspects of Australian working-class culture and its collectivist political traditions. Until Howard, Australian Liberals had left the legend to Labor. Labor was the party of 'mates', committed to egalitarianism, the fair go and an assertive Australian nationalism. Liberals spoke a language of respectability, deference to Britain, and support for the institutions of the state. But, as John Hirst pointed out, the Australian Legend was never as inherently radical as Ward had argued; it had a conservative version, 'the Pioneer Legend' of land-holding rural Australia.

During the 1980s the Australian Legend experienced a revival in Australian popular culture as globalisation and growing international tourism focused attention on the uniqueness of Australia's natural environment and on the people who lived outside its cities. This revival can be seen in the popularity of films such as *The Man from Snowy River*, the transformation of rural work clothes like Driza-Bones, akubras and riding boots into fashion items, the confidence of Australian country music, the explosion of domestic outback tourism.

Labor benefited from aspects of this revival. Republican anti-Britishness was used against the Liberal and National parties' support for the monarchy. But its rural provenance also presented Labor with difficulties: the men from Snowy River and the heroes of the outback were probably racists. And the Australian Legend clearly had stronger roots in Australian working-class than middle-class experience. Its revival thus added an overlay of obvious cultural difference to the tensions that already existed between the ALP's historically labourist working-class base and its new cohort of urban middle-class supporters. The legend seemed to be about Australia's past, with little to offer its multicultural present and future.

In his 1997 Australia Day speech, Howard reflected on the sources of Australia's national identity – 'The symbols we hold dear as Australians and the beliefs that we have about what it is to be an Australian … are feelings and attitudes that grow out of the spirit of the people.' Howard posited two sources for these: great traumatic events such as Gallipoli; and 'long usage and custom', such as our tradition of 'informal mateship and egalitarianism'. Howard was staking out the traditional symbols of Australian nationalism for the Liberal Party and the speech continued by listing a few of Howard's favourite things about Australians: their 'tremendous spirit and versatility', their 'adaptability', their 'tolerance and openness', their 'scepticism and irreverence'.

Howard's speeches since 1997 are filled with characterisations of what he variously calls the Australian Way, Australian values, the Australian identity or the Australian character. A few examples:

Our society is underpinned by those uniquely Australian concepts of a fair go and practical mateship.

Being Australian means doing the decent thing in a pragmatic and respectable society which lives up to its creed of practical mateship … Australians are a down-to-earth people. It is part of our virtue. Rooted deep in our psyche is a sense of fair play and a strong egalitarian streak.

The openness and unpretentious character of Australians has given us a well-deserved reputation for tolerance and hospitality.

In speeches like these, Howard re-works Australian Liberals' under-standing of the virtues on which the nation is built and attaches them to the broad popular forms of the Australian Legend. Like many Australian men, Howard is fascinated by the lessons of war, both for individuals and nations. In speech after speech he has embraced the national myth of Gallipoli 'where our nation's spirit was born'. The death of the last veteran of that campaign, Tasmanian Alec Campbell, became an occasion of national mourning, with Howard himself delivering a eulogy at the state funeral in which he presented Campbell's life as 'contain[ing] the richness of our nation's history'. Campbell had spent six weeks at Gallipoli as an under-age boy soldier. For most of his life he was a radical trade unionist and office bearer, and so to Liberal eyes a bearer of the various vices of militant unionism. Howard passed lightly over Campbell's radical politics to present him as an exemplar of the virtues of the legend.

The death of sporting hero Sir Donald Bradman in the previous year provided Howard with another occasion to reflect on the history of Australia's national spirit. Bradman's phenomenal cricketing success in the Test matches against Britain in the 1930s and 40s, claimed Howard, 'reinforced the national spirit, which was born out of the Australian sacrifice during World War I and helped to display the independence and self-reliance of a young nation barely decades old'.

Bradman spent longer at the crease than Campbell did at the front, but he too had another life, as an Adelaide stockbroker and company director, and a long-serving cricket administrator. Throwing the lives of these two men, the radical trade unionist and the stockbroker cricketer, into the powerful solvent of the Australian Legend, their class differences blur and they are reborn as nation-building comrades-in-arms, decent Australians and equally plausible representatives of the consensual centre.

Howard has also raided the Australian Legend to restate Australian Liberals' long-standing belief that they are the party which best allows Australia's civic spirit to flourish. He has revived the concept of the volunteer as the embodiment of the Liberals' founding belief that society is based on the actions and qualities of individuals. In a statement of fundamental principles published in 1954 under the title 'We Believe', the Liberal Party asserted that 'We Believe in the spirit of the Volunteer ... the greatest community efforts can be made only when voluntary co-operation and self-sacrifice come in aid of and lend character to the performance of legal duties.' Howard now describes Australia as 'the greatest volunteer society in the world'. With the language of citizenship now captured by ideas of entitlement, the concept of the volunteer reclaims active civic involvement as a core Liberal value. Volunteers are the people who 'when the chips are down hold our society and our community together'. Volunteering is a flexible description of people's engagement with civic activities, from fire brigades to helping out at the local football club or school to the great 'volunteer Army' of World War One. And in yet another brilliant move, Howard links volunteering to the Australian Legend by describing it as an expression of mateship: 'The great Australian capacity to work together in adversity – I call it mateship.' So citizens have become volunteers have become mates, and Howard has planted the Liberals' flag firmly in Labor's territory of vernacular egalitarianism.

Howard has been astonishingly successful in linking contemporary Australian Liberalism to the Australian Legend. It has given him a flexible language of social cohesion which is distinctively Australian and which enables him to generate a convincing contemporary rhetoric. It enables him to talk to rural Australia, where aspects of the legend still inform people's daily lives, as well as to families in the suburbs where it connects with a deeply held commitment to ordinariness. And it can be turned, for state occasions, into a modest national story. His moving of the volunteer from the relative invisibility of local community good works into the centre of national life has restored a meaningful civic identity to Liberal rhetoric.

Howard's opponents have been misled by his own description of himself as a social conservative and so missed his takeover of the symbolic repertoire of Australia's radical nationalist past to reconnect Australian Liberalism with ordinary Australian experience. His critics, many of them people who value skill with words, have also been misled by his rhetorical dullness. Certainly, Howard is no great orator, his language is plain and repetitive. There are no striking metaphors, no rolling cadences, no flights of fancy. Once he has hit on a form of words – like 'practical mateship' – he repeats it, without embellishment, in speech after speech. This may be dull, boring even, but it does not follow from this that Howard has no vision, nor that he is unable to strike chords with aspects of Australian experience.

There are still obvious tensions between Howard's commitment to radical economic policies, which bring change and anxiety into people's lives, and his professed social conservatism. After all, the trade unionists whose rights he attacks with industrial relations reform, the small-business owners struggling to implement the GST or sent broke by extended trading hours, the young people working all hours in the deregulated service industry, also have families and want security. But there is nothing new in this. Politicians in capitalist democracies have always allowed big business and financial interests considerable room to move against people's established entitlements and ways of living. This after all is progress. The problem for the Liberals before Howard was that they had no plausible way of talking about anything other than economics. Now they do, with the language of the consensual centre reworked into a flexible vernacular nationalism.

Howard has not gone back to the 1950s to mine Robert Menzies and Australian suburbia for past certainties but has re-worked the symbolic resources of the Liberal Party's rhetorical traditions to create a persuasive political language for the present. Party rhetoric is always most successful when it disables the opponent at the same time as it rallies supporters. Howard's renewal of Liberal traditions has done both. It has reconnected the Liberal Party with its traditional claims to the consensual centre and to civic life; and it has done this in a way that has depleted Labor's symbolic resources.

THE FIG, THE OLIVE AND THE POMEGRANATE TREE

Ghassan Hage

2008

I was heading to a birthday party in western New South Wales with my wife and daughters when we drove past Bathurst. My grandparents had arrived there in the late 1930s and opened a clothing factory. My mother went to school, then began helping her parents run the factory. She has good memories of many years spent zigzagging New South Wales in the family Studebaker as she delivered clothes to shops across Bathurst and as far afield as Lithgow and Young.

But in the mid-1950s, when she was thirty, she left Australia for Lebanon. I'm not sure if she did so specifically to find herself a husband, but she says she was introduced to my father – an influential gendarmerie officer at the time – fell in love and stayed.

Although I never visited Australia as a youth, Bathurst was a familiar name to me. It was often on my mother's lips. It was the sender's address of the many large boxes that came by ship to Beirut's port; inside, among many other things, were those furry koala and kangaroo toys that were everywhere in our house. These clearly marked our household's Australian connections. So did the distinctness of my mother's accent when speaking English. I remember Carla, the blonde German-Lebanese neighbour, and the secret object of my passions in my early teens, asking me: 'Why does your mother always say "aahy" instead of "eehy"?'

But far more important to me than the stuffed toys or the accent were the pictures of my grandparents in Bathurst that my mother kept in her drawer and that I took out and examined carefully every now and then. It was primarily these photos that constituted the portal through which I stared to imagine what life in Australia was like.

The adventures of Sandy and his friend Hoppy the kangaroo in my favourite French comic journal, *Spirou*, helped extend my imagining. Courtesy of the excellent drawings of Willy Lambil, the series' Belgian creator, Sandy and Hoppy were my first introduction to images of the Australian outback and its culture, albeit in a European, clichéd way.

Sandy and Hoppy's adventures happened in various places, although mostly somewhere on the border between Victoria and New South Wales; *Poursuite sur la Murray* was the title of one suspenseful adventure. Yet somehow these drawings fused with the family photos to create my own particular idea of Bathurst.

When I finally came to Australia during the Lebanese civil war, I lived in Sydney but visited my grandparents in Bathurst. By then, they were old. The clothing factory was no more and all that remained was a frock shop that my grandmother kept going to make a few dollars that she spent during short telephone conversations with what was referred to, quite obscurely to me, as the bookmaker. Soon after I arrived, my grandparents sold the Bathurst house and the shop and moved to Sydney where their children could look after them.

Despite having visited the Bathurst house several times, I had no memory of it twenty-five years later when we stopped on our way to that birthday party in Cowra.

This is not surprising, as I spent much of my first couple of years in Australia in a state of almost total detachment from reality. My most distinct feeling was of living in a state of suspension produced by an acute sense not only of displacement, but also of directionlessness. As a kid I dreamed of what it was like to be in Australia, but never with a desire to live there. Australia was simply not in a zone where I envisaged my life would unfold. In the back of my mind was a pre-Galilean image: the earth was flat and soon after people got to Australia they would start falling off a gigantic cliff.

So, when my parents insisted I go to Australia to escape the civil war and continue my university education, I felt I was positioned at the edge of the universe with no task other than to wait … for whatever.

This made Australia, for me, a transitional space unsuitable for purpose of settlement or long-term planning: what French sociologist Pierre Bourdieu calls a space of 'zero social gravity'. For Bourdieu, if one has no interest in the social reality in which one exists, then reality in turn fails to impose itself on one's senses and fails to pull one in. Reality loses its importance and, because of this, it loses its consistency, and even the materiality of the physical environment diminishes. This was certainly the way I experienced Australia to begin with, and more so Bathurst. It did not really leave much of an imprint on my mind. I did not particularly miss anything about Bathurst when I stopped visiting. But on that day, on our way to Cowra, my wife, Caroline, and the kids were eager to see where Teita (Granny) grew up.

So I tried to locate the house, remembering that it was towards the Mt Panorama side of a long shopping street. Indeed, with Mt Panorama in sight, it was not hard to locate what to me clearly looked like the house. Next to it, I was almost certain, stood my grandmother's old frock shop. Nonetheless, I still had some doubts, and when we all got out of the car I was still trying to convince myself that I was not mistaken about it all. That's when a woman came out of the shop, locking the door behind her. She was about to go down the street, but she noticed us all standing there.

'Are you looking for something, love?' she said.

'Is that the Debs' house?' I replied. (Debs is my mother's maiden name.)

'Well, yes,' she said, 'but it hasn't been the Debs' house for a very long time.'

She inquired a bit more and I told her my mother had grown up there. She said she remembered her, then asked: 'Would you like to go in and have a look?'

'Yes, thank you,' said Caroline, before I had the time to say anything.

And so we all went in and looked around. I could not remember a thing, not the house's layout, not the shop's interior – although we were told that nothing had changed – not the furniture, nothing. I was a bit disappointed. The woman even showed us some garments that were still there from 'Mrs Debs' time', but I was unaffected.

Then I went to the backyard, and there something quite spectacular happened to me. The backyard was unkempt. There was no lawn but a chaotic entanglement of high and low vegetation. Nonetheless, there, amid the chaos, I could discern three unmistakable forms: a fig tree, an olive tree and a pomegranate tree, the holy Mediterranean trinity, or one of them at least.

At the very sight of them a complex web of emotions as wild as the vegetation that was before my eyes welled in me.

I glimpsed a moment in my past when my mother, sitting on a long chair in front of our beach house to the north of Beirut, was telling someone the story of how my grandmother had an argument with my grandfather because she felt that he was wasting his time planting these trees.

I am not sure why the sight of the trees affected me so much, especially since, even though I had no memory of it, I must have seen them before on my early visits.

Perhaps it was because I am pulled by the social gravity of Australia, now that I am as seriously immersed and interested in Australia as can be. Or perhaps it was simply because I am older, more existential and more appreciative of whatever memory and feeling comes my way.

But the thought of me on my way from Sydney to Cowra, standing in the middle of this backyard in Bathurst, next to a couple of trees that my grandfather had planted more than fifty years ago, was awesome, as my teenage daughter would say. Roots, routes, Lebanon, family, the cosmos, Heidegger and much more, all came racing into my mind.

But among all of the above there was one feeling that was particularly discernible and that I want to highlight here: next to these very Lebanese trees, planted by my very Lebanese grandfather, I stood feeling rooted, feeling more Australian than ever. What was surprising about this feeling was not its paradoxical nature. Rather, it was how non-paradoxical – or, to use the equivalent of paradox in the emotional realm, it was how non-ambivalent – this feeling of rootedness in Australia was.

The Lebanese trees did not make me feel Australian and Lebanese, although I do feel both at many moments of life. Nor did they make me feel torn between my Lebaneseness and my Australianness. They simply made me feel, as I said, more Australian.

Reflecting, I came to understand that this was because it was not the trees themselves or the presence of my grandfather in Bathurst that made me feel rooted there. If I had seen those trees simply as Lebanese trees on Australian soil, I probably would have felt nostalgic for Lebanon. But this was not the case. Nor did the trees represent a memory of my grandfather that would have carried me back to the time when he lived there. What seemed to me to be crucial to my experience was the memory of my grandfather planting the trees. It was the practice that symbolised a specific relation to the land that made me feel rooted. And the trees stood there as a metonymic extension of that practice and that relation.

Now, despite the elevating feeling that overwhelmed me, I knew Australia's history too well to forget that I was in a town that was at the heart of the white settlement of Australia. I was also in a backyard: as quintessentially Anglo a mode of marking and shaping and rooting oneself in the land as can be. So I was well aware that others have come at different times and, through their practices, rooted themselves in this space. And, of course, I am too politically correct, and proudly so, to have missed the fact that my Lebanese trees and the Anglo backyard in which they were planted were both on Aboriginal land.

So I was fully conscious at the time – indeed, at the moment when I was experiencing a high, admiring my grandfather's trees – of the colonial histories of violence, domination and appropriation, of heroism and overcoming, of resistance, defeat and perseverance that marks the land on which these trees have grown.

But, again, this awareness did not diminish the sense of rootedness with which they infused me, for this was not – nor could it afford to be – a possessive rootedness that claimed monopoly over the space of its emergence.

It is this open, non-exclusivist, rootedness that allows for a superposed multiplicity of roots that I want to highlight.

Roots have a bad name in certain intellectual circles. They are associated with stasis, conservatism and narrow-mindedness. There is no doubt that roots can be experienced in this way. Some people end up burying themselves in their roots and their rootedness becomes a territorial and a claustrophobic one. So there is certainly a good reason to acknowledge the negativity that is part of such a conception of roots.

But there is no reason to universalise this. For many people, a greater sense of rootedness does not mean a sense of being locked in the ground, unable to move. On the contrary, roots are often paradoxically experienced as being like an extra pair of wings. And this was exactly how I experienced my trees. I felt them propelling me. It is important to comprehend what propelling means here. When we are pushed by a force, it can make us go forward. The same goes with a force that is propelling us. Yet there is one important difference: when we are propelled, the force that pushes us stays with us.

There, it seems to me, lies the importance and the power of the roots that I am referring to: they are not roots that keep you grounded, they are roots that stay with you as you move. They are of the same order as the 'with' we offer someone when we wish them, 'May God be with you' or 'May the Force be with you'. It is a Heideggerian withness that gives strength to our being.

I want to emphasise this mode of rootedness and its positive character because in it I glimpsed not just a way of being rooted, but a mode of belonging that can stand in opposition to the narrow territorial way of being rooted that I referred to earlier, and that has often generated sadness and paranoia.

The latter inherits colonialism's exclusivist mentality, which operates with an either-or logic: either my roots or yours, either this land is mine or yours, either you belong here or there, either you are sovereign or I am.

The experience of rootedness that I found so uplifting seems to offer a path to a different mode of belonging. But this is not an anti-colonial belonging, which pits the belonging of the colonised against that of the coloniser while conserving colonialism's either-or logic.

Nor is it a post-colonialism, which prematurely sees colonial culture as something superseded. If anything, it is a supra-counter-colonialism: it counters colonial culture from a space outside of and beyond it. This is what some theorists today refer to as the event: that which comes from an outer plane and carries with it multiple possibilities of transforming the existing.

Given the many dead-ends that various forms of multiculturalism have led to, it is important to look for such a novel space, and from it to rethink the interaction of cultures in Australia. This is an important challenge, one that was elided by the 'Help! Our core values are in danger' brigade that the Howard government represented. And it would be a mistake if the Rudd government is to continue to shy away from it.

For let there be no mistake: Australia's future culture will be plural. And there is no other way forward but to think about how all of us can learn to embrace it in its plurality.

Sources

'Overture', Miles Franklin: extract from *My Brilliant Career*,
William Blackwood & Sons, 1901

'The Workers' Paradise', Albert Metin: edited extract from
Le Socialisme sans Doctrines, 1901 [*Socialism without Doctrine*,
Alternative Publishing Cooperative Ltd, 1977, tr. Russel Ward]

'The Anzac Landing', Ellis Ashmead-Bartlett: extract from cabled
report, published in Australia on 8 May 1915

'The Gallipoli Letter', Keith Murdoch: edited extract,
23 September 1915

'Women in Australia', Maybanke Anderson: edited extract from
M. Atkinson (ed.), *Australia – Economic and Political Studies*, 1920
[*Maybanke: A Woman's Voice*, Jan Roberts and Beverley Kingston
(eds), Ruskin Rowe Press, 2001]

'Kangaroo', D.H. Lawrence: edited extract from *Kangaroo*,
Martin Secker, 1923

'The Australian Democracy', W.K. Hancock: extract from
Australia, Ernest Benn Limited, 1930

'The Foundations of Culture in Australia', P.R. Stephensen: edited extract from *The Foundations of Culture in Australia*, W.J. Miles, 1936

'What Is Significant in Us Will Survive', Vance Palmer, *Meanjin*, No. 8, March 1942

'The Forgotten People', R.G. Menzies: speech broadcast on 2UE in Sydney and 3AW in Melbourne, 22 May 1942 [*The Forgotten People*, Angus and Robertson, 1943]

'The Cultural Cringe', A.A. Phillips: *Meanjin*, No. 4, 1950. Reproduced by permission of MUP, publisher of the latest edition *A.A. Phillips on the Cultural Cringe*, A.A. Phillips, Melbourne, 2006

'Re-writing Australian History', Manning Clark: *Australian Signpost*, Cheshire, 1956. Courtesy of Manning Clark House

'The Australian Legend', Russel Ward: edited extract from *The Australian Legend*, Oxford University Press, 1958. Print book: Reproduced by permission of Oxford University Press Australia & New Zealand, from *The Australian Legend*, by Russel Ward, 1958. Reprinted in 2005. ISBN: 9780195502862. Ebook: By arrangement with the Licensor, The Russel Ward Estate, c/- Curtis Brown (Aust) Pty Ltd

'A Nice Night's Entertainment', Barry Humphries: *Wild Life in Suburbia*, 1958 [*A Nice Night's Entertainment*, Barry Humphries, Currency Press, 1981]

'The Australian Ugliness', Robin Boyd: edited extract from *The Australian Ugliness*, Cheshire, 1960. Reproduced by permission of the Text Publishing Company, publisher of the latest edition *The Australian Ugliness*, Robin Boyd, Melbourne, 2012. Courtesy Robin Boyd Foundation www.robinboyd.org.au

'The Lucky Country', Donald Horne: edited extract from *The Lucky Country*, Penguin, 1964. Reproduced with permission by Penguin Group (Australia)

'After the Dreaming', W.E.H. Stanner: edited extract from
After the Dreaming, Boyer Lectures, ABC, 1968

'Racists', Humphrey McQueen: extract from *A New Britannia*,
Penguin, 1970

'Australia as a Suburb', Hugh Stretton, edited extract from
Ideas for Australian Cities, self-published, 1970

'Manzone Country', Anne Summers: edited extract from
Damned Whores and God's Police, Penguin, 1975.
Damned Whores and God's Police is out of print, but an ebook version
can be obtained by contacting the author at drannesummers@me.com

'The Real Matilda', Miriam Dixson: edited extract from
The Real Matilda, Penguin, 1976

'The Spectre of Truganini', Bernard Smith: edited extract from
The Spectre of Truganini, Boyer Lectures, ABC, 1980

'The End of Certainty', Paul Kelly: edited extract from
The End of Certainty: Power, Politics and Business in Australia,
Sydney: Allen & Unwin, 1993

'From Three Cheers to the Black Armband', Geoffrey Blainey:
The John Latham Memorial Lecture, Sydney, 28 April 1993
['Drawing up a Balance Sheet of Our History',
Quadrant, July–August, 1993]

'The Future Eaters', Tim Flannery: edited extract from
The Future Eaters, Reed New Holland, 1994

'A Spirit of Play', David Malouf: extract from *A Spirit of Play*,
Boyer Lectures, ABC Books, 1998

'Home-Grown Traditions', Inga Clendinnen: extract from
True Stories, Boyer Lectures, ABC Books, 1999

'Our Right to Take Responsibility', Noel Pearson: edited extract from *Our Right to Take Responsibility*, Noel Pearson & Associates, 2000

'The New Liberalism', Judith Brett: extract from Robert Manne (ed.), *The Howard Years*, Black Inc., 2004

'The Fig, the Olive and the Pomegranate Tree', Ghassan Hage: *The Australian*, 23 April 2008